Praise for *Spring Boot: Up and Running*

This book is a must read for new and existing Spring Boot users. Mark has done a stellar job at covering the intricate details of developing a Spring Boot application. The code samples are relatable and easy to follow, provide a reference guide to developers, and as a bonus they cover many aspects of coffee!

—*Nikhil Nanivadekar, Java Champion*

I approached this book hoping for Mark Heckler's unique blend of technical insight and charm, and I was not disappointed! Mark's gone from beginner to winner since he joined our Spring advocacy team more than half a decade ago. I knew that his decades in industry and relatively fresh perspective to Spring would make him uniquely qualified to sympathize with, and speak to, people who wanted to get up and running with Spring Boot. This book belongs on your bookshelf if you want the "make it wiggle" experience. It belongs on your bookshelf if you want to validate what you know and want to flesh out the gaps in your knowledge. It belongs on your bookshelf if you want a good reference. It belongs on your bookshelf.

—*Josh Long (@starbuxman), Spring Developer Advocate*

This book and its author have to be the friendliest companions out there for those getting started with Spring Boot. I hope you enjoy their company as much as I have.

—*Dr. David Syer, VMware*

Mark offers a fresh perspective on what it takes to build apps with Spring Boot. Don't pass this up.

—*Greg L. Turnquist, Spring teammate, host of* Spring Boot Learning *on YouTube*

Spring Boot: Up and Running

*Building Cloud Native Java
and Kotlin Applications*

Mark Heckler

Beijing · Boston · Farnham · Sebastopol · Tokyo

Spring Boot: Up and Running

by Mark Heckler

Published by O'Reilly Media, Inc., 1005 Gravenstein Highway North, Sebastopol, CA 95472.

This work is part of a collaboration between O'Reilly and VMWare Tanzu. See our statement of editorial independence (*https://oreil.ly/editorial-independence*).

O'Reilly books may be purchased for educational, business, or sales promotional use. Online editions are also available for most titles (*http://oreilly.com*). For more information, contact our corporate/institutional sales department: 800-998-9938 or *corporate@oreilly.com*.

Acquisitions Editor: Suzanne McQuade	**Indexer:** Potomac Indexing, LLC
Development Editor: Corbin Collins	**Interior Designer:** David Futato
Production Editor: Caitlin Ghegan	**Cover Designer:** Karen Montgomery
Copyeditor: Kim Sandoval	**Illustrator:** Kate Dullea
Proofreader: Scarlett Lindsay	

February 2021:   First Edition

Revision History for the First Edition

2021-02-04:   First Release

See *http://oreilly.com/catalog/errata.csp?isbn=9781492076988* for release details.

978-1-098-10339-2

[LSI]

Table of Contents

Preface

Welcome

"Kites rise against not with the wind."

—John Neal, *from Enterprise and Perseverance (The Weekly Mirror)*

Welcome to *Spring Boot: Up and Running*. I'm glad you're here.

There are other Spring Boot books available today. Good books, written by good people. But every author makes decisions on what to include in their material, what to exclude, how to present what makes the cut, and so many more decisions large and small that make their book unique. What feels like optional material to one author may seem absolutely essential to another. We're all developers, and like all developers, we have opinions.

My opinion was that there were some missing pieces, things I felt were either necessary or just incredibly helpful to share with devs new to Spring Boot. This list of missing pieces has grown as I interact with more and more developers around the world, at various stages in their Spring Boot journey. We're all learning different things at different times in different ways. Thus this book.

If you're new to Spring Boot, or if you feel it would be useful to strengthen your knowledge of the fundamentals — and let's face it, when is it *not* useful to do that? — this book was written with you in mind. It is a gentle introduction that covers the key capabilities of Spring Boot while advancing into useful application of those capabilities *in the real world*.

Thank you for joining me on this journey. Let's begin!

Conventions Used in This Book

The following typographical conventions are used in this book:

Italic
> Indicates new terms, URLs, email addresses, filenames, and file extensions.

`Constant width`
> Used for program listings, as well as within paragraphs to refer to program elements such as variable or function names, databases, data types, environment variables, statements, and keywords.

`Constant width bold`
> Shows commands or other text that should be typed literally by the user.

`Constant width italic`
> Shows text that should be replaced with user-supplied values or by values determined by context.

 This element signifies a tip or suggestion.

 This element signifies a general note.

 This element indicates a warning or caution.

Using Code Examples

Supplemental material (code examples, exercises, etc.) is available for download at *https://resources.oreilly.com/examples/0636920338727*.

If you have a technical question or a problem using the code examples, please send email to *bookquestions@oreilly.com*.

This book is here to help you get your job done. In general, if example code is offered with this book, you may use it in your programs and documentation. You do not need to contact us for permission unless you're reproducing a significant portion of the code. For example, writing a program that uses several chunks of code from this book does not require permission. Selling or distributing examples from O'Reilly books does require permission.

Answering a question by citing this book and quoting example code does not require permission. Incorporating a significant amount of example code from this book into your product's documentation does require permission.

We appreciate, but generally do not require, attribution. An attribution usually includes the title, author, publisher, and ISBN. For example: "*Spring Boot: Up and Running* by Mark Heckler (O'Reilly). Copyright 2021 Mark Heckler, 978-1-098-10339-1."

If you feel your use of code examples falls outside fair use or the permission given above, feel free to contact us at *permissions@oreilly.com*.

O'Reilly Online Learning

 For more than 40 years, *O'Reilly Media* has provided technology and business training, knowledge, and insight to help companies succeed.

Our unique network of experts and innovators share their knowledge and expertise through books, articles, and our online learning platform. O'Reilly's online learning platform gives you on-demand access to live training courses, in-depth learning paths, interactive coding environments, and a vast collection of text and video from O'Reilly and 200+ other publishers. For more information, visit *http://oreilly.com*.

How to Contact Us

Please address comments and questions concerning this book to the publisher:

O'Reilly Media, Inc.
1005 Gravenstein Highway North
Sebastopol, CA 95472
800-998-9938 (in the United States or Canada)
707-829-0515 (international or local)
707-829-0104 (fax)

We have a web page for this book, where we list errata, examples, and any additional information. You can access this page at *https://oreil.ly/springboot_UR*.

Email *bookquestions@oreilly.com* to comment or ask technical questions about this book.

For news and information about our books and courses, visit *http://oreilly.com*.

Find us on Facebook: *http://facebook.com/oreilly*

Follow us on Twitter: *http://twitter.com/oreillymedia*

Watch us on YouTube: *http://www.youtube.com/oreillymedia*

Acknowledgments

I can't say thank you enough to everyone who encouraged me to write this book and who encouraged me while I was writing it. If you read early releases and offered feedback or even a kind word on Twitter, you've no idea how much it meant to me. You have my deepest thanks.

There are a few people who made it all possible, and not just a hopeful plan to write this book someday:

To my boss, mentor, and friend Tasha Isenberg. Tasha, you worked with me to accommodate timelines and when push came to shove, cleared a path for me to sprint through and hit key deadlines. I'm truly grateful to have such an understanding champion and fierce advocate within VMware.

To Dr. David Syer, founder of Spring Boot, Spring Cloud, Spring Batch, and contributor to countless Spring projects. Your insights and feedback were truly exceptional and incredibly thoughtful, and I can't thank you enough for everything.

To Greg Turnquist, Spring Data team member. Thanks for your critical eye and unfiltered feedback; you provided an invaluable additional perspective and made the book markedly better by doing so.

To my editors, Corbin Collins and Suzanne (Zan) McQuade. You were supportive in the extreme from concept to completion, encouraging me to produce my best work and somehow meet deadlines that outside circumstances seemed intent on crushing. I couldn't have asked for better.

To Rob Romano, Caitlin Ghegan, Kim Sandoval, and the entire O'Reilly production team. You got me across the finish line, stepping in to fuel that all-important last mile and literally and figuratively get this book *into production*.

Finally and most importantly, to my brilliant, loving, and exceedingly patient wife Kathy. To say that you inspire and enable me to do all that I do is the greatest of understatements. From the depths of my heart, thank you for *everything*.

## CHAPTER 1

Spring Boot in a Nutshell

This chapter explores the three core features of Spring Boot and how they are force multipliers for you as a developer.

Spring Boot's Three Foundational Features

The three core features of Spring Boot upon which everything else builds are simplified dependency management, simplified deployment, and autoconfiguration.

Starters for Simplified Dependency Management

One of the genius aspects of Spring Boot is that it makes dependency management… manageable.

If you've been developing software of any import for any length of time, you've almost certainly had to contend with several headaches surrounding dependency management. Any capability you provide in your application typically requires a number of "frontline" dependencies. For example, if you want to provide a RESTful web API, you must provide a way to expose endpoints over HTTP, listen for requests, tie those endpoints to methods/functions that will process those requests, and then build and return appropriate responses.

Almost invariably, each primary dependency incorporates numerous other secondary dependencies in order to fulfill its promised functionality. Continuing with our example of providing a RESTful API, we might expect to see a collection of dependencies (in some sensible but debatable structure) that includes code to supply responses in a particular format, e.g., JSON, XML, HTML; code to marshal/unmarshal objects to requested format(s); code to listen for and process requests and return responses to same; code to decode complex URIs used to create versatile APIs; code to support various wire protocols; and more.

Even for this fairly simple example, we're already likely to require a large number of dependencies in our build file. And we haven't even considered what functionality we may wish to include in our application at this point, only its outward interactions.

Now, let's talk versions. Of each and every one of those dependencies.

Using libraries together requires a certain degree of rigor, as one version of a particular dependency may have been tested (or even function correctly) only with a specific version of another dependency. When these issues inevitably arise, it leads to what I refer to as "Dependency Whack-a-Mole."

Like its namesake carnival game, Dependency Whack-a-Mole can be a frustrating experience. Unlike its namesake, when it comes to chasing down and bashing bugs stemming from mismatches that pop up between dependencies, there are no prizes, only elusive conclusive diagnoses and *hours* wasted pursuing them.

Enter Spring Boot and its starters. Spring Boot starters are Bills of Materials (BOMs) built around the proven premise that the vast majority of times you provide a particular capability, you do it in nearly the same way, nearly every time.

In the previous example, each time we build an API, we expose endpoints, listen for requests, process requests, convert to and from objects, exchange information in 1+ standard formats, send and receive data over the wire using a particular protocol, and more. This design/development/usage pattern doesn't vary much; it's an approach adopted industry-wide, with few variations. And like other similar patterns, it's handily captured in a Spring Boot starter.

Adding a single starter, e.g., `spring-boot-starter-web`, provides all of those related functionalities in a *single application dependency*. All dependencies encompassed by that single starter are version-synchronized too, meaning that they've been tested successfully together and the included version of library A is proven to function properly with the included version of library B...and C...and D...etc. This dramatically simplifies your dependency list and your life, as it practically eliminates any chance you'll have difficult-to-identify version conflicts among dependencies you need to provide your application's critical capabilities.

In those rare cases when you must incorporate functionality provided by a different version of an included dependency, you can simply override the tested version.

 If you must override the default version of a dependency, do so... but you should probably increase your level of testing to mitigate risks you introduce by doing so.

You can also exclude dependencies if they are unnecessary for your application, but the same cautionary note applies.

All in all, Spring Boot's concept of starters greatly streamlines your dependencies and reduces the work required to add whole sets of capabilities to your applications. It also dramatically diminishes the overhead you incur testing, maintaining, and upgrading them.

Executable JARs for Simplified Deployment

Long ago, in the days when application servers roamed the earth, deployments of Java applications were a complex affair.

In order to field a working application with, say, database access—like many micro-services today and nearly all monoliths then and now—you would need to do the following:

1. Install and configure the Application Server.
2. Install database drivers.
3. Create a database connection.
4. Create a connection pool.
5. Build and test your application.
6. Deploy your application and its (usually numerous) dependencies to the Application Server.

Note that this list assumes you had administrators to configure the machine/virtual machine and that at some point you had created the database independently of this process.

Spring Boot turned much of this cumbersome deployment process on its head and collapsed the previous steps into one, or perhaps two, if you count copying or `cf` push-ing a single file to a destination as an actual *step*.

Spring Boot wasn't the origin of the so-called über JAR, but it revolutionized it. Rather than teasing out every file from the application JAR and all dependent JARs, then combining them into a single destination JAR—sometimes referred to as *shading* —the designers of Spring Boot approached things from a truly novel perspective: what if we could *nest JARs*, retaining their intended and delivered format?

Nesting JARs instead of shading them alleviates *many* potential problems, as there are no potential version conflicts to be encountered when dependency JAR A and dependency JAR B each use a different version of C; it also removes potential legal issues due to repackaging software and combining it with other software using a different license. Keeping all dependent JARs in their original format cleanly avoids those and other issues.

It is also trivial to extract the contents of a Spring Boot executable JAR, should you wish to do that. There are some good reasons for doing so in some circumstances, and I'll discuss those in this book as well. For now, just know that the Spring Boot executable JAR has you covered.

That single Spring Boot JAR with all dependencies makes deployment a breeze. Rather than collecting and verifying all dependencies are deployed, the Spring Boot plug-in ensures they're all zipped into the output JAR. Once you have that, the application can be run anywhere there is a Java Virtual Machine (JVM) just by executing a command like `java -jar <SpringBootAppName.jar>`.

There's more.

By setting a single property in your build file, the Spring Boot build plug-in can also make that single JAR entirely (self) executable. Still assuming a JVM is present, rather than having to type or script that entire bothersome line of `java -jar <SpringBoo tAppName.jar>`, you could simply type `<SpringBootAppName.jar>` (replacing with your filename, of course), and Bob's your uncle—you're up and running. It doesn't get any easier than that.

Autoconfiguration

Sometimes called "magic" by those new to Spring Boot, autoconfiguration is perhaps the greatest "force multiplier" that Spring Boot brings to developers. I often refer to it as a developer's superpower: Spring Boot gives you *insane productivity* by bringing opinions to widely used and -repeated use cases.

Opinions in software? How does that help?!?

If you've been a developer for very long at all, you'll doubtless have noticed that some patterns repeat themselves frequently. Not perfectly, of course, but in the high percentages; perhaps 80–90% of the time things fall within a certain range of design, development, or activity.

I alluded earlier to this repetition within software, as this is what makes Spring Boot's starters amazingly consistent and useful. The repetition also means that these activities, when it comes to the code that must be written to complete a particular task, are ripe for streamlining.

To borrow an example from Spring Data, a Spring Boot–related and –enabled project, we know that every time we need to access a database, we need to open some manner of connection to that database. We also know that when our application completes its tasks, that connection must be closed to avoid potential issues. In between, we are likely to make numerous requests to the database using queries—simple and complex, read-only and write-enabled—and those queries will require some effort to create properly.

Now imagine we could streamline all of that. Automatically open a connection when we specify the database. Automatically close the connection when the application terminates. Follow a simple and expected convention to create queries *automatically* with minimal effort from you, the developer. Enable easy customization of even that minimal code, again by simple convention, to create complex bespoke queries that are reliably consistent and efficient.

This approach to code is sometimes referred to as *convention over configuration*, and if you're new to a particular convention, it can appear mildly jarring (no pun intended) at first glance. But if you've implemented similar features before, writing often hundreds of repetitive, mind-numbing lines of setup/teardown/configuration code to accomplish even the simplest of tasks, it's like a gust of fresh air. Spring Boot (and most Spring projects) follow the *convention over configuration* mantra, providing the assurance that if you follow simple, well-established and -documented conventions to do something, the configuration code you must write is minimal, or none at all.

Another way in which autoconfiguration gives you superpowers is the Spring team's laserlike focus on "developer-first" environment configuration. As developers, we are most productive when we can focus on the task at hand and not a million setup chores. How does Spring Boot make that happen?

Let's borrow an example from another Spring Boot–related project, Spring Cloud Stream: when connecting to a messaging platform like RabbitMQ or Apache Kafka, a developer typically must specify certain settings for said messaging platform in order to connect to and use it—hostname, port, credentials, and more. Focusing on the development experience means that defaults are provided when none are specified that *favor the developer working locally*: localhost, default port, etc. This makes sense as an *opinion* because it's nearly 100% consistent for development environments, while it isn't so in production. In prod, you would need to provide specific values due to widely varying platform and hosting environments.

Shared development projects using those defaults also eliminate a great deal of time required for developer environment setup. Win for you, win for your team.

There are occasions when your specific use cases don't exactly match the 80–90% of use cases that are typical, when you fall into the other 10–20% of valid use cases. In those instances, autoconfiguration can be selectively overridden, or even disabled entirely, but you lose all of your superpowers then, of course. Overriding certain opinions is typically a matter of setting one or more properties as you wish them to be or providing one or more beans to accomplish something that Spring Boot would normally autoconfigure on your behalf. In other words, this is often a very simple matter to accomplish on those rare occasions when you must do so. In the end, autoconfiguration is a powerful tool that silently and tirelessly works on your behalf to make your life easier and you insanely productive.

Summary

The three core features of Spring Boot upon which everything else builds are simplified dependency management, simplified deployment, and autoconfiguration. All three are customizable, but you'll seldom need to do so. And all three work hard to make you a better, more productive developer. Spring Boot gives you wings!

In the next chapter, we'll take a look at some of the great options you have when getting started creating Spring Boot applications. Choices are good!

## CHAPTER 2

Choosing Your Tools and Getting Started

Getting started creating Spring Boot apps is easy, as you'll soon see. The most difficult part might be deciding which of the available options you'd like to choose.

In this chapter, we'll examine some of the excellent choices you have available to create Spring Boot applications: build systems, languages, toolchains, code editors, and more.

Maven or Gradle?

Historically, Java application developers have had a few options for project build tools. Some have fallen out of favor over time—for good reason—and now we've coalesced as a community around two: Maven and Gradle. Spring Boot supports both with equal aplomb.

Apache Maven

Maven is a popular and solid choice for a build automation system. It has been around for quite some time, having had its beginning in 2002 and becoming a top-level project at the Apache Software Foundation in 2003. Its declarative approach was (and is) conceptually simpler than the alternatives of the time and of now: simply create an XML-formatted file named *pom.xml* with desired dependencies and plug-ins. When you execute the mvn command, you can specify a "phase" to complete, which accomplishes a desired task like compiling, removing prior output(s), packaging, running an application, and more:

```
<?xml version="1.0" encoding="UTF-8"?>
<project xmlns="http://maven.apache.org/POM/4.0.0"
         xmlns:xsi="http://www.w3.org/2001/XMLSchema-instance"
         xsi:schemaLocation="http://maven.apache.org/POM/4.0.0
         https://maven.apache.org/xsd/maven-4.0.0.xsd">
```

```xml
<modelVersion>4.0.0</modelVersion>
<parent>
        <groupId>org.springframework.boot</groupId>
        <artifactId>spring-boot-starter-parent</artifactId>
        <version>2.4.0</version>
        <relativePath/> <!-- lookup parent from repository -->
</parent>
<groupId>com.example</groupId>
<artifactId>demo</artifactId>
<version>0.0.1-SNAPSHOT</version>
<name>demo</name>
<description>Demo project for Spring Boot</description>

<properties>
        <java.version>11</java.version>
</properties>

<dependencies>
        <dependency>
                <groupId>org.springframework.boot</groupId>
                <artifactId>spring-boot-starter</artifactId>
        </dependency>

        <dependency>
                <groupId>org.springframework.boot</groupId>
                <artifactId>spring-boot-starter-test</artifactId>
                <scope>test</scope>
        </dependency>
</dependencies>

<build>
        <plugins>
                <plugin>
                        <groupId>org.springframework.boot</groupId>
                        <artifactId>spring-boot-maven-plugin</artifactId>
                </plugin>
        </plugins>
</build>

</project>
```

Maven also creates and expects a particular project structure by convention. You typically shouldn't deviate much—if at all—from that structure unless you are prepared to fight your build tool, a counterproductive quest if there ever was one. For the vast majority of projects, the conventional Maven structure works perfectly, so it isn't something you'll likely need to change. Figure 2-1 shows a Spring Boot application with the typical Maven project structure.

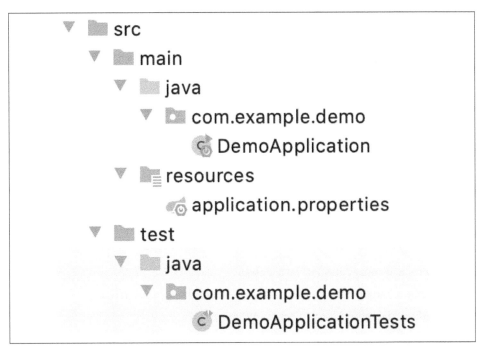

Figure 2-1. Maven project structure within a Spring Boot application

For more details about Maven's expected project structure, refer to The Maven Project's Introduction to the Standard Directory Layout (*https://oreil.ly/mavenprojintro*).

If there comes a time when Maven's project conventions and/or tightly structured approach to builds become too constrictive, there is another excellent option.

Gradle

Gradle is another popular option for building Java Virtual Machine (JVM) projects. First released in 2008, Gradle leverages a Domain Specific Language (DSL) to produce a *build.gradle* build file that is both minimal and flexible. An example of a Gradle build file for a Spring Boot application follows.

```
plugins {
        id 'org.springframework.boot' version '2.4.0'
        id 'io.spring.dependency-management' version '1.0.10.RELEASE'
        id 'java'
}

group = 'com.example'
version = '0.0.1-SNAPSHOT'
```

```
sourceCompatibility = '11'

repositories {
        mavenCentral()
}

dependencies {
        implementation 'org.springframework.boot:spring-boot-starter'
        testImplementation 'org.springframework.boot:spring-boot-starter-test'
}

test {
        useJUnitPlatform()
}
```

Gradle allows you, the developer, to choose to use either the Groovy or the Kotlin programming languages for a DSL. It also offers several features meant to reduce your time waiting for a project to build, such as the following:

- Incremental compilation of Java classes
- Compile avoidance for Java (in cases where no changes occurred)
- A dedicated daemon for project compilation

Choosing Between Maven and Gradle

Your choice of build tool may not sound like much of a choice at this point. Why not simply choose Gradle?

Maven's more rigid declarative (some might say opinionated) approach keeps things incredibly consistent from project to project, environment to environment. If you follow the Maven way, few issues typically crop up, leaving you to focus on your code with little fussing with the build.

As a build system built around programming/scripting, Gradle also occasionally has issues digesting initial releases of new language versions. The Gradle team is responsive and typically dispatches these issues with great haste, but if you prefer to (or must) dive immediately into early access language releases, this warrants consideration.

Gradle can be faster for builds—and sometimes *significantly* faster, especially in larger projects. That said, for your typical microservices-based project, build times aren't likely to differ by that much between similar Maven and Gradle projects.

Gradle's flexibility can be a breath of fresh air for simple projects and projects with very complex build requirements. But especially in those complex projects, Gradle's additional flexibility can result in more time spent tweaking and troubleshooting when things aren't working the way you might expect. TANSTAAFL (There Ain't No Such Thing as a Free Lunch).

Spring Boot supports both Maven and Gradle, and if you use the Initializr (to be covered in a section that follows), the project and desired build file are created for you, to get you up and running quickly. In short, try both, then choose what works best for you. Spring Boot will happily support you either way.

Java or Kotlin?

While there are many languages available for use on the JVM, two enjoy the most widespread use. One is the original JVM language, Java; the other is a relative newcomer to the space, Kotlin. Both are full first-class citizens in Spring Boot.

Java

Depending on whether you consider the public 1.0 release or the project origin as its official birthdate, Java has been around for 25 or 30 years, respectively. It's anything but stagnant, though. Since September 2017, Java has been on a six-month release cycle, resulting in more frequent feature improvements than before. The maintainers have cleaned up the codebase and have pruned features obviated by new ones, as well as introduced vital features driven by the Java community. Java is more vibrant than ever.

That lively pace of innovation, combined with Java's longevity and consistent focus on backward compatibility, means that there are countless Java shops maintaining and creating critical Java applications daily around the world. Many of those applications use Spring.

Java forms the bedrock-solid foundation of nearly the entire Spring codebase, and as such, it's a great choice to use for building your Spring Boot applications. Examining the code for Spring, Spring Boot, and all related projects is a simple matter of visiting GitHub where it's hosted and viewing it there or cloning the project to review offline. And with the availability of an abundance of example code, sample projects, and "Getting Started" guides written using Java, writing Spring Boot apps using Java may be better supported than any other toolchain combination on the market.

Kotlin

Relatively speaking, Kotlin is the new kid on the block. Created by JetBrains in 2010 and made public in 2011, Kotlin was created to address perceived gaps in Java's usability. Kotlin was designed from the beginning to be:

Concise
Kotlin requires minimal code to clearly communicate intent to the compiler (and oneself and other developers).

Safe

Kotlin eliminates null-related errors by eliminating the possibility of null values *by default*, unless the developer specifically overrides behavior to allow for them.

Interoperable

Kotlin aims for frictionless interoperability with all existing JVM, Android, and browser libraries.

Tool-friendly

Build Kotlin applications in numerous Integrated Development Environments (IDEs) or from the command line, just like Java.

Kotlin's maintainers extend the language's capabilities with great care but also with great velocity. Without 25+ years of language compatibility as a core design focus, they've moved quickly to add very useful capabilities that are likely to appear in Java some versions later.

In addition to being concise, Kotlin is also a very fluent language. Without diving into too many details yet, several language features contribute to this linguistic elegance, among them `extension functions` and `infix notation`. I'll discuss this idea in more depth later, but Kotlin makes syntax options like this possible:

```
infix fun Int.multiplyBy(x: Int): Int { ... }

// calling the function using the infix notation
1 multiplyBy 2

// is the same as
1.multiplyBy(2)
```

As you might imagine, the ability to define your own, more fluent "language within a language" can be a boon to API design. Combined with Kotlin's concision, this can make Spring Boot applications written in Kotlin even shorter and more readable than their Java counterparts, with no loss in communication of intent.

Kotlin has been a full first-class citizen in Spring Framework since version 5.0 was released in autumn of 2017, with full support propagating through Spring Boot (spring 2018) and other component projects ever since. Additionally, all Spring documentation is being expanded to include examples in both Java *and* Kotlin. This means that effectively, you can write entire Spring Boot applications with Kotlin as easily as with Java.

Choosing Between Java and Kotlin

The amazing thing is that you don't actually have to choose. Kotlin compiles to the same bytecode output that Java does; and since Spring projects can be created that include both Java source files and Kotlin, and can call both compilers with ease, you

---

can use whichever makes more sense to you even *within the same project*. How's that for having your cake and eating it too?

Of course, if you prefer one over the other or have other personal or professional strictures, you're obviously able to develop entire applications in one or the other. It's good to have choices, no?

Choosing a Version of Spring Boot

For production applications, you should always use the current version of Spring Boot with the following temporary and narrow exceptions:

- You're currently running an older version but are upgrading, retesting, and deploying your applications in some order such that you simply haven't reached this particular app yet.

- You're currently running an older version, but there is an identified conflict or bug you've reported to the Spring team and are instructed to wait for an update to Boot or a dependency in question.

- You need to utilize features in a snapshot, milestone, or release candidate pre-GA (General Availability) version and are willing to accept the risks inherent with code that hasn't yet been declared GA, i.e., "ready for production use."

 Snapshot, milestone, and Release Candidate (RC) versions are extensively tested prior to publication, so a great deal of rigor has already gone into ensuring their stability. Until the full GA version is approved and published, though, there is always the potential for API changes, fixes, etc. The risks to your application are low, but you'll have to decide for yourself (and test and confirm) if those risks are manageable when you consider using *any* early-access software.

The Spring Initializr

There are many ways to create a Spring Boot application, but most lead back to a single starting point: the Spring Initializr, shown in Figure 2-2.

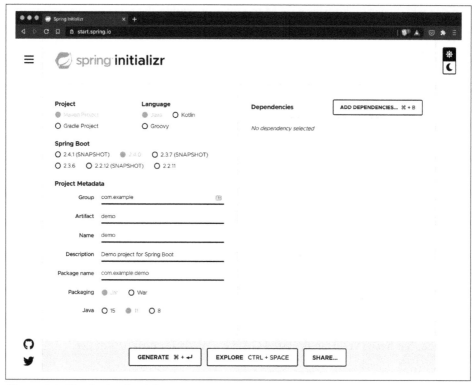

Figure 2-2. The Spring Initializr

Sometimes referred to simply by its URL, `start.spring.io`, the Spring Initializr can be accessed from project creation wizards within prominent IDEs, via the command line, or most often via a web browser. Using the web browser provides a few extra useful features that can't (yet) be accessed via other avenues.

To begin creating a Spring Boot project in the "Best Possible Way," point your browser to *https://start.spring.io*. From there, we'll choose a few options and get started.

Installing Java

I assume that if you've reached this point you've already installed a current version of the Java Development Kit (JDK)—sometimes referred to as *Java Platform, Standard Edition*—on your machine. If you haven't yet installed Java, you'll need to do so before proceeding.

Providing detailed instructions for how to do so lies outside the scope of this book, but a few recommendations wouldn't hurt either, right? :)

I've found that the easiest way to install and manage one or more JDKs on your machine is by using SDKMAN! (*https://sdkman.io*). This package manager also facilitates the installation of the Spring Boot Command Line Interface (CLI) you'll use later (and many, many other tools), so it's an incredibly useful utility app to have. Following the instructions at *https://sdkman.io/install* will get you ready to roll.

 SDKMAN! is written in bash (the Unix/Linux shell) script, and as such, it installs and works natively on MacOS and Linux as well as other operating systems with Unix or Linux foundations. SDKMAN! will run on Windows as well but not natively; in order to install and run SDKMAN! in a Windows environment, you must first install the Windows Subsystem for Linux (WSL) (*https://oreil.ly/WindowsSubL*), Git Bash for Windows (*https://oreil.ly/GitBashWin*) plus MinGW (*http://www.mingw.org*). Please see the SDKMAN! install page linked previously for details.

From SDKMAN!, it's a matter of installing the desired version of Java using `sdk list java` to view options, then `sdk install java <insert_desired_java_here>` to install. Numerous great options exist, but to start, I'd recommend you choose the current Long Term Support (LTS) version packaged by AdoptOpenJDK with the Hotspot JVM, e.g., `11.0.7.hs-adpt`.

If you prefer not to use SDKMAN! for whatever reason, you can also simply choose to download and install a JDK directly from *https://adoptopenjdk.net*. Doing so will get you up and running, but it makes updates more difficult and doesn't help you in the future with updating or if you need to manage multiple JDKs.

To get started with the Initializr, we first choose the build system we plan to use with our project. As mentioned previously, we have two great options: Maven and Gradle. Let's choose Maven for this example.

Next, we'll choose Java as the (language) basis for this project.

As you may have noticed already, the Spring Initializr selects enough defaults for the options presented to create a project with no input from you whatsoever. When you reached this web page, Maven and Java were both already preselected. The current version of Spring Boot is as well, and for this—and most—projects, that is what you'll want to select.

We can leave the options under Project Metadata as they are without issue, although we'll modify them for future projects.

And for now, we also don't include any dependencies. This way, we can focus on the mechanics of project creation, not any particular outcome.

Before generating that project, though, there are a couple of really nice features of the Spring Initializr I'd like to point out, along with one sidenote.

If you'd like to examine your project's metadata and dependency details prior to project generation based on your current selections, you can click the Explore button or use the keyboard shortcut, Ctrl+Space, to open Spring Initializr's Project Explorer (shown in Figure 2-3). The Initializr will then present you with the project structure and build file that will be included in the compressed (*.zip*) project you're about to download. You can review the directory/package structure, application properties file (more on this later), and the project properties and dependencies specified in your build file: since we're using Maven for this project, ours is *pom.xml*.

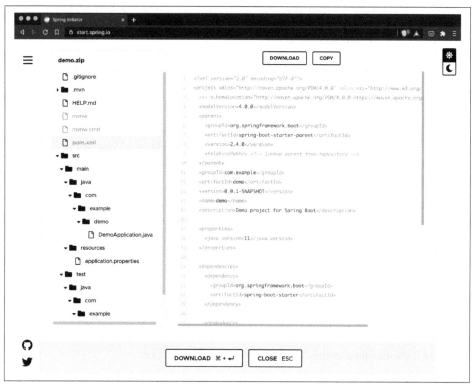

Figure 2-3. Spring Initializr's Project Explorer

This is a quick and handy way to verify project configuration and dependencies before downloading, extracting, and loading into your IDE your brand-new, empty project.

Another smaller feature of the Spring Initializr, but one that has been welcomed by numerous developers, is dark mode. By clicking on the Dark UI toggle at the top of the page as shown in Figure 2-4, you switch to Initializr's dark mode and make that the default each time you visit the page. It's a small feature, but if you keep your machine in dark mode everywhere else, it certainly makes loading the Initializr less jarring and more pleasant. You'll want to keep coming back!

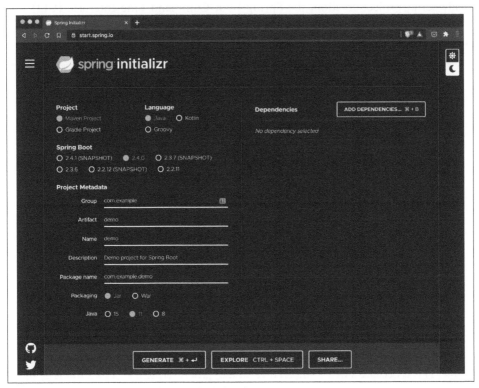

Figure 2-4. The Spring Initializr, in dark mode!

Other than the main application class and its main method, plus an empty test, the Spring Initializr doesn't generate code for you; it generates the *project* for you, per your guidance. It's a small distinction but a very important one: code generation has wildly varied results and often hamstrings you the moment you begin making changes. By generating the project structure, including the build file with specified dependencies, the Initializr provides you a running start to write the code you need to leverage Spring Boot's autoconfiguration. Autoconfig gives you superpowers without the straitjacket.

Next, click the Generate button to generate, package, and download your project, saving it to your chosen location on your local machine. Then navigate to that downloaded *.zip* file and unzip it to prepare to develop your application.

Straight Outta Commandline

If you happily spend as much time as possible on the command line or wish to eventually script project creation, the Spring Boot Command Line Interface (CLI) was made for you. The Spring Boot CLI has many powerful capabilities, but for now, we'll limit our focus to creating a new Boot project.

Installing the Spring Boot CLI

Perhaps the easiest way to install the Spring Boot CLI is via SDKMAN!, as with your JDK, Kotlin utilities, and more. From your terminal window, you can run

```
sdk list
```

to see all of the various packages available for installation; Figure 2-5 shows the Spring Boot CLI entry. Next, run

```
sdk list springboot
```

to see available versions of the Spring Boot CLI, then install the most recent (current) one with

```
sdk install springboot
```

If you don't provide a specific version identifier with the SDKMAN! command `sdk install <tool> <version_identifier>`, SDKMAN! typically installs the latest recommended production version of the language/tool. This has different meanings for different supported packages; as an example, the latest Long Term Support (LTS) version of Java will be installed, not a more recent (non-LTS) version that may be available. This is because a new numbered version of Java is released every six months, and periodically, a version is designated an LTS release—meaning that there are often one or more newer releases that are officially supported for only six months each (for feature evaluation, testing, or even production deployments), while a particular LTS release is fully supported with updates and bug fixes.

This note is a bit of a generalization that can vary somewhat between JDK providers, although most don't stray far (if at all) from the customary designations. Entire talks have been devoted to the details, but for our purposes here, they have no effect whatsoever.

```
--------------------------------------------------------------------------
Spring Boot (2.4.0)                           http://projects.spring.io/spring-boot/

Spring Boot takes an opinionated view of building production-ready Spring
applications. It favors convention over configuration and is designed to get you
up and running as quickly as possible.

                                              $ sdk install springboot
--------------------------------------------------------------------------
```

Figure 2-5. The Spring Boot CLI on SDKMAN!

Once you've installed the Spring Boot CLI, you can create the same project we just created with the following command:

```
spring init
```

To extract the zipped project into a directory named *demo*, you can execute the following command:

```
unzip demo.zip -d demo
```

Wait, how can it be so easy? In one word, defaults. The Spring CLI uses the same default settings as the Spring Initializr (Maven, Java, etc.), allowing you to provide arguments only for values you wish to change. Let's specifically provide values for a few of those defaults (and add a helpful twist for project extraction) just to better see what is involved:

```
spring init -a demo -l java --build maven demo
```

We're still initializing a project using the Spring CLI, but now we're providing the following arguments:

- `-a demo` (or `--artifactId demo`) allows us to provide an artifact ID for the project; in this case, we call it "demo."

- `-l java` (or `--language java`) lets us specify Java, Kotlin, or Groovy[1] as the primary language we'll use for this project.

- `--build` is the flag for the build system argument; valid values are `maven` and `gradle`.

- `-x demo` requests the CLI to extract the resultant project *.zip* file returned by the Initializr; note that the `-x` is optional, and specifying a text label without an extension (as we've done here) is helpfully inferred to be an extraction directory.

---

[1] Groovy support is still provided within Spring Boot but is nowhere near as widely used as Java or Kotlin.

All of these options can be reviewed further by executing `spring help init` from the command line.

Things get a bit more involved when specifying dependencies. As you might imagine, it's hard to beat the ease of choosing them from the "menu" presented by the Spring Initializr. But the flexibility of the Spring CLI is handy in the extreme for quick starts, scripting, and build pipelines.

One more thing: by default, the CLI leverages the Initializr to provide its project-building capabilities, which means projects created via either mechanism (CLI or via the Initializr web page) are identical. That consistency is absolutely essential in a shop that directly uses the Spring Initializr's capabilities.

Occasionally, though, an organization tightly controls what dependencies their developers can even use to create projects. To be completely honest, this approach saddens me and feels very timebound, impeding an organization's agility and user/market responsiveness. If you're in such an organization, this complicates your ability to "get the job done" on anything you set out to accomplish.

That being the case, it is possible to create your own project generator (even cloning the repository for the Spring Initializr) and use that directly via the resultant web page…or only expose the REST API portion and utilize that from the Spring CLI. To do so, just add this parameter to the commands shown earlier (replacing with your valid URL, of course):

```
--target https://insert.your.url.here.org
```

Staying In Integrated Development Environments (IDEs)

However you create your Spring Boot project, you'll need to open it and write some code to create a useful application.

There are three major IDEs and numerous text editors that do a respectable job of supporting you as a developer. IDEs include, but are not limited to, Apache NetBeans (*https://netbeans.apache.org*), Eclipse (*https://www.eclipse.org*), and IntelliJ IDEA (*https://www.jetbrains.com/idea*). All three are open source software (OSS), and all three are free in many circumstances.[2]

---

2 There are two options available: Community Edition (CE) and Ultimate Edition (UE). Community Edition supports Java and Kotlin app development, but to have access to all available Spring support, you must use Ultimate Edition. Certain use cases qualify for a free license for UE, or you can of course also purchase one. Additionally, all three provide excellent support for Spring Boot applications.

In this book, as in my daily life, I primarily use IntelliJ Ultimate Edition. There isn't really a wrong choice as much as a personal preference (or organizational mandate or preference) in choosing an IDE, so please use what fits you and your tastes best. Most concepts transfer pretty well among the major offerings.

There are also several editors that have garnered a large following among devs. Some, like Sublime Text (*https://www.sublimetext.com*), are paid applications that have fierce followings due to their quality and longevity. Other more recent entrants to the field, like Atom (*https://atom.io*) (created by GitHub, which is now owned by Microsoft) and Visual Studio Code (*https://code.visualstudio.com*) (shortened to VSCode, created by Microsoft) are gaining capabilities and loyal followings rapidly.

In this book, I occasionally use VSCode or its counterpart built from the same codebase but with telemetry/tracking disabled, VSCodium (*https://vscodium.com*). In order to support some of the features most developers expect and/or require from their development environment, I add the following extensions to VSCode/VSCodium:

Spring Boot Extension Pack (Pivotal) (https://oreil.ly/SBExtPack)
> This includes several other extensions, including `Spring Initializr Java Support`, `Spring Boot Tools`, and `Spring Boot Dashboard`, which facilitate the creation, editing, and management of Spring Boot applications within VSCode, respectively.

Debugger for Java (Microsoft) (https://oreil.ly/DebuggerJava)
> Dependency of the Spring Boot Dashboard.

IntelliJ IDEA Keybindings (Keisuke Kato) (https://oreil.ly/IntellijIDEAKeys)
> Because I primarily use IntelliJ, this makes it easier for me to switch between the two more easily.

Language Support for Java™ (Red Hat) (https://oreil.ly/JavaLangSupport)
> Dependency of Spring Boot Tools.

Maven for Java (Microsoft) (https://oreil.ly/MavenJava)
> Facilitates the use of Maven-based projects.

There are other extensions you may find useful for wrangling XML, Docker, or other ancillary technologies, but these are the essentials for our current purposes.

Continuing with our Spring Boot project, you'll next want to open it in your chosen IDE or text editor. For most of the examples in this book, we'll use IntelliJ IDEA, a very capable IDE (written in Java and Kotlin) produced by JetBrains. If you've already associated your IDE with project build files, you can double-click on the `pom.xml` file in your project's directory (using Finder on the Mac, File Explorer on Windows, or one of the various File Managers on Linux) and load the project into your IDE automatically. If not, you can open the project from within your IDE or editor in the manner recommended by its developers.

 Many IDEs and editors offer a way to create command line short-cuts to launch and load, bringing up your project with one short command. Examples include IntelliJ's idea, VSCode's/VSCodium's code, and Atom's atom shortcuts.

Cruising Down main()

Now that we've loaded the project in our IDE (or editor), let's take a look at what makes a Spring Boot project (Figure 2-6) just a bit different from a standard Java application.

```
DemoApplication.java ✕

src > main > java > com > example > demo > ⬤ DemoApplication.java > { } com.example.demo
  1    package com.example.demo;
  2
  3    import org.springframework.boot.SpringApplication;
  4    import org.springframework.boot.autoconfigure.SpringBootApplication;
  5
  6    @SpringBootApplication
  7    public class DemoApplication {
  8
       Run | Debug
  9        public static void main(String[] args) {
 10            SpringApplication.run(DemoApplication.class, args);
 11        }
 12
 13    }
 14
```

Figure 2-6. Our Spring Boot demo application's main application class

A standard Java application contains (by default) an empty public static void main method. When we execute a Java application, the JVM searches for this method as the app's starting point, and without it, application startup fails with an error like this one:

```
Error:
Main method not found in class PlainJavaApp, please define the main method as:
    public static void main(String[] args)
or a JavaFX application class must extend javafx.application.Application
```

Of course, you can place code to be executed upon application startup in a Java class's main method, and a Spring Boot application does exactly that. Upon startup, a Spring Boot app checks the environment, configures the application, creates the initial context, and launches the Spring Boot application. It does this via a single top-level annotation and a single line of code, as shown in Figure 2-7.

```java
DemoApplication.java
1         package com.example.demo;
2
3         import org.springframework.boot.SpringApplication;
4         import org.springframework.boot.autoconfigure.SpringBootApplication;
5
6    @SpringBootApplication
7    public class DemoApplication {
8
9        public static void main(String[] args) {
10           SpringApplication.run(DemoApplication.class, args);
11       }
12
13   }
```

Figure 2-7. The essence of a Spring Boot application

We'll dive under the covers of these mechanisms as the book unfolds. For now, suffice it to say that Boot takes a lot of tedious application setup off your hands during application startup *by design* and *by default* so that you can quickly get down to the business of writing meaningful code.

Summary

This chapter has examined some of the first-class choices you have in creating Spring Boot applications. Whether you prefer to build your projects using Maven or Gradle, write code in Java or Kotlin, or create projects from the web interface provided by the Spring Initializr or its command line partner, the Spring Boot CLI, you have the full power and ease of Spring Boot at your fingertips without compromise. You can also work with Boot projects using an impressive variety of IDEs and text editors with top-notch Spring Boot support.

As covered here and in Chapter 1, the Spring Initializr works hard for you in getting your project created quickly and easily. Spring Boot contributes meaningfully throughout the development life cycle with the following features:

- Simplified dependency management, which comes into play from project creation through development and maintenance
- Autoconfiguration that dramatically reduces/eliminates the boilerplate you might otherwise write before working on the problem domain
- Simplified deployment that makes packaging and deployment a breeze

And all of these capabilities are fully supported regardless of build system, language, or toolchain choices you make along the way. It's an amazingly flexible and powerful combination.

In the next chapter, we'll create our first really meaningful Spring Boot application: an app that provides a REST API.

## CHAPTER 3

Creating Your First Spring Boot REST API

In this chapter, I explain and demonstrate how to develop a basic working application using Spring Boot. Since most applications involve exposing backend cloud resources to users, usually via a frontend UI, an Application Programming Interface (API) is an excellent starting point for both understanding and practicality. Let's get started.

The Hows and Whys of APIs

The age of the monolithic application that does everything is over.

This isn't to say that monoliths no longer exist or that they won't still be created for ages to come. Under various circumstances, a monolithic application that provides numerous capabilities in one package still makes sense, especially in the following settings:

- The domain and thus domain boundaries are largely unknown.
- Provided capabilities are tightly coupled, and absolute performance of module interactions takes precedence over flexibility.
- Scaling requirements for all related capabilities are known and consistent.
- Functionality isn't volatile; change is slow, limited in scope, or both.

For everything else, there are microservices.

This is a gross oversimplification, of course, but I believe it to be a useful summary. By splitting capabilities into smaller, cohesive "chunks," we can decouple them, resulting in the potential for more flexible and robust systems that can be more rapidly deployed and more easily maintained.

In any distributed system—and make no mistake, a system comprising microservices is exactly that—communication is key. No service is an island. And while there are numerous mechanisms for connecting applications/microservices, we often begin our journey by emulating the very fabric of our daily lives: the internet.

The internet was built for communication. In fact, the designers of its precursor, the Advanced Research Projects Agency Network (ARPANET), anticipated a need to maintain intersystem communication even in the event of "significant interruption." It is reasonable to conclude that an HTTP-based approach similar to the one we use to conduct a great deal of our daily lives could also ably allow us to create, retrieve, update, and delete various resources "over the wire."

As much as I love history, I won't dive deeper into the history of REST APIs other than to say that Roy Fielding laid out their principles in his 2000 PhD dissertation, which built upon the *HTTP object model* from 1994.

What Is REST, and Why Does It Matter?

As mentioned earlier, an API is the specification/interface that we developers *write to* so our code can use other code: libraries, other applications, or services. But what does the *REST* in *REST API* represent?

REST is an acronym for *representational state transfer*, which is a somewhat cryptic way of saying that when one application communicates with another, Application A brings its current state with it; it doesn't expect Application B to maintain state—current and cumulative, process-based information—between communication calls. Application A supplies a representation of its relevant state with each request to Application B. You can easily see why this increases survivability and resilience, because if there is a communication issue or Application B crashes and is restarted, it doesn't lose the current state of its interactions with Application A; Application A can simply reissue the request and pick up where the two applications left off.

 This general concept is often referred to as *stateless* applications/ services, because each service maintains its own current state, even within a sequence of interactions, and doesn't expect others to do so on its behalf.

Your API, HTTP Verb Style

Now, about that REST API—sometimes called a RESTful API, which is a nice, relaxing take on things, isn't it?

There are a number of standardized HTTP verbs defined within a handful of Internet Engineering Task Force (IETF) requests for comments (RFCs). Of these, a small number are typically used consistently for building APIs, with a couple more that find occasional use. REST APIs are primarily built upon the following HTTP verbs:

- POST
- GET
- PUT
- PATCH
- DELETE

These verbs correspond with typical operations we perform on resources: create (POST), read (GET), update (PUT and PATCH), and delete (DELETE).

 I'm admittedly blurring the lines somewhat by loosely equating PUT with updating a resource, and a bit less so by equating POST with creating a resource. I would ask the reader to bear with me as I step through the implementation and provide clarifications.

Occasionally, the following two verbs are employed:

- OPTIONS
- HEAD

These can be used to retrieve the communication options available for request/response pairs (OPTIONS) and retrieve a response header minus its body (HEAD).

For this book, and indeed for most production use, I will focus on the first, heavily utilized group. To get (no pun intended) started, let's create a simple microservice that implements a very basic REST API.

Back to the Initializr

We begin as usual with the Spring Initializr, as shown in Figure 3-1. I've changed the Group and Artifact fields to reflect the details I use (please feel free to use your preferred nomenclature), selected Java 11 under Options (optional, any listed version will do nicely), and selected only the Spring Web dependency. As it indicates in the displayed description, this dependency brings with it several capabilities, including that of "[building] web, *including RESTful*, applications using Spring MVC" (emphasis added). This is exactly what we require for the task at hand.

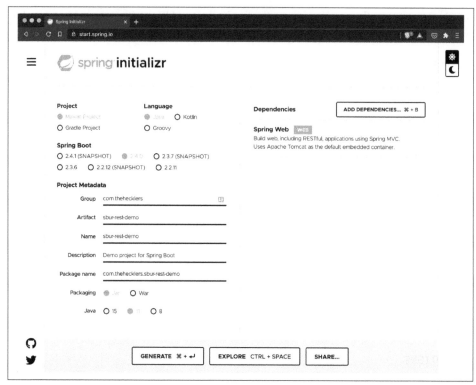

Figure 3-1. Creating a Spring Boot project to build a REST API

Once we've generated the project in the Initializr and saved the resultant *.zip* file locally, we'll extract the compressed project files—typically by double-clicking the *sbur-rest-demo.zip* file that was downloaded in your file browser or by using *unzip* from a shell/terminal window—and then open the now-extracted project in your chosen IDE or text editor for a view similar to Figure 3-2.

Figure 3-2. Our new Spring Boot project, just waiting for us to begin

Creating a Simple Domain

In order to *work with* resources, we'll need to write some code to *accommodate some* resources. Let's start by creating a very simple domain class that represents a resource we want to manage.

I'm somewhat of a coffee aficionado, as my good friends—this now includes you— know. With that in mind, I'll be using a coffee domain, with a class representing a particular type of coffee, as the domain for this example.

Let's begin by creating the `Coffee` class. This is essential to the example, as we need a resource of some kind to demonstrate how to manage resources via a REST API. But the domain simplicity or complexity is incidental to the example, so I'll keep it simple to focus on the objective: the resultant REST API.

As shown in Figure 3-3, the `Coffee` class has two member variables:

- An `id` field used to uniquely identify a particular kind of coffee
- A `name` field that describes the coffee by name

```
@SpringBootApplication
public class SburRestDemoApplication {

    public static void main(String[] args) {
        SpringApplication.run(SburRestDemoApplication.class, args);
    }

}

class Coffee {
    private final String id;
    private String name;

    public Coffee(String id, String name) {
        this.id = id;
        this.name = name;
    }

    public Coffee(String name) {
        this(UUID.randomUUID().toString(), name);
    }

    public String getId() {
        return id;
    }

    public String getName() {
        return name;
    }

    public void setName(String name) {
        this.name = name;
    }
}
```

Figure 3-3. The Coffee class: our domain class

I declare the id field as final so that it can be assigned only once and never modified; as such, this also requires that it is assigned when creating an instance of class Coffee and implies that it has no mutator method.

I create two constructors: one that takes both parameters and another that provides a unique identifier if none is provided upon creation of a Coffee.

Next, I create accessor and mutator methods—or getter and setter methods, if you prefer to call them that—for the name field, which is not declared final and is thus mutable. This is a debatable design decision, but it serves our upcoming needs for this example well.

With that, we now have a basic domain in place. Next it's time for a REST.

GET-ting

Perhaps the most-used of the most-used verbs is GET. So let's *get* (pun intended) started.

@RestController in a Nutshell

Without going too deep down the rabbit hole, Spring MVC (Model-View-Controller) was created to separate concerns between data, its delivery, and its presentation, assuming the views would be provided as a server-rendered web page. The @Control ler annotation helps tie the various pieces together.

@Controller is a stereotype/alias for the @Component annotation, meaning that upon application startup, a Spring Bean—an object created and managed by the Spring inversion of control (IoC) container within the app—is created from that class. @Controller-annotated classes accommodate a Model object to provide model-based data to the presentation layer and work with a ViewResolver to direct the application to display a particular view, as rendered by a view technology.

 Spring supports several view technologies and templating engines, covered in a later chapter.

It's also possible to instruct a Controller class to return a formatted response as Java-Script Object Notation (JSON) or as another data-oriented format such as XML simply by adding an @ResponseBody annotation to the class or method (JSON by default). This results in the Object/Iterable return value of a method being the *entire body* of the response to a web request, instead of being returned as a part of the Model.

The @RestController annotation is a convenience notation that combines @Control ler with @ResponseBody into a single descriptive annotation, simplifying your code and making intent more obvious. Once we've annotated a class as an @RestControl ler, we can begin creating our REST API.

Let's GET Busy

REST APIs deal with objects, and objects can come alone or as a group of related objects. To leverage our coffee scenario, you may want to retrieve a particular coffee; you may instead wish to retrieve all coffees, or all that are considered dark roast, fall within a range of identifiers, or include "Colombian" in the description, for example. To accommodate the need to retrieve one instance or more than one instance of an object, it is a good practice to create multiple methods in our code.

I'll begin by creating a list of `Coffee` objects to support the method returning multiple `Coffee` objects, as shown in the rudimentary class definition that follows. I define the variable holding this group of coffees as a `List` of `Coffee` objects. I choose `List` as the higher-level interface for my member variable type, but I'll actually assign an empty `ArrayList` for use within the `RestApiDemoController` class:

```
@RestController
class RestApiDemoController {
        private List<Coffee> coffees = new ArrayList<>();
}
```

It's a recommended practice to adopt the highest level of type (class, interface) that can cleanly satisfy internal and external APIs. These may not match in all cases, as they don't here. Internally, `List` provides the level of API that enables me to create the cleanest implementation based on my criteria; externally, we can define an even higher-level abstraction, as I'll demonstrate shortly.

It's always a good idea to have some data to retrieve in order to confirm that everything is working as expected. In the following code, I create a constructor for the `RestApiDemoController` class, adding code to populate the list of coffees upon object creation:

```
@RestController
class RestApiDemoController {
        private List<Coffee> coffees = new ArrayList<>();

        public RestApiDemoController() {
                coffees.addAll(List.of(
                                new Coffee("Café Cereza"),
                                new Coffee("Café Ganador"),
                                new Coffee("Café Lareño"),
                                new Coffee("Café Três Pontas")
                ));
        }
}
```

As shown in the following code, I create a method in the `RestApiDemoController` class that returns an iterable group of coffees represented by our member variable `coffees`. I choose to use an `Iterable<Coffee>` because any iterable type will satisfactorily provide this API's desired functionality:

.Using `@RequestMapping` to GET the list of coffees

```
@RestController
class RestApiDemoController {
        private List<Coffee> coffees = new ArrayList<>();

        public RestApiDemoController() {
                coffees.addAll(List.of(
                                new Coffee("Café Cereza"),
                                new Coffee("Café Ganador"),
                                new Coffee("Café Lareño"),
                                new Coffee("Café Três Pontas")
                ));
        }

        @RequestMapping(value = "/coffees", method = RequestMethod.GET)
        Iterable<Coffee> getCoffees() {
                return coffees;
        }
}
```

To the `@RequestMapping` annotation, I add a path specification of `/coffees` and a method type of `RequestMethod.GET`, indicating that the method will respond to requests with the path of `/coffees` and restrict requests to only HTTP GET requests. Retrieval of data is handled by this method, but updates of any kind are not. Spring Boot, via the Jackson dependencies included in Spring Web, performs the marshalling and unmarshalling of objects to JSON or other formats automatically.

We can streamline this even further using another convenience annotation. Using `@GetMapping` incorporates the direction to allow only GET requests, reducing boilerplate and requiring only the path to be specified, even omitting the `path` = since no parameter deconfliction is required. The following code clearly demonstrates the readability benefits of this annotation swap:

```
@GetMapping("/coffees")
Iterable<Coffee> getCoffees() {
    return coffees;
}
```

Helpful Hints About @RequestMapping

@RequestMapping has several specialized convenience annotations:

- @GetMapping

- @PostMapping

- @PutMapping

- @PatchMapping

- @DeleteMapping

Any of these mapping annotations can be applied at the class or method level, and paths are additive. For example, if I were to annotate the RestApiDemoController and its getCoffees() method as shown in the code, the application would respond exactly the same as it does with the following code shown in the previous two code snippets:

```
@RestController
@RequestMapping("/")
class RestApiDemoController {
        private List<Coffee> coffees = new ArrayList<>();

        public RestApiDemoController() {
                coffees.addAll(List.of(
                                new Coffee("Café Cereza"),
                                new Coffee("Café Ganador"),
                                new Coffee("Café Lareño"),
                                new Coffee("Café Três Pontas")
                ));
        }

        @GetMapping("/coffees")
        Iterable<Coffee> getCoffees() {
                return coffees;
        }
}
```

Retrieving all coffees in our makeshift datastore is useful, but it isn't enough. What if we want to retrieve one particular coffee?

Retrieving a single item works similarly to retrieving several items. I'll add another method called getCoffeeById to manage this for us, as shown in the next code segment.

The {id} portion of the specified path is a URI (uniform resource identifier) variable, and its value is passed to the getCoffeeById method via the id method parameter by annotating it with @PathVariable.

Iterating over the list of coffees, the method returns a populated `Optional<Coffee>` if it finds a match, or an empty `Optional<Coffee>` if the `id` requested isn't present in our small group of coffees:

```
@GetMapping("/coffees/{id}")
Optional<Coffee> getCoffeeById(@PathVariable String id) {
    for (Coffee c: coffees) {
        if (c.getId().equals(id)) {
            return Optional.of(c);
        }
    }

    return Optional.empty();
}
```

POST-ing

To create resources, an `HTTP POST` method is the preferred option.

A `POST` supplies details of a resource, typically in JSON format, and requests that the destination service creates that resource *under* the specified URI.

As shown in the next code fragment, a `POST` is a relatively simple affair: our service receives the specified coffee details as a `Coffee` object—thanks to Spring Boot's automatic marshalling—and adds it to our list of coffees. It then returns the `Coffee` object—automatically unmarshalled by Spring Boot to JSON by default—to the requesting application or service:

```
@PostMapping("/coffees")
Coffee postCoffee(@RequestBody Coffee coffee) {
    coffees.add(coffee);
    return coffee;
}
```

PUT-ting

Generally speaking, `PUT` requests are used to update existing resources with known URIs.

Per the IETF's document titled Hypertext Transfer Protocol (HTTP/1.1): Semantics and Content (*https://tools.ietf.org/html/ rfc7231*), `PUT` requests should update the specified resource if present; if the resource doesn't already exist, it should be created.

The following code operates in accordance with the specification: search for the coffee with the specified identifier, and if found, update it. If no such coffee is contained within the list, create it:

```
@PutMapping("/coffees/{id}")
Coffee putCoffee(@PathVariable String id, @RequestBody Coffee coffee) {
    int coffeeIndex = -1;

    for (Coffee c: coffees) {
        if (c.getId().equals(id)) {
            coffeeIndex = coffees.indexOf(c);
            coffees.set(coffeeIndex, coffee);
        }
    }

    return (coffeeIndex == -1) ? postCoffee(coffee) : coffee;
}
```

DELETE-ing

To delete a resource, we use an HTTP DELETE request. As shown in the next code fragment, we create a method that accepts a coffee's identifier as an @PathVariable and removes the applicable coffee from our list using the removeIf Collection method. removeIf accepts a Predicate, meaning we can provide a lambda to evaluate that will return a boolean value of true for the desired coffee to remove. Nice and tidy:

```
@DeleteMapping("/coffees/{id}")
void deleteCoffee(@PathVariable String id) {
    coffees.removeIf(c -> c.getId().equals(id));
}
```

And More

While there are many more things that could be done to improve this scenario, I'm going to focus on two in particular: reducing repetition and returning HTTP status codes where required by the specification.

To reduce repetition in the code, I'll elevate the portion of the URI mapping that is common to all methods within the RestApiDemoController class to the class-level @RequestMapping annotation, "/coffees". We can then remove that same portion of the URI from each method's mapping URI specification, reducing the textual noise level a bit, as the following code shows:

```
@RestController
@RequestMapping("/coffees")
class RestApiDemoController {
    private List<Coffee> coffees = new ArrayList<>();

    public RestApiDemoController() {
        coffees.addAll(List.of(
                        new Coffee("Café Cereza"),
```

```
                        new Coffee("Café Ganador"),
                        new Coffee("Café Lareño"),
                        new Coffee("Café Três Pontas")
            ));
    }

    @GetMapping
    Iterable<Coffee> getCoffees() {
            return coffees;
    }

    @GetMapping("/{id}")
    Optional<Coffee> getCoffeeById(@PathVariable String id) {
            for (Coffee c: coffees) {
                    if (c.getId().equals(id)) {
                            return Optional.of(c);
                    }
            }

            return Optional.empty();
    }

    @PostMapping
    Coffee postCoffee(@RequestBody Coffee coffee) {
            coffees.add(coffee);
            return coffee;
    }

    @PutMapping("/{id}")
    Coffee putCoffee(@PathVariable String id, @RequestBody Coffee coffee) {
            int coffeeIndex = -1;

            for (Coffee c: coffees) {
                    if (c.getId().equals(id)) {
                            coffeeIndex = coffees.indexOf(c);
                            coffees.set(coffeeIndex, coffee);
                    }
            }

            return (coffeeIndex == -1) ? postCoffee(coffee) : coffee;
    }

    @DeleteMapping("/{id}")
    void deleteCoffee(@PathVariable String id) {
            coffees.removeIf(c -> c.getId().equals(id));
    }
}
```

Next, I consult the IETF document referenced earlier and note that while HTTP status codes are not specified for GET and suggested for POST and DELETE methods, they are required for PUT method responses. To accomplish this, I modify the putCoffee method as shown in the following code segment. Instead of returning only the updated or created Coffee object, the putCoffee method will now return a ResponseEntity containing said Coffee and the appropriate HTTP status code: 201 (Created) if the PUT coffee didn't already exist, and 200 (OK) if it existed and was updated. We could do more, of course, but the current application code fulfills requirements and represents straightforward and clean internal and external APIs:

```
@PutMapping("/{id}")
ResponseEntity<Coffee> putCoffee(@PathVariable String id,
        @RequestBody Coffee coffee) {
    int coffeeIndex = -1;

    for (Coffee c: coffees) {
        if (c.getId().equals(id)) {
            coffeeIndex = coffees.indexOf(c);
            coffees.set(coffeeIndex, coffee);
        }
    }

    return (coffeeIndex == -1) ?
            new ResponseEntity<>(postCoffee(coffee), HttpStatus.CREATED) :
            new ResponseEntity<>(coffee, HttpStatus.OK);
}
```

Trust, but Verify

With all of the code in place, let's put this API through its paces.

 I use the HTTPie (*https://httpie.org*) command line HTTP client for nearly all of my HTTP-based chores. Occasionally I will also use curl (*https://curl.haxx.se*) or Postman (*https://www.post man.com*), but I find HTTPie to be a versatile client with a streamlined command-line interface and superb utility.

As shown in Figure 3-4, I query the *coffees* endpoint for all coffees currently in our list. HTTPie defaults to a GET request and assumes *localhost* if no hostname is provided, reducing unnecessary typing. As expected, we see all four coffees with which we prepopulated our list.

```
mheckler-a01 :: ~ » http :8080/coffees
HTTP/1.1 200
Connection: keep-alive
Content-Type: application/json
Date: Thu, 19 Nov 2020 00:04:42 GMT
Keep-Alive: timeout=60
Transfer-Encoding: chunked

[
    {
        "id": "41ba3a26-b94c-4ab2-84ff-71a8ab63aad9",
        "name": "Café Cereza"
    },
    {
        "id": "686ed31a-0719-4907-b4ec-d79f41c8be2d",
        "name": "Café Ganador"
    },
    {
        "id": "f96da5f2-ede8-4862-aa81-ea4c3a5b626a",
        "name": "Café Lareño"
    },
    {
        "id": "11f1dcef-7808-4971-99fc-0cc1458baff2",
        "name": "Café Três Pontas"
    }
]
```

Figure 3-4. GET-ting all coffees

Next, I copy the id field for one of the coffees just listed and paste it into another GET request. Figure 3-5 displays the correct response.

```
mheckler-a01 :: ~ » http :8080/coffees/41ba3a26-b94c-4ab2-84ff-71a8ab63aad9
HTTP/1.1 200
Connection: keep-alive
Content-Type: application/json
Date: Thu, 19 Nov 2020 00:09:10 GMT
Keep-Alive: timeout=60
Transfer-Encoding: chunked

{
    "id": "41ba3a26-b94c-4ab2-84ff-71a8ab63aad9",
    "name": "Café Cereza"
}
```

Figure 3-5. GET-ting a coffee

To execute a POST request with HTTPie is simple: just pipe a plaintext file containing a JSON representation of a Coffee object with id and name fields, and HTTPie assumes that a POST operation is in order. Figure 3-6 shows the command and its successful outcome.

```
mheckler-a01 :: ~/dev » http :8080/coffees < coffee.json
HTTP/1.1 200
Connection: keep-alive
Content-Type: application/json
Date: Thu, 19 Nov 2020 00:10:48 GMT
Keep-Alive: timeout=60
Transfer-Encoding: chunked

{
    "id": "99999",
    "name": "Kaldi's Coffee"
}
```

Figure 3-6. POST-ing a new coffee to the list

As mentioned earlier, a `PUT` command should allow for updating an existing resource or adding a new one if the requested resource doesn't already exist. In Figure 3-7, I specify the `id` of the coffee I just added and pass another JSON object with a different name to the command. The result is that the coffee with `id` of "99999" now has a name of "Caribou Coffee" instead of "Kaldi's Coffee" as before. The return code is 200 (OK), as expected as well.

```
mheckler-a01 :: ~/dev » http PUT :8080/coffees/99999 < coffee2.json
HTTP/1.1 200
Connection: keep-alive
Content-Type: application/json
Date: Thu, 19 Nov 2020 00:12:13 GMT
Keep-Alive: timeout=60
Transfer-Encoding: chunked

{
    "id": "99999",
    "name": "Caribou Coffee"
}
```

Figure 3-7. PUT-ting an update to an existing coffee

In Figure 3-8 I initiate a `PUT` request in the same manner but reference an `id` in the URI that doesn't exist. The application dutifully adds it in compliance with IETF-specified behavior and correctly returns an HTTP status of 201 (Created).

```
mheckler-a01 :: ~/dev » http PUT :8080/coffees/88888 < coffee3.json
HTTP/1.1 201
Connection: keep-alive
Content-Type: application/json
Date: Thu, 19 Nov 2020 00:13:35 GMT
Keep-Alive: timeout=60
Transfer-Encoding: chunked

{
    "id": "88888",
    "name": "Motor Oil Coffee"
}
```

Figure 3-8. PUT-ting a new coffee

Creating a DELETE request with HTTPie is very similar to creating a PUT request: the HTTP verb must be specified, and the resource's URI must be complete. Figure 3-9 shows the result: an HTTP status code of 200 (OK), indicating the resource was successfully deleted and with no shown value, since the resource no longer exists.

```
mheckler-a01 :: ~/dev » http DELETE :8080/coffees/99999
HTTP/1.1 200
Connection: keep-alive
Content-Length: 0
Date: Thu, 19 Nov 2020 00:14:47 GMT
Keep-Alive: timeout=60
```

Figure 3-9. DELETE-ing a coffee

Finally, we re-query our full list of coffees to confirm the expected final state. As Figure 3-10 demonstrates, we now have one additional coffee that wasn't in our list before, as expected: Mötor Oil Coffee. API validation is a success.

```
mheckler-a01 :: ~/dev » http :8080/coffees
HTTP/1.1 200
Connection: keep-alive
Content-Type: application/json
Date: Thu, 19 Nov 2020 00:15:50 GMT
Keep-Alive: timeout=60
Transfer-Encoding: chunked

[
    {
        "id": "41ba3a26-b94c-4ab2-84ff-71a8ab63aa09",
        "name": "Café Cereza"
    },
    {
        "id": "686cd31a-0719-4907-b4ec-a79f41c83c2d",
        "name": "Café Ganador"
    },
    {
        "id": "f96da5f2-ede8-4862-aa81-ea4c3a5b626a",
        "name": "Café Lareño"
    },
    {
        "id": "11f1dcef-7808-4971-99fc-0cc1458baff2",
        "name": "Café Três Pontas"
    },
    {
        "id": "88888",
        "name": "Mötor Oil Coffee"
    }
]
```

Figure 3-10. GET-ting all coffees now in the list

Summary

This chapter demonstrated how to develop a basic working application using Spring Boot. Since most applications involve exposing backend cloud resources to users, usually via a frontend user interface, I showed how to create and evolve a useful REST API that can be consumed in numerous, consistent ways to provide needed functionality for creating, reading, updating, and deleting resources central to nearly every critical system.

I examined and explained the `@RequestMapping` annotation and its various convenience annotation specializations that align with defined HTTP verbs:

- `@GetMapping`
- `@PostMapping`
- `@PutMapping`
- `@PatchMapping`
- `@DeleteMapping`

After creating methods that addressed many of these annotations and their associated actions, I then refactored the code a bit to streamline it and provide HTTP response codes where required. Validating the API confirmed its correct operation.

In the next chapter, I discuss and demonstrate how to add database access to our Spring Boot application to make it increasingly useful and ready for production.

## CHAPTER 4

Adding Database Access to Your Spring Boot App

As discussed in the previous chapter, applications often expose stateless APIs for many very good reasons. Behind the scenes, however, very few useful applications are entirely ephemeral; state of some kind is usually stored for *something*. For example, every request to an online store's shopping cart may well include its state, but once the order is placed, that order's data is kept. There are many ways to do this, and many ways to share or route this data, but invariably there are one or more databases involved within nearly all systems of sufficient size.

In this chapter, I'll demonstrate how to add database access to the Spring Boot application created in the previous chapter. This chapter is meant to be a short primer on Spring Boot's data capabilities, and subsequent chapters will dive much deeper. But in many cases, the basics covered here still apply well and provide a fully sufficient solution. Let's dig in.

Code Checkout Checkup

Please check out branch *chapter4begin* from the code repository to begin.

Priming Autoconfig for Database Access

As demonstrated earlier, Spring Boot aims to simplify to the maximum extent possible the so-called 80–90% use case: the patterns of code and process that developers do over and over and over again. Once patterns are identified, Boot springs into action to initialize the required beans automatically, with sensible default configurations. Customizing a capability is as simple as providing one or more property values or creating a tailored version of one or more beans; once autoconfig detects the changes, it backs off and follows the developer's guidance. Database access is a perfect example.

What Do We Hope to Gain?

In our earlier example application, I used an `ArrayList` to store and maintain our list of coffees. This approach is straightforward enough for a single application, but it does have its drawbacks.

First, it isn't resilient at all. If your application or the platform running it fails, all changes made to the list while the app was running—whether for seconds or months—disappear.

Second, it doesn't scale. Starting another instance of the application results in that second (or subsequent) app instance having its own distinct list of coffees it maintains. Data isn't shared between the multiple instances, so changes to coffees made by one instance—new coffees, deletions, update—aren't visible to anyone accessing a different app instance.

Clearly this is no way to run a railroad.

I cover a few different ways to fully solve these very real problems in upcoming chapters. But for now, let's lay some groundwork that will serve as useful steps on the path there.

Adding a Database Dependency

In order to access a database from your Spring Boot application, you need a few things:

- A running database, whether initiated by/embedded within your application or simply accessible to your application
- Database drivers enabling programmatic access, usually provided by the database vendor
- A Spring Data module for accessing the target database

Certain Spring Data modules include the appropriate database drivers as a single selectable dependency from within the Spring Initializr. In other cases, such as when Spring uses the Java Persistence API (JPA) to access JPA-compliant datastores, it's necessary to choose the Spring Data JPA dependency *and* a dependency for the target database's specific driver, e.g., PostgreSQL.

To take the first step forward from memory constructs to persistent database, I'll begin by adding dependencies, and thus capabilities, to our project's build file.

H2 is a fast database written completely in Java that has some interesting and useful features. For one thing, it's JPA-compliant, so we can connect our application to it in the same manner we would to any other JPA database like Microsoft SQL, MySQL, Oracle, or PostgreSQL. It also has in-memory and disk-based modes. This allows us some useful options after we convert from our in-memory `ArrayList` to an in-memory database: we can either change H2 to disk-based persistence or—since we're now using a JPA database—change to a different JPA database. Either option becomes much simpler at that point.

To enable our application to interact with the H2 database, I'll add the following two dependencies to the `<dependencies>` section of our project's *pom.xml*:

```
<dependency>
    <groupId>org.springframework.boot</groupId>
    <artifactId>spring-boot-starter-data-jpa</artifactId>
</dependency>
<dependency>
    <groupId>com.h2database</groupId>
    <artifactId>h2</artifactId>
    <scope>runtime</scope>
</dependency>
```

The H2 database driver dependency's scope of `runtime` indicates that it will be present in the runtime and test classpath but not in the compile classpath. This is a good practice to adopt for libraries that are not required for compilation.

Once you save your updated *pom.xml* and (if necessary) reimport/refresh your Maven dependencies, you have access to the functionality included within the added dependencies. Next, it's time to write a bit of code to use it.

Adding Code

Since we already have code in place to manage coffees in some fashion, we'll need to refactor a bit while we add our new database capabilities. I find the best place to begin is with the domain class(es), in this case, `Coffee`.

The @Entity

As mentioned earlier, H2 is a JPA-compliant database, so I'll add JPA annotations to connect the dots. To the `Coffee` class itself I add an `@Entity` annotation from `javax.persistence` that indicates `Coffee` is a persistable entity, and to the existing `id` member variable, I add the `@Id` annotation (also from `javax.persistence`) to mark it as the database table's ID field.

If the class name—Coffee in this case—doesn't match the desired database table name, the @Entity annotation accepts a name parameter for specifying the data table name to match the annotated entity.

If your IDE is helpful enough, it may provide you feedback that something is still missing in the Coffee class. For example, IntelliJ underlines the class name in red and provides the helpful pop-up upon mouseover shown in Figure 4-1.

```
@Entity
class Coffee {
    @Id
    privat        Class 'Coffee' should have [public, protected] no-arg constructor    ⋮
    private String name;
```

Figure 4-1. Missing constructor in the JPA Coffee class

Java Persistence API requires a no-argument constructor for use when creating objects from database table rows, so I'll add that next. This results in our next IDE warning, as displayed in Figure 4-2: in order to have a no-arg constructor, we must make all member variables mutable, i.e., nonfinal.

```
@Entity
class Coffee {
    @Id
    private final String id;
    private Str   Variable 'id' might not have been initialized           ⋮
    public Coff   Add constructor parameter  ⌥⇧↵      More actions...  ⌥↵
    }
```

Figure 4-2. With a no-arg constructor, id cannot be final

Removing the final keyword from the declaration for the id member variable solves that. Making id mutable also requires our Coffee class to have a mutator method for id for JPA to be able to assign a value to that member, so I add the setId() method as well, as shown in Figure 4-3.

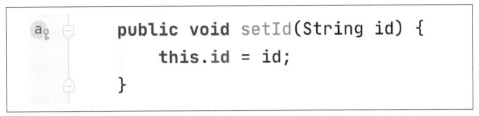

```
public void setId(String id) {
    this.id = id;
}
```

Figure 4-3. The new setId() method

The Repository

With `Coffee` now defined as a valid JPA entity able to be stored and retrieved, it's time to make the connection to the database

For such a simple concept, configuring and establishing a database connection in the Java ecosystem has long been a rather cumbersome affair. As mentioned in Chapter 1, using an application server to host a Java application required developers to perform several tedious steps just to get things ready. Once you started interacting with the database, or if you were accessing a datastore directly from a Java utility or client application, you would be expected to perform additional steps involving `Persisten ceUnit`, `EntityManagerFactory`, and `EntityManager` APIs (and possibly `DataSource` objects), open and close the database, and more. It's a lot of repetitive ceremony for something developers do so often.

Spring Data introduces the concept of repositories. A `Repository` is an interface defined in Spring Data as a useful abstraction above various databases. There are other mechanisms for accessing databases from Spring Data that will be explained in subsequent chapters, but the various flavors of `Repository` are arguably the most useful in the most cases.

`Repository` itself is a mere placeholder for the following types:

- The object stored in the database
- The object's unique ID/primary key field

There is a lot more to repositories, of course, and I cover a great deal of that in Chapter 6. For now, let's focus on two that are directly relevant to our current example: `CrudRepository` and `JpaRepository`.

Recall my earlier mention of the preferred practice of writing code to use the highest-level interface suited to purpose? While `JpaRepository` extends a handful of interfaces and thus incorporates broader functionality, `CrudRepository` covers all of the key CRUD capabilities and is sufficient for our (so far) simple application.

The first thing to do to enable repository support for our application is to define an interface specific to our application by extending a Spring Data `Repository` interface: .interfaceCoffeeRepo

```
interface CoffeeRepository extends CrudRepository<Coffee, String> {}
```

 The two types defined are the object type to store and the type of its unique ID.

This represents the simplest expression of repository creation within a Spring Boot app. It's possible, and very useful at times, to define queries for a repository; I'll dive into that in a future chapter as well. But here is the "magical" part: Spring Boot's auto-configuration takes into account the database driver on the classpath (in this case, H2), the repository interface defined in our application, and the JPA entity `Coffee` class definition and creates a database proxy bean *on our behalf*. No need to write lines of nearly identical boilerplate for every application when the patterns are this clear and consistent, which frees the developer to work on new, requested functionality.

The utility, aka "Springing" into action

Now to put that repository to work. I'll approach this step by step as in previous chapters, introducing functionality first and polishing afterward.

First, I'll autowire/inject the repository bean into `RestApiDemoController` so the controller can access it when receiving requests via the external API, as shown in Figure 4-4.

First I declare the member variable with:

```
private final CoffeeRepository coffeeRepository;
```

Next, I add it as a parameter to the constructor with:

```
public RestApiDemoController(CoffeeRepository coffeeRepository){}
```

 Prior to Spring Framework 4.3, it was necessary in all cases to add the `@Autowired` annotation above the method to indicate when a parameter represented a Spring bean to be autowired/injected. From 4.3 onward, a class with a single constructor doesn't require the annotation for autowired parameters, a useful time-saver.

```
@RestController
@RequestMapping("/coffees")
class RestApiDemoController {
    private final CoffeeRepository coffeeRepository;

    private List<Coffee> coffees = new ArrayList<>();

    public RestApiDemoController(CoffeeRepository coffeeRepository) {
        this.coffeeRepository = coffeeRepository;

        this.coffeeRepository.saveAll(List.of(
                new Coffee( name: "Café Cereza"),
                new Coffee( name: "Café Ganador"),
                new Coffee( name: "Café Lareño"),
                new Coffee( name: "Café Três Pontas")
        ));

        coffees.addAll(List.of(
                new Coffee( name: "Café Cereza"),
                new Coffee( name: "Café Ganador"),
                new Coffee( name: "Café Lareño"),
                new Coffee( name: "Café Três Pontas")
        ));
    }
```

Figure 4-4. Autowire repository into `RestApiDemoController`

With the repository in place, I delete the List<Coffee> member variable and change
the initial population of that list in the constructor to instead save the same coffees to
the repository, as in Figure 4-4.

Per Figure 4-5, removing the coffees variable immediately flags all references to it as
unresolvable symbols, so the next task is replacing those with appropriate repository
interactions.

```
@GetMapping
Iterable<Coffee> getCoffees() {
    return coffees;
}
            Cannot resolve symbol 'coffees'                    ⋮

            Create local variable 'coffees'  ⌥⇧↵    More actions...  ⌥↵
```

Figure 4-5. Replacing the removed *coffees* *member variable*

As a simple retrieval of all coffees with no parameters, the `getCoffees()` method is a great place to begin. Using the `findAll()` method built into `CrudRepository`, it isn't even necessary to change the return type of `getCoffees()` as it also returns an `Itera ble` type; simply calling `coffeeRepository.findAll()` and returning its result does the job, as shown here:

```
@GetMapping
Iterable<Coffee> getCoffees() {
    return coffeeRepository.findAll();
}
```

Refactoring the `getCoffeeById()` method presents some insights into how much simpler your code can be, thanks to the functionality that repositories bring to the mix. We no longer have to manually search the list of coffees for a matching `id`; `Cru dRepository`'s `findById()` method handles it for us, as demonstrated in the following code snippet. And since `findById()` returns an `Optional` type, no changes whatsoever are required for our method signature:

```
@GetMapping("/{id}")
Optional<Coffee> getCoffeeById(@PathVariable String id) {
    return coffeeRepository.findById(id);
}
```

Converting the `postCoffee()` method to use the repository is also a fairly straightforward endeavor, as shown here:

```
@PostMapping
Coffee postCoffee(@RequestBody Coffee coffee) {
    return coffeeRepository.save(coffee);
}
```

With the `putCoffee()` method, we again see some of the substantial time- and code-saving functionality of the `CrudRepository` on display. I use the built-in `exist sById()` repository method to determine if this is a new or existing `Coffee` and return the appropriate HTTP status code along with the saved `Coffee`, as shown in this listing:

```
@PutMapping("/{id}")
ResponseEntity<Coffee> putCoffee(@PathVariable String id,
                                  @RequestBody Coffee coffee) {

    return (!coffeeRepository.existsById(id))
            ? new ResponseEntity<>(coffeeRepository.save(coffee),
                HttpStatus.CREATED)
            : new ResponseEntity<>(coffeeRepository.save(coffee), HttpStatus.OK);
}
```

Finally, I update the `deleteCoffee()` method to use `CrudRepository`'s built-in `deleteById()` method, as shown here:

```
@DeleteMapping("/{id}")
void deleteCoffee(@PathVariable String id) {
    coffeeRepository.deleteById(id);
}
```

Leveraging a repository bean created using the fluent API of `CrudRepository` streamlines the code for the `RestApiDemoController` and makes it much clearer, in terms of both readability and understandability, as evidenced by the complete code listing:

```
@RestController
@RequestMapping("/coffees")
class RestApiDemoController {
    private final CoffeeRepository coffeeRepository;

    public RestApiDemoController(CoffeeRepository coffeeRepository) {
        this.coffeeRepository = coffeeRepository;

        this.coffeeRepository.saveAll(List.of(
                new Coffee("Café Cereza"),
                new Coffee("Café Ganador"),
                new Coffee("Café Lareño"),
                new Coffee("Café Três Pontas")
        ));
    }

    @GetMapping
    Iterable<Coffee> getCoffees() {
        return coffeeRepository.findAll();
    }

    @GetMapping("/{id}")
    Optional<Coffee> getCoffeeById(@PathVariable String id) {
        return coffeeRepository.findById(id);
    }

    @PostMapping
    Coffee postCoffee(@RequestBody Coffee coffee) {
        return coffeeRepository.save(coffee);
    }

    @PutMapping("/{id}")
    ResponseEntity<Coffee> putCoffee(@PathVariable String id,
                                     @RequestBody Coffee coffee) {

        return (!coffeeRepository.existsById(id))
                ? new ResponseEntity<>(coffeeRepository.save(coffee),
                HttpStatus.CREATED)
                : new ResponseEntity<>(coffeeRepository.save(coffee), HttpStatus.OK);
    }

    @DeleteMapping("/{id}")
    void deleteCoffee(@PathVariable String id) {
```

```
        coffeeRepository.deleteById(id);
    }
}
```

Now all that remains is to verify that our application works as expected and external functionality remains the same.

 An alternative approach to testing functionality—and a recommended practice—is to create unit tests first, a la Test Driven Development (TDD). I strongly recommend this approach in real-world software development environments, but I've found that when the goal is to demonstrate and explain discrete software development concepts, less is better; showing as little as possible to clearly communicate key concepts increases signal and decreases noise, even if the noise is useful later. As such, I cover testing in a dedicated chapter later in this book.

Saving and Retrieving Data

Once more unto the breach, dear friends, once more: accessing the API from the command line using HTTPie. Querying the *coffees* endpoint results in the same four coffees being returned from our H2 database as before, as shown in Figure 4-6.

Copying the id field for one of the coffees just listed and pasting it into a coffee-specific GET request produces the output shown in Figure 4-7.

```
mheckler-a01 :: ~ » http :8080/coffees
HTTP/1.1 200
Connection: keep-alive
Content-Type: application/json
Date: Wed, 25 Nov 2020 21:08:48 GMT
Keep-Alive: timeout=60
Transfer-Encoding: chunked

[
    {
        "id": "ff3d96e0-236e-4157-8b45-9e9699276d6d",
        "name": "Café Cereza"
    },
    {
        "id": "d7a0f2a1-38f7-46ef-a884-8beb43e655cf",
        "name": "Café Ganador"
    },
    {
        "id": "d5458c8c-f480-47dc-9926-42fcb1f4051d",
        "name": "Café Lareño"
    },
    {
        "id": "1726fcdf-94f9-4f7b-9e60-e6e1b453f56f",
        "name": "Café Três Pontas"
    }
]
```

Figure 4-6. GET-ting all coffees

```
mheckler-a01 :: ~ » http :8080/coffees/ff3d96e0-236e-4157-8b45-9e9699276d6d
HTTP/1.1 200
Connection: keep-alive
Content-Type: application/json
Date: Wed, 25 Nov 2020 21:20:18 GMT
Keep-Alive: timeout=60
Transfer-Encoding: chunked

{
    "id": "ff3d96e0-236e-4157-8b45-9e9699276d6d",
    "name": "Café Cereza"
}
```

Figure 4-7. GET-ting a coffee

In Figure 4-8, I POST a new coffee to the application and its database.

```
mheckler-a01 :: ~/dev » http :8080/coffees < coffee.json
HTTP/1.1 200
Connection: keep-alive
Content-Type: application/json
Date: Wed, 25 Nov 2020 21:22:17 GMT
Keep-Alive: timeout=60
Transfer-Encoding: chunked

{
    "id": "99999",
    "name": "Kaldi's Coffee"
}
```

Figure 4-8. POST-ing a new coffee to the list

As discussed in the previous chapter, a PUT command should allow for updating an existing resource or adding a new one if the requested resource doesn't already exist. In Figure 4-9, I specify the id of the coffee just added and pass to the command a JSON object with a change to that coffee's name. After the update, the coffee with the id of "99999" now has a name of "Caribou Coffee" instead of "Kaldi's Coffee", and the return code is 200 (OK), as expected.

```
mheckler-a01 :: ~/dev » http PUT :8080/coffees/99999 < coffee2.json
HTTP/1.1 200
Connection: keep-alive
Content-Type: application/json
Date: Wed, 25 Nov 2020 21:24:04 GMT
Keep-Alive: timeout=60
Transfer-Encoding: chunked

{
    "id": "99999",
    "name": "Caribou Coffee"
}
```

Figure 4-9. PUT-ting an update to an existing coffee

Next I initiate a similar `PUT` request but specify an `id` in the URI that doesn't exist. The application adds a new coffee to the database in compliance with IETF-specified behavior and correctly returns an HTTP status of 201 (Created), as shown in Figure 4-10.

```
mheckler-a01 :: ~/dev » http PUT :8080/coffees/88888 < coffee3.json
HTTP/1.1 201
Connection: keep-alive
Content-Type: application/json
Date: Wed, 25 Nov 2020 21:25:28 GMT
Keep-Alive: timeout=60
Transfer-Encoding: chunked

{
    "id": "88888",
    "name": "Mötor Oil Coffee"
}
```

Figure 4-10. PUT-ting a new coffee

Finally, I test deletion of a specified coffee by issuing a `DELETE` request, which returns only an HTTP status code of 200 (OK), indicating the resource was successfully deleted and nothing else, since the resource no longer exists, per Figure 4-11. To check our end state, we once again query the full list of coffees (Figure 4-12).

```
mheckler-a01 :: ~/dev » http DELETE :8080/coffees/99999
HTTP/1.1 200
Connection: keep-alive
Content-Length: 0
Date: Wed, 25 Nov 2020 21:26:55 GMT
Keep-Alive: timeout=60
```

Figure 4-11. DELETE-ing a coffee

```
mheckler-a01 :: ~/dev » http :8080/coffees
HTTP/1.1 200
Connection: keep-alive
Content-Type: application/json
Date: Wed, 25 Nov 2020 21:28:20 GMT
Keep-Alive: timeout=60
Transfer-Encoding: chunked

[
    {
        "id": "ff3d96e0-236e-4157-8b45-9e9699276d6d",
        "name": "Café Cereza"
    },
    {
        "id": "d7a0f2a1-38f7-46ef-a884-8beb43e655cf",
        "name": "Café Ganador"
    },
    {
        "id": "d5458c8c-f480-47dc-9926-42fcb1f4051d",
        "name": "Café Lareño"
    },
    {
        "id": "1726fcdf-94f9-4f7b-9e60-e6e1b453f56f",
        "name": "Café Três Pontas"
    },
    {
        "id": "88888",
        "name": "Mötor Oil Coffee"
    }
]
```

Figure 4-12. GET-ting all coffees now in the list

As before, we now have one additional coffee that wasn't initially in our repository: Mötor Oil Coffee.

A Bit of Polishing

As always, there are many areas that could benefit from additional attention, but I'll confine the focus to two: extracting the initial population of sample data to a separate component and a bit of condition reordering for clarity.

Last chapter I populated the list of coffees with some initial values in the `RestApiDemo`
`Controller` class, so I maintained that same structure—until now—in this chapter
after converting to a database with repository access. A better practice is to extract
that functionality to a separate component that can be enabled or disabled quickly
and easily.

There are many ways to execute code automatically upon application startup, including using a `CommandLineRunner` or `ApplicationRunner` and specifying a lambda to
accomplish the desired goal: in this case, creating and saving sample data. But I prefer
using an `@Component` class and an `@PostConstruct` method to accomplish the same
thing for the following reasons:

- When `CommandLineRunner` and `ApplicationRunner` bean-producing methods
  autowire a repository bean, unit tests that mock the repository bean within the
  test (as is typically the case) break.

- If you mock the repository bean within the test or wish to run the application
  without creating sample data, it's quick and easy to disable the actual data-
  populating bean simply by commenting out its `@Component` annotation.

I recommend creating a `DataLoader` class similar to the one shown in the following
code block. Extracting the logic to create sample data to the `DataLoader` class's `load`
`Data()` method and annotating it with `@PostContruct` restores `RestApiDemoControl`
`ler` to its intended single purpose of providing an external API and makes the
`DataLoader` responsible for *its* intended (and obvious) purpose:

```java
@Component
class DataLoader {
    private final CoffeeRepository coffeeRepository;

    public DataLoader(CoffeeRepository coffeeRepository) {
        this.coffeeRepository = coffeeRepository;
    }

    @PostConstruct
    private void loadData() {
        coffeeRepository.saveAll(List.of(
                new Coffee("Café Cereza"),
                new Coffee("Café Ganador"),
                new Coffee("Café Lareño"),
                new Coffee("Café Três Pontas")
        ));
    }
}
```

The other dab of polishing is an admittedly small adjustment to the boolean condition of the ternary operator within the `putCoffee()` method. After refactoring the
method to use a repository, no compelling justification remains for evaluating the
negative condition first. Removing the not (!) operator from the condition slightly

improves clarity; swapping the true and false values of the ternary operator are of course required to maintain the original outcomes, as reflected in the following code:

```
@PutMapping("/{id}")
ResponseEntity<Coffee> putCoffee(@PathVariable String id,
                                @RequestBody Coffee coffee) {

    return (coffeeRepository.existsById(id))
            ? new ResponseEntity<>(coffeeRepository.save(coffee),
                HttpStatus.OK)
            : new ResponseEntity<>(coffeeRepository.save(coffee),
                HttpStatus.CREATED);
}
```

Code Checkout Checkup

For complete chapter code, please check out branch *chapter4end* from the code repository.

Summary

This chapter demonstrated how to add database access to the Spring Boot application created in the last chapter. While it was meant to be a concise introduction to Spring Boot's data capabilities, I provided an overview of the following:

- Java database access
- The Java Persistence API (JPA)
- The H2 database
- Spring Data JPA
- Spring Data repositories
- Mechanisms to create sample data via repositories

Subsequent chapters will dive much deeper into Spring Boot database access, but the basics covered in this chapter supply a solid foundation upon which to build and, in many cases, are sufficient by themselves.

In the next chapter, I'll discuss and demonstrate useful tools Spring Boot provides to gain insights into your applications when things aren't functioning as expected or when you need to verify that they are.

## CHAPTER 5

Configuring and Inspecting Your Spring Boot App

There are many things that can go wrong with any application, and some of these many things may even have simple solutions. With the rare exception of an occasional good guess, however, one must determine the root cause of a problem before it is possible to truly solve it.

Debugging Java or Kotlin applications—or any other applications, for that matter—is a fundamental skill that every developer should learn very early on in their career and refine and expand throughout. I don't find that to be the case universally, so if you haven't already become handy with the debugging capabilities of your language and tools of choice, please explore the options at your disposal as soon as possible. It really is important in everything you develop and can save you inordinate amounts of time.

That said, debugging code is only one level of establishing, identifying, and isolating behaviors manifested within your application. As applications become more dynamic and distributed, developers often need to do the following:

- Configure and reconfigure applications dynamically
- Determine/confirm current settings and their origins
- Inspect and monitor application environment and health indicators
- Temporarily adjust logging levels of live apps to identify root causes

This chapter demonstrates how to use Spring Boot's built-in configuration capabilities, its Autoconfiguration Report, and Spring Boot Actuator to create, identify, and modify application environment settings flexibly and dynamically.

Code Checkout Checkup

Please check out branch *chapter5begin* from the code repository to begin.

Application Configuration

No app is an island.

Most times when I say that, it's to point out the truism that in nearly every case, an application doesn't provide all of its utility without interaction with other applications/services. But there is another meaning that is just as true: no application can be as useful without access to its environment, in one form or another. A static, unconfigurable app is rigid, inflexible, and hobbled.

Spring Boot applications supply a variety of powerful mechanisms for developers to dynamically configure and reconfigure their applications, even while the app is running. These mechanisms leverage the Spring Environment to manage configuration properties from all sources, including the following:

- Spring Boot Developer Tools (devtools) global settings properties in the *$HOME/.config/spring-boot* directory when devtools is active.
- @TestPropertySource annotations on tests.
- properties attribute on tests, available on @SpringBootTest and the various test annotations for testing an application slice.
- Command line arguments.
- Properties from SPRING_APPLICATION_JSON (inline JSON embedded in an environment variable or system property).
- ServletConfig init parameters.
- ServletContext init parameters.
- JNDI attributes from *java:comp/env*.
- Java System properties (System.getProperties()).
- OS environment variables.
- A RandomValuePropertySource that has properties only in random.*.
- Profile-specific application properties outside of the packaged jar (*application-{profile}.properties* and YAML variants).
- Profile-specific application properties packaged inside the jar (*application-{profile}.properties* and YAML variants).

- Application properties outside of the packaged jar (*application.properties* and YAML variants).

- Application properties packaged inside the jar (*application.properties* and YAML variants).

- @PropertySource annotations on @Configuration classes; note that such property sources are not added to the Environment until the application context is refreshed, which is too late to configure certain properties read before refresh begins, such as logging.* and spring.main.*.

- Default properties specified by setting SpringApplication.setDefaultProperties. NOTE: The preceding property sources are listed in decreasing order of precedence: properties from sources higher in the list supersede identical properties from lower sources.[1]

All of these can be extremely useful, but I'll choose a few in particular for the code scenarios in this chapter:

- Command line arguments
- OS environment variables
- Application properties packaged inside the jar (*application.properties* and YAML variants)

Let's begin with properties defined in the app's *application.properties* file and work our way up the food chain.

@Value

The @Value annotation is perhaps the most straightforward approach to ingesting configuration settings into your code. Built around pattern-matching and the Spring Expression Language (SpEL), it's simple and powerful.

I'll start by defining a single property in our application's *application.properties* file, as shown in Figure 5-1.

---

1 Order of precedence for Spring Boot PropertySources (*https://oreil.ly/OrderPredSB*).

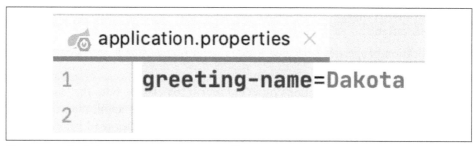

Figure 5-1. Defining `greeting-name` *in application.properties*

To show how to put this property to use, I create an additional `@RestController` within the application to handle tasks related to greeting application users, as demonstrated in Figure 5-2.

```
@RestController
@RequestMapping("/greeting")
class GreetingController {
    @Value("${greeting-name: Mirage}")
    private String name;

    @GetMapping
    String getGreeting() {
        return name;
    }
}
```

Figure 5-2. Greeting `@RestController` *class*

Note that the `@Value` annotation applies to the `name` member variable and accepts a single parameter of type `String` called `value`. I define the `value` using SpEL, placing the variable name (as the expression to evaluate) between the delimiters `${` and `}`. One other thing of note: SpEL allows for a default value after the colon—in this example, "Mirage"—for cases in which the variable isn't defined in the app `Environ ment`.

Upon executing the application and querying the *greeting* endpoint, the app responds with "Dakota" as expected, shown in Figure 5-3.

```
mheckler-a01 :: ~/dev » http :8080/greeting
HTTP/1.1 200
Connection: keep-alive
Content-Length: 6
Content-Type: text/plain;charset=UTF-8
Date: Fri, 27 Nov 2020 15:24:32 GMT
Keep-Alive: timeout=60

Dakota
```

Figure 5-3. Greeting response with defined property value

To verify the default value is being evaluated, I comment out the following line in *application.properties* with a # as follows and restart the application:

```
#greeting-name=Dakota
```

Querying the *greeting* endpoint now results in the response shown in Figure 5-4. Since greeting-name is no longer defined in any source for the application's Environment, the default value of "Mirage" kicks in, as expected.

```
mheckler-a01 :: ~/dev » http :8080/greeting
HTTP/1.1 200
Connection: keep-alive
Content-Length: 7
Content-Type: text/plain;charset=UTF-8
Date: Fri, 27 Nov 2020 15:28:28 GMT
Keep-Alive: timeout=60

Mirage
```

Figure 5-4. Greeting response with default value

Using @Value with roll-your-own properties provides another useful capability: the value of one property can be derived/built using the value of another.

To demonstrate how property nesting works, we'll need at least two properties. I create a second property greeting-coffee in *application.properties*, as in Figure 5-5.

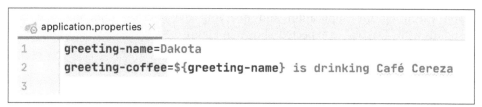

```
  application.properties  ×
1     greeting-name=Dakota
2     greeting-coffee=${greeting-name} is drinking Café Cereza
3
```

Figure 5-5. Property value feeding another property

Next, I add a bit of code to our `GreetingController` to represent a coffee-fied greeting and an endpoint we can access to see the results. Note that I provide a default value for `coffee`'s value as well, per Figure 5-6.

```
@RestController
@RequestMapping("/greeting")
class GreetingController {
    @Value("${greeting-name: Mirage}")
    private String name;

    @Value("${greeting-coffee: ${greeting-name} is drinking Café Ganador}")
    private String coffee;

    @GetMapping
    String getGreeting() {
        return name;
    }


    @GetMapping("/coffee")
    String getNameAndCoffee() {
        return coffee;
    }
}
```

Figure 5-6. Adding a coffee greeting to `GreetingController`

To verify the proper outcome, I restart the application and query the new */greeting/coffee* endpoint, resulting in the output shown in Figure 5-7. Note that since both properties in question are defined in *application.properties*, the values displayed are consistent with those values' definitions.

```
mheckler-a01 :: ~/dev » http :8080/greeting/coffee
HTTP/1.1 200
Connection: keep-alive
Content-Length: 30
Content-Type: text/plain;charset=UTF-8
Date: Fri, 27 Nov 2020 15:36:51 GMT
Keep-Alive: timeout=60

Dakota is drinking Cafe Cereza
```

Figure 5-7. Querying the coffee greeting endpoint

As with all things in life and software development, @Value does have some limitations. Since we provided a default value for the greeting-coffee property, we can
comment out its definition in *application.properties*, and the @Value annotation still
properly processes its (default) value using the coffee member variable within Gree
tingController. However, commenting out both greeting-name and greeting-
coffee in the properties file results in no Environment source actually defining them,
further resulting in the following error when the application attempts to initialize the
GreetingController bean using a reference to (now-undefined) greeting-name
within greeting-coffee:

```
org.springframework.beans.factory.BeanCreationException:
    Error creating bean with name 'greetingController':
        Injection of autowired dependencies failed; nested exception is
        java.lang.IllegalArgumentException:
            Could not resolve placeholder 'greeting-name' in value
            "greeting-coffee: ${greeting-name} is drinking Cafe Ganador"
```

Full stacktrace removed for brevity and clarity.

Another limitation with properties defined in *application.properties* and used solely
via @Value: they aren't recognized by the IDE as being used by the application, as
they're only referenced in the code within quote-delimited String variables; as such,
there is no direct tie-in to code. Of course, developers can visually check for correct
spelling of property names and usage, but this is entirely manual and thus more
prone to error.

As you might imagine, a typesafe and tool-verifiable mechanism for property use and
definition would be a better all-around option.

@ConfigurationProperties

Appreciating the flexibility of `@Value` but recognizing its shortcomings, the Spring team created `@ConfigurationProperties`. Using `@ConfigurationProperties`, a developer can define properties, group related properties, and reference/use them in a tool-verifiable and typesafe way.

For example, if a property is defined in an app's *application.properties* file that isn't used in code, the developer will see the name highlighted to flag it as a confirmed unused property. Similarly, if the property is defined as a `String` but associated with a differently typed member variable, the IDE will point out the type mismatch. These are valuable helps that catch simple, but frequent, mistakes.

To demonstrate how to put `@ConfigurationProperties` to work, I'll start by defining a POJO to encapsulate the desired related properties: in this case, our `greeting-name` and `greeting-coffee` properties previously referenced. As shown in the code that follows, I create a `Greeting` class to hold both:

```
class Greeting {
    private String name;
    private String coffee;

    public String getName() {
        return name;
    }

    public void setName(String name) {
        this.name = name;
    }

    public String getCoffee() {
        return coffee;
    }

    public void setCoffee(String coffee) {
        this.coffee = coffee;
    }
}
```

In order to register `Greeting` to manage configuration properties, I add the `@Configu rationProperties` annotation shown in Figure 5-8 and specify the `prefix` to use for all `Greeting` properties. This annotation prepares the class for use only with configuration properties; the application also must be told to process classes annotated in such manner for properties to include in the application `Environment`. Note the helpful error message that results:

```
@ConfigurationProperties(prefix = "greeting")
class Greetin   Not registered via @EnableConfigurationProperties, marked as Spring component, or  ⋮
    private S   scanned via @ConfigurationPropertiesScan
    private S
                org.springframework.boot.context.properties
    public St   @Target({ElementType.TYPE,ElementType.METHOD})
        retur   @Retention(RetentionPolicy.RUNTIME)
                @Documented
    }           public interface ConfigurationProperties
                extends annotation.Annotation
    public vo   ▓ Maven: org.springframework.boot:spring-boot:2.4.0                               ⋮
        this...
    }

    public String getCoffee() {
        return coffee;
    }

    public void setCoffee(String coffee) {
        this.coffee = coffee;
    }
}
```

Figure 5-8. Annotation and error

Instructing the application to process @ConfigurationProperties classes and add their properties to the app's Environment is, in most cases, best accomplished by adding the @ConfigurationPropertiesScan annotation to the main application class, as demonstrated here:

```
@SpringBootApplication
@ConfigurationPropertiesScan
public class SburRestDemoApplication {

    public static void main(String[] args) {
        SpringApplication.run(SburRestDemoApplication.class, args);
    }

}
```

The exceptions to the rule of having Boot scan for @Configuration Properties classes are if you need to enable certain @Configura tionProperties classes conditionally or if you are creating your own autoconfiguration. In all other cases, however, @Configura tionPropertiesScan should be used to scan for and enable @Con figurationProperties classes in like manner to Boot's component scanning mechanism.

In order to generate metadata using the annotation processor, enabling the IDE to connect the dots between @ConfigurationProperties classes and related properties defined in the *application.properties* file, I add the following dependency to the project's *pom.xml* build file:

```
<dependency>
    <groupId>org.springframework.boot</groupId>
    <artifactId>spring-boot-configuration-processor</artifactId>
    <optional>true</optional>
</dependency>
```

 This dependency also can be selected and added automatically from the Spring Initializr at the time of project creation.

Once the configuration processor dependency is added to the build file, it's necessary to refresh/reimport the dependencies and rebuild the project to take advantage of them. To reimport deps, I open the Maven menu in IntelliJ and click the Reimport button at the top left, as shown in Figure 5-9.

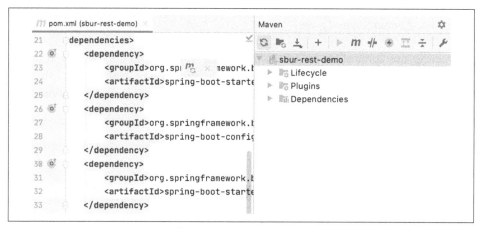

Figure 5-9. Reimporting project dependencies

 Unless the option is disabled, IntelliJ also presents a small button over the changed *pom.xml* to allow for a quick reimport without needing to open the Maven menu. The overlaid reimport button, a small *m* with a circular arrow on its bottom left portion, can be seen in Figure 5-9 hovering over the first dependency's `<groupid>` entry; it disappears when reimport is complete.

Once dependencies are updated, I rebuild the project from the IDE to incorporate the configuration processor.

Now, to define some values for these properties. Returning to *application.properties*, when I begin typing `greeting`, the IDE helpfully shows property names that match, as demonstrated in Figure 5-10.

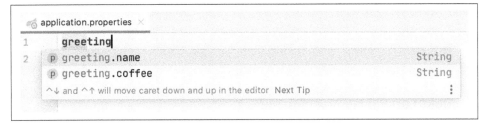

Figure 5-10. Full IDE property support for @ConfigurationProperties

To use these properties instead of the ones we were using before, a bit of refactoring is required.

I can do away entirely with `GreetingController`'s own member variables `name` and `coffee` along with their `@Value` annotations; instead, I create a member variable for the `Greeting` bean that now manages `greeting.name` and `greeting.coffee` properties and inject it into `GreetingController` via constructor injection, as shown in the following code:

```
@RestController
@RequestMapping("/greeting")
class GreetingController {
    private final Greeting greeting;

    public GreetingController(Greeting greeting) {
        this.greeting = greeting;
    }

    @GetMapping
    String getGreeting() {
        return greeting.getName();
    }

    @GetMapping("/coffee")
    String getNameAndCoffee() {
        return greeting.getCoffee();
    }
}
```

Running the application and querying the *greeting* and *greeting/coffee* endpoints results in the outcomes captured in Figure 5-11.

```
mheckler-a01 :: ~/dev » http :8080/greeting
HTTP/1.1 200
Connection: keep-alive
Content-Length: 6
Content-Type: text/plain;charset=UTF-8
Date: Fri, 27 Nov 2020 16:37:52 GMT
Keep-Alive: timeout=60

Dakota

mheckler-a01 :: ~/dev » http :8080/greeting/coffee
HTTP/1.1 200
Connection: keep-alive
Content-Length: 30
Content-Type: text/plain;charset=UTF-8
Date: Fri, 27 Nov 2020 16:37:57 GMT
Keep-Alive: timeout=60

Dakota is drinking Cafe Cereza
```

Figure 5-11. Retrieving Greeting properties

Properties managed by an @ConfigurationProperties bean still obtain their values from the Environment and all of its potential sources; the only significant thing missing in comparison to @Value-based properties is the ability to specify a default value at the annotated member variable. That is less of a sacrifice than it might appear to be at first glance because the app's *application.properties* file typically serves as the place for defining sensible defaults for an application. If there is a need for different property values to accommodate different deployment environments, those environment-specific values are ingested into the application's Environment via other sources, e.g., environment variables or command line parameters. In short, @ConfigurationProperties simply enforces the better practice for default property values.

Potential Third-Party Option

A further extension to the already impressive usefulness of @ConfigurationProperties is the ability to wrap third-party components and incorporate their properties into the application's Environment. To demonstrate how, I create a POJO to simulate a component that might be incorporated into the application. Note that in typical use cases where this feature is handiest, one would add an external dependency to the project and consult the component's documentation to determine the class from which to create a Spring bean, rather than creating one by hand as I do here.

In the code listing that follows, I create the simulated third-party component called Droid with two properties—id and description—and their associated accessor and mutator methods:

```
class Droid {
    private String id, description;

    public String getId() {
        return id;
    }

    public void setId(String id) {
        this.id = id;
    }

    public String getDescription() {
        return description;
    }

    public void setDescription(String description) {
        this.description = description;
    }
}
```

The next step falls into place the same way a true third-party component would: instantiating the component as a Spring bean. Spring beans can be created from defined POJOs in several ways, but the one most appropriate to this particular use case is to create an @Bean-annotated method within a class annotated with @Configuration, either directly or via a meta-annotation.

One meta-annotation that incorporates @Configuration within its definition is @SpringBootApplication, which is found on the main application class. That's why developers often place bean creation methods there.

 Within IntelliJ and most other IDEs and advanced text editors with solid Spring support, it's possible to drill into Spring meta-annotations to explore the annotations nested within. In IntelliJ, Cmd+LeftMouseClick (on MacOS) will expand the annotation. @SpringBootApplication includes @SpringBootConfiguration, which includes @Configuration, making only two degrees of separation from Kevin Bacon.

In the following code listing I demonstrate the bean creation method and the requisite @ConfigurationProperties annotation and prefix parameter, indicating that Droid properties should be incorporated within the Environment under the top-level property grouping droid:

```
@SpringBootApplication
@ConfigurationPropertiesScan
public class SburRestDemoApplication {

    public static void main(String[] args) {
        SpringApplication.run(SburRestDemoApplication.class, args);
    }

    @Bean
    @ConfigurationProperties(prefix = "droid")
    Droid createDroid() {
        return new Droid();
    }
}
```

As before, it is necessary to rebuild the project for the configuration processor to detect the properties exposed by this new source of configuration properties. After executing a build, we can return to *application.properties* and see that both droid properties have now surfaced complete with type information, as per Figure 5-12.

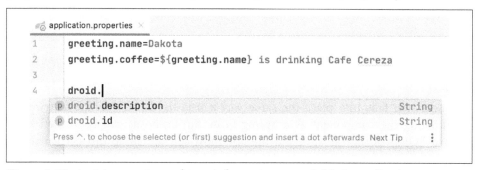

Figure 5-12. droid properties and type information now visible in application.properties

I assign some default values to droid.id and droid.description for use as defaults, as shown in Figure 5-13. This is a good habit to adopt for all Environment properties, even those obtained from third parties.

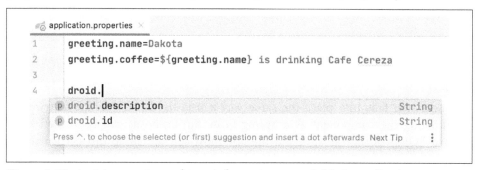

Figure 5-13. droid properties with default values assigned in application.properties

In order to verify that everything works as expected with the Droid's properties, I create a very simple @RestController with a single @GetMapping method, as shown in the code that follows:

```
@RestController
@RequestMapping("/droid")
class DroidController {
    private final Droid droid;

    public DroidController(Droid droid) {
        this.droid = droid;
    }

    @GetMapping
    Droid getDroid() {
        return droid;
    }
}
```

After building and running the project, I query the new */droid* endpoint and confirm the appropriate response, as indicated in Figure 5-14.

```
mheckler-a01 :: ~/dev » http :8080/droid
HTTP/1.1 200
Connection: keep-alive
Content-Type: application/json
Date: Fri, 27 Nov 2020 17:29:29 GMT
Keep-Alive: timeout=60
Transfer-Encoding: chunked

{
    "description": "Small, rolling android. Probably doesn't drink coffee.",
    "id": "BB-8"
}
```

Figure 5-14. Querying the /droid endpoint to retrieve properties from the Droid

Autoconfiguration Report

As mentioned previously, Boot does a *lot* on behalf of developers via autoconfiguration: setting up the application with the beans it needs to fulfill the functionalities that are part and parcel to chosen capabilities, dependencies, and code. Also mentioned earlier is the ability to override any bit of autoconfiguration necessary to implement functionality in a more specific (to your use case) manner. But how can one see what beans are created, what beans aren't created, and what conditions prompted either outcome?

It's a simple matter to produce the autoconfiguration report using the debug flag in one of several ways, owing to the flexibility of the JVM:

- Executing the application's jar file with the --debug option: java -jar bootap plication.jar --debug

- Executing the application's jar file with a JVM parameter: java -Ddebug=true -jar bootapplication.jar

- Adding debug=true to your application's *application.properties* file
- Executing export DEBUG=true in your shell (Linux or Mac) or adding it to your Windows environment, then running java -jar bootapplication.jar

 Any way to add an affirmative value for debug to the application's Environment, as discussed earlier, will provide the same results. These are just more frequently used options.

The autoconfiguration report's section listing positive matches—those conditions that evaluated to true and caused an action to take place—are listed within a section headed by "Positive matches." I've copied that section header here, along with one example of a positive match and its resultant autoconfiguration action:

```
=============================
CONDITIONS EVALUATION REPORT
=============================

Positive matches:
-----------------
    DataSourceAutoConfiguration matched:
        - @ConditionalOnClass found required classes 'javax.sql.DataSource',
        'org.springframework.jdbc.datasource.embedded.EmbeddedDatabaseType'
        (OnClassCondition)
```

This particular match demonstrates what we expected to happen, although it's always good to confirm the following:

- JPA and H2 are application dependencies.
- JPA works with SQL datasources.
- H2 is an embedded database.
- Classes were found that support embedded SQL datasources.

As a result, DataSourceAutoConfiguration is invoked.

Similarly, the "Negative matches" section displays actions not taken by Spring Boot's autoconfiguration and why, as illustrated in the following:

```
Negative matches:
-----------------
    ActiveMQAutoConfiguration:
        Did not match:
            - @ConditionalOnClass did not find required class
            'javax.jms.ConnectionFactory' (OnClassCondition)
```

In this case, `ActiveMQAutoConfiguration` was not performed because the application didn't find the JMS `ConnectionFactory` class upon startup.

Another useful tidbit is the section listing "Unconditional classes," which are created without having to satisfy any conditions. I've listed one next that is of particular interest given the previous section:

```
Unconditional classes:
---------------------
    org.springframework.boot.autoconfigure.context
    .ConfigurationPropertiesAutoConfiguration
```

As you can see, `ConfigurationPropertiesAutoConfiguration` is always instantiated to manage any `ConfigurationProperties` created and referenced within a Spring Boot application; it's integral to every Spring Boot app.

Actuator

actuator
> n. One that actuates specifically: a mechanical device for moving or controlling something

The original version of Spring Boot Actuator reached General Availability (GA) in 2014 and was hailed for providing valuable insights into production Boot applications. Providing monitoring and management capabilities of running apps via HTTP endpoints or Java Management Extensions (JMX), Actuator encompasses and exposes all of Spring Boot's production-ready features.

Completely retooled with the 2.0 version of Spring Boot, Actuator now leverages the Micrometer instrumentation library to provide metrics via a consistent façade from numerous leading monitoring systems, similar to how SLF4J operates with regard to various logging mechanisms. This dramatically extends the scope of things that can be integrated, monitored, and exposed via Actuator within any given Spring Boot application.

To get started with Actuator, I add another dependency to the current project's `pom.xml` dependencies section. As shown in the following snippet, the `spring-boot-starter-actuator` dependency provides the necessary capabilities; to do so, it brings with it both Actuator itself and Micrometer, along with autoconfiguration capabilities to slide into place within a Spring Boot application with nearly zero effort:

```
<dependencies>
    ... (other dependencies omitted for brevity)
    <dependency>
        <groupId>org.springframework.boot</groupId>
        <artifactId>spring-boot-starter-actuator</artifactId>
    </dependency>
</dependencies>
```

After refreshing/reimporting dependencies once more, I rerun the application. With the application running, we can see what information Actuator exposes by default by accessing its primary endpoint. Again, I use HTTPie to accomplish this, as per Figure 5-15.

```
mheckler-a01 :: ~/dev » http :8080/actuator
HTTP/1.1 200
Connection: keep-alive
Content-Type: application/vnd.spring-boot.actuator.v3+json
Date: Fri, 27 Nov 2020 17:34:29 GMT
Keep-Alive: timeout=60
Transfer-Encoding: chunked

{
    "_links": {
        "health": {
            "href": "http://localhost:8080/actuator/health",
            "templated": false
        },
        "health-path": {
            "href": "http://localhost:8080/actuator/health/{*path}",
            "templated": true
        },
        "info": {
            "href": "http://localhost:8080/actuator/info",
            "templated": false
        },
        "self": {
            "href": "http://localhost:8080/actuator",
            "templated": false
        }
    }
}
```

Figure 5-15. Accessing Actuator endpoint, default configuration

 All Actuator information is grouped together under the app's */actuator* endpoint by default, but this too is configurable.

This doesn't seem like much information for the fanfare (and fanbase) that Actuator has created. But this terseness is intentional.

Actuator has access to and can expose a great deal of information about running applications. This information can be incredibly useful to developers, operational personnel, and also nefarious individuals who might desire to threaten your application's security. Following Spring Security's de facto goal of *secure by default*, Actuator's autoconfiguration exposes very limited *health* and *info* responses—in fact, *info* defaults to an empty set—that provide an application heartbeat and little else out of the box (OOTB).

As with most things Spring, you can create some pretty sophisticated mechanisms for controlling access to various Actuator data feeds, but there are fast, consistent, and low-friction options available as well. Let's take a look at those now.

It's possible to easily configure Actuator via properties with either a set of included endpoints or a set of excluded endpoints. For simplicity's sake, I choose the inclusion route, adding the following to *application.properties*:

```
management.endpoints.web.exposure.include=env, info, health
```

In this example, I direct the app (and Actuator) to expose only the */actuator/env*, */actuator/info*, and */actuator/health* endpoints (and any subordinate endpoints).

Figure 5-16 confirms the expected outcome upon rerunning the application and querying its */actuator* endpoint.

In order to fully demonstrate Actuator's OOTB capabilities, I can go a step further and disable security entirely *for demonstration purposes only* by using a wildcard with the aforementioned *application.properties* setting:

```
management.endpoints.web.exposure.include=*
```

 This point is impossible to overstate: security mechanisms for sensitive data should be disabled only for demonstration or verification purposes. *NEVER DISABLE SECURITY FOR PRODUCTION APPLICATIONS.*

```
mheckler-a01 :: ~/dev » http :8080/actuator
HTTP/1.1 200
Connection: keep-alive
Content-Type: application/vnd.spring-boot.actuator.v3+json
Date: Fri, 27 Nov 2020 17:38:30 GMT
Keep-Alive: timeout=60
Transfer-Encoding: chunked

{
    "_links": {
        "env": {
            "href": "http://localhost:8080/actuator/env",
            "templated": false
        },
        "env-toMatch": {
            "href": "http://localhost:8080/actuator/env/{toMatch}",
            "templated": true
        },
        "health": {
            "href": "http://localhost:8080/actuator/health",
            "templated": false
        },
        "health-path": {
            "href": "http://localhost:8080/actuator/health/{*path}",
            "templated": true
        },
        "info": {
            "href": "http://localhost:8080/actuator/info",
            "templated": false
        },
        "self": {
            "href": "http://localhost:8080/actuator",
            "templated": false
        }
    }
}
```

Figure 5-16. Accessing the Actuator after specifying endpoints to include

For verification when starting the application, Actuator dutifully reports the number of endpoints it is currently exposing and the root path to reach them—in this case, the default of */actuator*—as shown in the startup report fragment that follows. This is a useful reminder/warning to provide a quick visual check that no more endpoints are being exposed than desired before advancing the application to a target deployment:

```
INFO 22115 --- [           main] o.s.b.a.e.web.EndpointLinksResolver      :
     Exposing 13 endpoint(s) beneath base path '/actuator'
```

To examine all mappings currently accessible via Actuator, simply query the provided Actuator root path to retrieve a full listing:

```
mheckler-a01 :: ~/dev » http :8080/actuator
HTTP/1.1 200
Connection: keep-alive
Content-Type: application/vnd.spring-boot.actuator.v3+json
Date: Fri, 27 Nov 2020 17:43:27 GMT
Keep-Alive: timeout=60
Transfer-Encoding: chunked

{
    "_links": {
        "beans": {
            "href": "http://localhost:8080/actuator/beans",
            "templated": false
        },
        "caches": {
            "href": "http://localhost:8080/actuator/caches",
            "templated": false
        },
        "caches-cache": {
            "href": "http://localhost:8080/actuator/caches/{cache}",
            "templated": true
        },
        "conditions": {
            "href": "http://localhost:8080/actuator/conditions",
            "templated": false
        },
        "configprops": {
            "href": "http://localhost:8080/actuator/configprops",
            "templated": false
        },
        "env": {
            "href": "http://localhost:8080/actuator/env",
            "templated": false
        },
        "env-toMatch": {
            "href": "http://localhost:8080/actuator/env/{toMatch}",
            "templated": true
        },
        "health": {
            "href": "http://localhost:8080/actuator/health",
            "templated": false
        },
        "health-path": {
            "href": "http://localhost:8080/actuator/health/{*path}",
            "templated": true
        },
        "heapdump": {
            "href": "http://localhost:8080/actuator/heapdump",
            "templated": false
        },
        "info": {
            "href": "http://localhost:8080/actuator/info",
            "templated": false
        },
        "loggers": {
            "href": "http://localhost:8080/actuator/loggers",
```

```
                    "templated": false
            },
            "loggers-name": {
                "href": "http://localhost:8080/actuator/loggers/{name}",
                "templated": true
            },
            "mappings": {
                "href": "http://localhost:8080/actuator/mappings",
                "templated": false
            },
            "metrics": {
                "href": "http://localhost:8080/actuator/metrics",
                "templated": false
            },
            "metrics-requiredMetricName": {
                "href": "http://localhost:8080/actuator/metrics/{requiredMetricName}",
                "templated": true
            },
            "scheduledtasks": {
                "href": "http://localhost:8080/actuator/scheduledtasks",
                "templated": false
            },
            "self": {
                "href": "http://localhost:8080/actuator",
                "templated": false
            },
            "threaddump": {
                "href": "http://localhost:8080/actuator/threaddump",
                "templated": false
            }
        }
    }
}
```

The listing of Actuator endpoints provides a good idea of the scope of information captured and exposed for examination, but of particular usefulness to actors good and bad are the following:

/actuator/beans

All Spring beans created by the application

/actuator/conditions

Conditions met (or not) to create Spring beans; similar to the Conditions Evaluation Report discussed previously

/actuator/configprops

All Environment properties accessible by the application

/actuator/env

Myriad aspects of the environment in which the application is operating; especially useful to see where each individual configprop value originates

/actuator/health

Health info (basic or expanded, depending on settings)

/actuator/heapdump
Initiates heap dump for troubleshooting and/or analysis

/actuator/loggers
Logging levels for every component

/actuator/mappings
All endpoint mappings and supporting details

/actuator/metrics
Metrics currently being captured by the application

/actuator/threaddump
Initiates thread dump for troubleshooting and/or analysis

These, and all of the remaining preconfigured Actuator endpoints, are handy when needed and easy to access for examination. Continuing to focus on the application's environment, even among these endpoints there are firsts among peers.

Getting Actuator to Open Up

As mentioned, Actuator's default security posture intentionally exposes only very limited *health* and *info* responses. In fact, the */actuator/health* endpoint provides a rather utilitarian "UP" or "DOWN" application status out of the box.

With most applications, however, there are dependencies for which Actuator tracks health information; it simply doesn't expose that additional information unless authorized to do so. To show expanded health information for preconfigured dependencies, I add the following property to *application.properties*:

```
management.endpoint.health.show-details=always
```

 There are three possible values for the health indicator's show-details property: never (default), when_authorized, and always. For this example, I choose always simply to demonstrate the possible, but for every application put into production, the correct choices would be either never or when_authorized in order to limit visibility to the application's expanded health information.

Restarting the application results in the addition of health information for the application's primary components to the overall application health summary when accessing the */actuator/health* endpoint, per Figure 5-17.

```
mheckler-a01 :: ~/dev » http :8080/actuator/health
HTTP/1.1 200
Connection: keep-alive
Content-Type: application/vnd.spring-boot.actuator.v3+json
Date: Fri, 27 Nov 2020 17:47:32 GMT
Keep-Alive: timeout=60
Transfer-Encoding: chunked

{
    "components": {
        "db": {
            "details": {
                "database": "H2",
                "validationQuery": "isValid()"
            },
            "status": "UP"
        },
        "diskSpace": {
            "details": {
                "exists": true,
                "free": 133346631680,
                "threshold": 10485760,
                "total": 499963174912
            },
            "status": "UP"
        },
        "ping": {
            "status": "UP"
        }
    },
    "status": "UP"
}
```

Figure 5-17. Expanded health information

Becoming More Environmentally Aware Using Actuator

One malady that often afflicts developers—present company included—is an assumption of complete knowledge of current application environment/state when behavior
doesn't match expectations. This isn't entirely unexpected, especially if one wrote the
anomalous code oneself. A relatively quick and invaluable first step is to *check all
assumptions*. Do you *know* what that value is? Or are you just really certain you
know?

Have you checked?

Especially in code in which outcomes are driven by inputs, this should be a required starting point. Actuator helps make this painless. Querying the application's *actuator/env* endpoint returns all environmental information; following is the portion of that result that shows only the properties set in the application to this point:

```
{
    "name": "Config resource 'classpath:/application.properties' via location
    'optional:classpath:/'",
    "properties": {
        "droid.description": {
            "origin": "class path resource [application.properties] - 5:19",
            "value": "Small, rolling android. Probably doesn't drink coffee."
        },
        "droid.id": {
            "origin": "class path resource [application.properties] - 4:10",
            "value": "BB-8"
        },
        "greeting.coffee": {
            "origin": "class path resource [application.properties] - 2:17",
            "value": "Dakota is drinking Cafe Cereza"
        },
        "greeting.name": {
            "origin": "class path resource [application.properties] - 1:15",
            "value": "Dakota"
        },
        "management.endpoint.health.show-details": {
            "origin": "class path resource [application.properties] - 8:41",
            "value": "always"
        },
        "management.endpoints.web.exposure.include": {
            "origin": "class path resource [application.properties] - 7:43",
            "value": "*"
        }
    }
}
```

Actuator shows not only the current value for each defined property but also its source, down to the line and column number where each value is defined. But what happens if one or more of those values is overridden by another source, e.g., an external environment variable or command line argument when executing the application?

To demonstrate a typical production-bound application scenario, I run `mvn clean package` from the application's directory at the command line, then execute the app with the following command:

```
java -jar target/sbur-rest-demo-0.0.1-SNAPSHOT.jar --greeting.name=Sertanejo
```

Querying *actuator/env* once more, you can see that there is a new section for command line arguments with a single entry for `greeting.name`:

```
{
    "name": "commandLineArgs",
    "properties": {
        "greeting.name": {
            "value": "Sertanejo"
        }
    }
}
```

Following the order of precedence for `Environment` inputs that was referenced earlier, command line arguments should override the value set from within *application.properties*. Querying the */greeting* endpoint returns "Sertanejo" as expected; querying */greeting/coffee* likewise results in the overridden value being incorporated into that response via the SpEL expression as well: `Sertanejo is drink ing Cafe Cereza`.

Trying to get to the bottom of errant, data-driven behavior just got a lot simpler thanks to Spring Boot Actuator.

Turning Up the Volume on Logging with Actuator

Like many other choices in developing and deploying software, choosing logging levels for production applications involves tradeoffs. Opting for more logging results in more system-level work and storage consumption and the capture of both more relevant and irrelevant data. This in turn can make it considerably more difficult to find an elusive issue.

As part of its mission of providing Boot's production-ready features, Actuator addresses this as well, allowing developers to set a typical logging level like "INFO" for most or all components and change that level temporarily when a critical issue surfaces…all in live, production Spring Boot applications. Actuator facilitates the setting and resetting of logging levels with a simple `POST` to the applicable endpoint. For example, Figure 5-18 shows the default logging level for `org.springframe work.data.web`.

```
mheckler-a01 :: ~/dev » http :8080/actuator/loggers/org.springframework.data.web

HTTP/1.1 200
Connection: keep-alive
Content-Disposition: inline;filename=f.txt
Content-Type: application/vnd.spring-boot.actuator.v3+json
Date: Fri, 27 Nov 2020 18:01:15 GMT
Keep-Alive: timeout=60
Transfer-Encoding: chunked

{
    "configuredLevel": null,
    "effectiveLevel": "INFO"
}
```

Figure 5-18. Default logging level for `org.springframework.data.web`

Of particular interest is that since a logging level wasn't configured for this component, an effective level of "INFO" is used. Again, Spring Boot provides a sensible default when specifics aren't provided.

If I'm notified of an issue with a running app and would like to increase logging to help diagnose and resolve it, all that is necessary to do so for a particular component is to POST a new JSON-formatted value for configuredLevel to its */actuator/loggers* endpoint, as shown here:

```
echo '{"configuredLevel": "TRACE"}'
  | http :8080/actuator/loggers/org.springframework.data.web
```

Requerying the logging level now returns confirmation that the logger for org.springframework.data.web is now set to "TRACE" and will provide intensive diagnostic logging for the application, as shown in Figure 5-19.

"TRACE" can be essential in pinning down an elusive issue, but it is a rather heavyweight level of logging, capturing even finer-grained information than "DEBUG"—use in production applications can provide essential information, but be mindful of the impact.

```
mheckler-a01 :: ~/dev » http :8080/actuator/loggers/org.springframework.data.web

HTTP/1.1 200
Connection: keep-alive
Content-Disposition: inline;filename=f.txt
Content-Type: application/vnd.spring-boot.actuator.v3+json
Date: Fri, 27 Nov 2020 18:05:34 GMT
Keep-Alive: timeout=60
Transfer-Encoding: chunked

{
    "configuredLevel": "TRACE",
    "effectiveLevel": "TRACE"
}
```

Figure 5-19. New "TRACE" Logging Level for org.springframework.data.web

Code Checkout Checkup

For complete chapter code, please check out branch *chapter5end* from the code repository.

Summary

It's critical for a developer to have useful tools to establish, identify, and isolate behaviors manifested within production applications. As applications become more dynamic and distributed, there is often a need to do the following:

- Configure and reconfigure applications dynamically
- Determine/confirm current settings and their origins
- Inspect and monitor application environment and health indicators
- Temporarily adjust logging levels of live apps to identify root causes

This chapter demonstrated how to use Spring Boot's built-in configuration capabilities, its Autoconfiguration Report, and Spring Boot Actuator to create, identify, and modify application environment settings flexibly and dynamically.

In the next chapter, I dive deep into data: how to define its storage and retrieval using various industry standards and leading database engines and the Spring Data projects and facilities that enable their use in the most streamlined and powerful ways possible.

## CHAPTER 6

Really Digging into Data

Data can be a complex topic, with so much to consider: its structure and relationships with other data; handling, storage, and retrieval options; various applicable standards; database providers and mechanisms; and more. Data may be the most complex aspect of development to which devs are exposed so early in their careers and when learning a new toolchain.

The reason this is often the case is that without data in some form, nearly all applications are meaningless. Very few apps provide any value at all without storing, retrieving, or correlating data.

As something that forms the underpinning for nearly all application value, *data* has attracted a great deal of innovation from database providers and platform vendors. But in many cases, complexity remains: it is a topic with great depth and breadth, after all.

Enter Spring Data. Spring Data's stated mission (*https://spring.io/projects/spring-data*) is "to provide a familiar and consistent, Spring-based programming model for data access while still retaining the special traits of the underlying data store." Regardless of database engine or platform, Spring Data's goal is to make the developer's access to data as simple and as powerful as humanly possible.

This chapter demonstrates how to define data storage and retrieval using various industry standards and leading database engines and the Spring Data projects and facilities that enable their use in the most streamlined and powerful ways possible: via Spring Boot.

Defining Entities

In nearly every case when dealing with data, some form of domain entity is involved. Whether it's an invoice, an automobile, or something else entirely, data is rarely dealt with as a collection of unrelated properties. Inevitably, what we consider useful data are cohesive pools of elements that together constitute a meaningful whole. An automobile—in data or in real life—is really only a useful concept if it's a unique, fully attributed thing.

Spring Data provides several different mechanisms and data access options for Spring Boot applications to use, at a variety of abstraction levels. Regardless of which level of abstraction a developer settles on for any given use case, the first step is defining any domain classes that will be used to handle applicable data.

While a full exploration of Domain-Driven Design (DDD) is beyond the scope of this book, I'll use the concepts as a foundation for defining applicable domain classes for the example applications built in this and subsequent chapters. For a full exploration of DDD I would refer the reader to Eric Evans's seminal work on the topic, *Domain-Driven Design: Tackling Complexity in the Heart of Software* (*https://oreil.ly/Domain DrivDes*).

By way of a cursory explanation, a *domain class* encapsulates a primary domain entity that has relevance and significance independently of other data. This doesn't mean it doesn't relate to other domain entities, only that it can stand alone and make sense as a unit, even when unassociated with other entities.

To create a domain class in Spring using Java, you can create a class with member variables, applicable constructors, accessors/mutators, and `equals()`/`hash Code()`/`toString()` methods (and more). You can also employ Lombok with Java or data classes in Kotlin to create domain classes for data representation, storage, and retrieval. I do all of these things in this chapter to demonstrate just how easy it is to work with domains using Spring Boot and Spring Data. It's great to have options.

For the examples in this chapter, once I've defined a domain class, I'll decide on a database and level of abstraction based on goals for data usage and exposed APIs for or by the database provider. Within the Spring ecosystem, this typically boils down to one of two options, with minor variations: templates or repositories.

Template Support

In order to provide a set of "just high enough" coherent abstractions, Spring Data defines an interface of type `Operations` for most of its various data sources. This `Oper ations` interface—examples include `MongoOperations`, `RedisOperations`, and `Cas sandraOperations`—specifies a foundational set of operations that can be used

---

directly for greatest flexibility or upon which higher-level abstractions can be constructed. `Template` classes provide direct implementations of `Operations` interfaces.

Templates can be thought of as a Service Provider Interface (SPI) of sorts—directly usable and extremely capable but with many repetitive steps required each time they're used to accomplish the more common use cases developers face. For those scenarios in which data access follows common patterns, repositories may be a better choice. And the best part is that repositories build upon templates, so you lose nothing by stepping up to the higher abstraction.

Repository Support

Spring Data defines the `Repository` interface from which all other types of Spring Data repository interfaces derive. Examples include `JPARepository` and `MongoReposi tory` (providing JPA-specific and Mongo-specific capabilities, respectively) and more versatile interfaces like `CrudRepository`, `ReactiveCrudRepository`, and `PagingAnd SortingRepository`. These various repository interfaces specify useful higher-level operations like `findAll()`, `findById()`, `count()`, `delete()`, `deleteAll()`, and more.

Repositories are defined for both blocking and nonblocking interactions. Additionally, creating queries using convention over configuration, and even literal query statements, is supported by Spring Data's repositories. Using Spring Data's repositories with Spring Boot makes building complex database interactions an almost trivial exercise.

I demonstrate all of these capabilities at some point in this book. In this chapter, I plan to cover the key elements across a number of database options by incorporating various implementation details: Lombok, Kotlin, and more. In that way, I provide a broad and stable base upon which to build in subsequent chapters.

@Before

As much as I love coffee and rely on it to drive my application development, in order to better explore the concepts covered throughout the rest of this book, I felt a more versatile domain was in order. As both a software developer and pilot, I see the increasingly complex and data-driven world of aviation as offering no shortage of interesting scenarios (and fascinating data) to explore as we delve deeper into Spring Boot's facility in numerous use cases.

To deal with data, we must *have* data. I've developed a small Spring Boot RESTful web service called `PlaneFinder` (available within this book's code repositories) to serve as an API gateway that I can poll for current aircraft and positions within range of a small device on my desk. This device receives Automatic Dependent Surveillance—Broadcast (ADS-B) data from airplanes within a certain distance and shares them with a service online, PlaneFinder.net (*https://planefinder.net*). It also exposes an HTTP API that my gateway service consumes, simplifies, and exposes to other downstream services like the ones in this chapter.

More details throughout, but for now, let's create some database-connected services.

Creating a Template-Based Service Using Redis

Redis is a database that is typically used as an in-memory datastore for sharing state among instances of a service, caching, and brokering messages between services. Like all major databases, Redis does more, but the focus for this chapter is simply using Redis to store and retrieve from memory aircraft information our service obtains from the `PlaneFinder` service referred to previously.

Initializing the Project

To begin, we return to the Spring Initializr. From there, I choose the following options:

- Maven project
- Java
- Current production version of Spring Boot
- Packaging: Jar
- Java: 11

And for dependencies:

- Spring Reactive Web (`spring-boot-starter-webflux`)
- Spring Data Redis (Access+Driver) (`spring-boot-starter-data-redis`)
- Lombok (`lombok`)

Notes About Project Options

Artifact IDs are in parentheses after Initializr's menu name for the shown capabilities/libraries above. The first two have a common Group ID—`org.springframework.boot`—while Lombok's is `org.projectlombok`.

Although I don't specifically target any nonblocking, reactive capabilities for this chapter's applications, I include the dependency for Spring Reactive Web instead of that of Spring Web in order to gain access to `WebClient`, the preferred client for both blocking and nonblocking service interactions for applications built using Spring Boot 2.x and onward. From the perspective of a developer building a basic web

---

service, the code is the same regardless of which dependency I include: code, annotations, and properties for this chapter's examples are fully consistent between the two. I'll point out the differences as the two paths begin to diverge in future chapters.

Next, I generate the project and save it locally, unzip it, and open it in the IDE.

Developing the Redis Service

Let's begin with the domain.

Currently, the `PlaneFinder` API gateway exposes a single REST endpoint:

```
http://localhost:7634/aircraft
```

Any (local) service can query this endpoint and receive a JSON response of all aircraft within range of the receiver in the following format (with representative data):

```
[
    {
        "id": 108,
        "callsign": "AMF4263",
        "squawk": "4136",
        "reg": "N49UC",
        "flightno": "",
        "route": "LAN-DFW",
        "type": "B190",
        "category": "A1",
        "altitude": 20000,
        "heading": 235,
        "speed": 248,
        "lat": 38.865905,
        "lon": -90.429382,
        "barometer": 0,
        "vert_rate": 0,
        "selected_altitude": 0,
        "polar_distance": 12.99378,
        "polar_bearing": 345.393951,
        "is_adsb": true,
        "is_on_ground": false,
        "last_seen_time": "2020-11-11T21:44:04Z",
        "pos_update_time": "2020-11-11T21:44:03Z",
        "bds40_seen_time": null
    },
    {<another aircraft in range, same fields as above>},
    {<final aircraft currently in range, same fields as above>}
]
```

Defining the domain class

In order to ingest and manipulate these aircraft reports, I create an `Aircraft` class as follows:

```java
package com.thehecklers.sburredis;

import com.fasterxml.jackson.annotation.JsonIgnoreProperties;
import com.fasterxml.jackson.annotation.JsonProperty;
import lombok.AllArgsConstructor;
import lombok.Data;
import lombok.NoArgsConstructor;
import org.springframework.data.annotation.Id;

import java.time.Instant;

@Data
@NoArgsConstructor
@AllArgsConstructor
@JsonIgnoreProperties(ignoreUnknown = true)
public class Aircraft {
    @Id
    private Long id;
    private String callsign, squawk, reg, flightno, route, type, category;
    private int altitude, heading, speed;
    @JsonProperty("vert_rate")
    private int vertRate;
    @JsonProperty("selected_altitude")
    private int selectedAltitude;
    private double lat, lon, barometer;
    @JsonProperty("polar_distance")
    private double polarDistance;
    @JsonProperty("polar_bearing")
    private double polarBearing;
    @JsonProperty("is_adsb")
    private boolean isADSB;
    @JsonProperty("is_on_ground")
    private boolean isOnGround;
    @JsonProperty("last_seen_time")
    private Instant lastSeenTime;
    @JsonProperty("pos_update_time")
    private Instant posUpdateTime;
    @JsonProperty("bds40_seen_time")
    private Instant bds40SeenTime;

    public String getLastSeenTime() {
        return lastSeenTime.toString();
    }

    public void setLastSeenTime(String lastSeenTime) {
        if (null != lastSeenTime) {
            this.lastSeenTime = Instant.parse(lastSeenTime);
        } else {
            this.lastSeenTime = Instant.ofEpochSecond(0);
        }
    }

    public String getPosUpdateTime() {
        return posUpdateTime.toString();
    }
```

```java
        public void setPosUpdateTime(String posUpdateTime) {
            if (null != posUpdateTime) {
                this.posUpdateTime = Instant.parse(posUpdateTime);
            } else {
                this.posUpdateTime = Instant.ofEpochSecond(0);
            }
        }

        public String getBds40SeenTime() {
            return bds40SeenTime.toString();
        }

        public void setBds40SeenTime(String bds40SeenTime) {
            if (null != bds40SeenTime) {
                this.bds40SeenTime = Instant.parse(bds40SeenTime);
            } else {
                this.bds40SeenTime = Instant.ofEpochSecond(0);
            }
        }
    }
```

This domain class includes a few helpful annotations that streamline the necessary code and/or increase its flexibility. Class-level annotations include the following:

`@Data`:: Instructs Lombok to create getter, setter, `equals()`, `hashCode()`, and `toString()` methods, creating a so-called data class `@NoArgsConstructor`:: Instructs Lombok to create a zero-parameter constructor, thus requiring no arguments `@AllArgsConstructor`:: Instructs Lombok to create a constructor with a parameter for each member variable, requiring an argument be provided for all `@JsonIgnorePro perties(ignoreUnknown = true)`:: Informs Jackson deserialization mechanisms to ignore fields within JSON responses for which there is no corresponding member variable

Field-level annotations provide more specific guidance where appropriate. Examples of field-level annotations include the two used for this class:

`@Id`:: Designates the annotated member variable as holding the unique identifier for a database entry/record `@JsonProperty("vert_rate")`:: Connects a member variable with its differently named JSON field

You may be wondering why I created explicit accesssors and mutators for the three member variables of type `Instant` if the `@Data` annotation results in the creation of getter and setter methods for all member variables. In the case of these three, the JSON value must be parsed and transformed from a `String` to a complex data type by calling a method: `Instant::parse`. If that value is entirely absent (null), different logic must be performed to avoid passing a null to `parse()` and to assign some mean- ingful substitute value to the corresponding member variable via setter. Additionally, serialization of `Instant` values is best done by conversion to a `String`—thus the explicit getter methods.

With a domain class defined, it's time to create and configure the mechanism for accessing a Redis database.

Adding template support

Spring Boot provides basic `RedisTemplate` capabilities via autoconfiguration, and if you only need to manipulate `String` values using Redis, very little work (or code) is required from you. Dealing with complex domain objects necessitates a bit more configuration but not too much.

The `RedisTemplate` class extends the `RedisAccessor` class and implements the `Redis Operations` interface. Of particular interest for this application is `RedisOperations`, as it specifies the functionality needed to interact with Redis.

As developers, we should prefer to write code against interfaces, not implementations. Doing so allows one to provide the most appropriate concrete implementation for the task at hand without code/API changes or excessive and unnecessary violations of the DRY (Don't Repeat Yourself) principle; as long as the interface is fully implemented, any concrete implementation will function just as well as any other.

In the following code listing, I create a bean of type `RedisOperations`, returning a `RedisTemplate` as the bean's concrete implementation. I perform the following steps in order to configure it properly to accommodate inbound `Aircraft`:

1. I create a `Serializer` to be used when converting between objects and JSON records. Since Jackson is used for marshalling/unmarshalling (serialization/ deserialization) of JSON values and is already present in Spring Boot web applications, I create a `Jackson2JsonRedisSerializer` for objects of type `Aircraft`.

2. I create a `RedisTemplate` that accepts keys of type `String` and values of type `Air craft` to accommodate the inbound `Aircraft` with `String` IDs. . I plug the `Redis ConnectionFactory` bean that was helpfully and automatically autowired into this bean-creation method's sole parameter—`RedisConnectionFactory factory` —into the `template` object so it can create and retrieve a connection to the Redis database.

3. I supply the `Jackson2JsonRedisSerializer<Aircraft>` serializer to the `tem plate` object in order to be used as the default serializer. `RedisTemplate` has a number of serializers that are assigned the default serializer in the absence of specific assignment, a useful touch.

4. I create and specify a different serializer to be used for keys so that the template doesn't attempt to use the default serializer—which expects objects of type `Air craft`—to convert to/from key values of type `String`. A `StringRedisSerializer` does the trick nicely.

5. Finally, I return the created and configured `RedisTemplate` as the bean to use when some implementation of a `RedisOperations` bean is requested within the application:

```
import org.springframework.boot.SpringApplication;
import org.springframework.boot.autoconfigure.SpringBootApplication;
import org.springframework.context.annotation.Bean;
import org.springframework.data.redis.connection.RedisConnectionFactory;
import org.springframework.data.redis.core.RedisOperations;
import org.springframework.data.redis.core.RedisTemplate;
import org.springframework.data.redis.serializer.Jackson2JsonRedisSerializer;
import org.springframework.data.redis.serializer.StringRedisSerializer;

@SpringBootApplication
public class SburRedisApplication {
    @Bean
    public RedisOperations<String, Aircraft>
    redisOperations(RedisConnectionFactory factory) {
        Jackson2JsonRedisSerializer<Aircraft> serializer =
                new Jackson2JsonRedisSerializer<>(Aircraft.class);

        RedisTemplate<String, Aircraft> template = new RedisTemplate<>();
        template.setConnectionFactory(factory);
        template.setDefaultSerializer(serializer);
        template.setKeySerializer(new StringRedisSerializer());

        return template;
    }

    public static void main(String[] args) {
        SpringApplication.run(SburRedisApplication.class, args);
    }
}
```

Bringing it all together

Now that the underlying wiring is in place for accessing the Redis database using a template, it's time for the payoff. As shown in the code listing that follows, I create a Spring Boot @Component class to poll the `PlaneFinder` endpoint and handle the resultant `Aircraft` records it receives using Redis template support.

To initialize the `PlaneFinderPoller` bean and prepare it for action, I create a `WebClient` object and assign it to a member variable, pointing it to the destination endpoint exposed by the external `PlaneFinder` service. `PlaneFinder` currently runs on my local machine and listens on port 7634.

The `PlaneFinderPoller` bean requires access to two other beans to perform its duties: a `RedisConnectionFactory` (supplied by Boot's autoconfiguration due to Redis being an app dependency) and an implementation of `RedisOperations`, the `RedisTemplate` created earlier. Both are assigned to properly defined member variables via constructor injection (autowired):

```
import org.springframework.data.redis.connection.RedisConnectionFactory;
import org.springframework.data.redis.core.RedisOperations;
import org.springframework.scheduling.annotation.EnableScheduling;
import org.springframework.stereotype.Component;
import org.springframework.web.reactive.function.client.WebClient;

@EnableScheduling
@Component
class PlaneFinderPoller {
    private WebClient client =
            WebClient.create("http://localhost:7634/aircraft");

    private final RedisConnectionFactory connectionFactory;
    private final RedisOperations<String, Aircraft> redisOperations;

    PlaneFinderPoller(RedisConnectionFactory connectionFactory,
                RedisOperations<String, Aircraft> redisOperations) {
        this.connectionFactory = connectionFactory;
        this.redisOperations = redisOperations;
    }
}
```

Next, I create the method that does the heavy lifting. In order to have it poll on a fixed schedule, I leverage the @EnableScheduling annotation I previously placed at the class level and annotate the pollPlanes() method I create with @Scheduled, supplying a parameter of fixedDelay=1000 to specify a polling frequency of once per 1,000 ms—once per second. The rest of the method consists of only three declarative statements: one to clear any previously saved Aircraft, one to retrieve and save current positions, and one to report the results of the latest capture.

For the first task I use the autowired ConnectionFactory to obtain a connection to the database, and via that connection, I execute the server command to clear all keys present: flushDb().

The second statement uses the WebClient to call the PlaneFinder service and retrieve a collection of aircraft within range, along with their current position information. The response body is converted to a Flux of Aircraft objects, filtered to remove any Aircraft that don't include registration numbers, converted to a Stream of Aircraft, and saved to the Redis database. The save is performed on each valid Aircraft by setting a key/value pair to the Aircraft registration number and the Aircraft object itself, respectively, using Redis's operations tailored to manipulating data values.

 A Flux is a reactive type covered in upcoming chapters, but for now, simply think of it as a collection of objects delivered without blocking.

The final statement in `pollPlanes()` again leverages a couple of Redis's defined value operations to retrieve all keys (via the wildcard parameter *) and, using each key, to retrieve each corresponding `Aircraft` value, which is then printed. Here is the `pollPlanes()` method in finished form:

```
@Scheduled(fixedRate = 1000)
private void pollPlanes() {
    connectionFactory.getConnection().serverCommands().flushDb();

    client.get()
            .retrieve()
            .bodyToFlux(Aircraft.class)
            .filter(plane -> !plane.getReg().isEmpty())
            .toStream()
            .forEach(ac -> redisOperations.opsForValue().set(ac.getReg(), ac));

    redisOperations.opsForValue()
            .getOperations()
            .keys("*")
            .forEach(ac ->
                System.out.println(redisOperations.opsForValue().get(ac)));
}
```

The final version (for now) of the `PlaneFinderPoller` class is shown in the following listing:

```
import org.springframework.data.redis.connection.RedisConnectionFactory;
import org.springframework.data.redis.core.RedisOperations;
import org.springframework.scheduling.annotation.EnableScheduling;
import org.springframework.scheduling.annotation.Scheduled;
import org.springframework.stereotype.Component;
import org.springframework.web.reactive.function.client.WebClient;

@EnableScheduling
@Component
class PlaneFinderPoller {
    private WebClient client =
            WebClient.create("http://localhost:7634/aircraft");

    private final RedisConnectionFactory connectionFactory;
    private final RedisOperations<String, Aircraft> redisOperations;

    PlaneFinderPoller(RedisConnectionFactory connectionFactory,
                    RedisOperations<String, Aircraft> redisOperations) {
        this.connectionFactory = connectionFactory;
        this.redisOperations = redisOperations;
    }

    @Scheduled(fixedRate = 1000)
    private void pollPlanes() {
        connectionFactory.getConnection().serverCommands().flushDb();

        client.get()
                .retrieve()
                .bodyToFlux(Aircraft.class)
```

```
                    .filter(plane -> !plane.getReg().isEmpty())
                    .toStream()
                    .forEach(ac ->
                        redisOperations.opsForValue().set(ac.getReg(), ac));

            redisOperations.opsForValue()
                    .getOperations()
                    .keys("*")
                    .forEach(ac ->
                        System.out.println(redisOperations.opsForValue().get(ac)));
        }
    }
```

With polling mechanisms fully fleshed out, let's run the application and see the results.

The results

With the `PlaneFinder` service already running on my machine, I start the *sbur-redis* application to obtain, store and retrieve in Redis, and display the results of each poll of `PlaneFinder`. What follows is an example of the results, edited for brevity and formatted a bit for readability:

```
Aircraft(id=1, callsign=EDV5015, squawk=3656, reg=N324PQ, flightno=DL5015,
route=ATL-OMA-ATL, type=CRJ9, category=A3, altitude=35000, heading=168,
speed=485, vertRate=-64, selectedAltitude=0, lat=38.061808, lon=-90.280629,
barometer=0.0, polarDistance=53.679699, polarBearing=184.333345, isADSB=true,
isOnGround=false, lastSeenTime=2020-11-27T18:34:14Z,
posUpdateTime=2020-11-27T18:34:11Z, bds40SeenTime=1970-01-01T00:00:00Z)

Aircraft(id=4, callsign=AAL500, squawk=2666, reg=N839AW, flightno=AA500,
route=PHX-IND, type=A319, category=A3, altitude=36975, heading=82, speed=477,
vertRate=0, selectedAltitude=36992, lat=38.746399, lon=-90.277644,
barometer=1012.8, polarDistance=13.281347, polarBearing=200.308663, isADSB=true,
isOnGround=false, lastSeenTime=2020-11-27T18:34:50Z,
posUpdateTime=2020-11-27T18:34:50Z, bds40SeenTime=2020-11-27T18:34:50Z)

Aircraft(id=15, callsign=null, squawk=4166, reg=N404AN, flightno=AA685,
route=PHX-DCA, type=A21N, category=A3, altitude=39000, heading=86, speed=495,
vertRate=0, selectedAltitude=39008, lat=39.701611, lon=-90.479309,
barometer=1013.6, polarDistance=47.113195, polarBearing=341.51817, isADSB=true,
isOnGround=false, lastSeenTime=2020-11-27T18:34:50Z,
posUpdateTime=2020-11-27T18:34:50Z, bds40SeenTime=2020-11-27T18:34:50Z)
```

Working with databases via Spring Data's template support provides a lower-level API with excellent flexibility. If you're looking for minimum friction and maximum productivity and repeatability, however, repository support is the better choice. Next, I show how to convert from using templates to interact with Redis to using a Spring Data repository. It's great to have options.

Converting from Template to Repository

Before we can use a repository, it's necessary to define one, and Spring Boot's auto-configuration helps considerably with this. I create a repository interface as follows, extending Spring Data's `CrudRepository` and providing the type of object to store along with its key: `Aircraft` and `Long`, in this case:

```
public interface AircraftRepository extends CrudRepository<Aircraft, Long> {}
```

As explained in Chapter 4, Spring Boot detects the Redis database driver on the application classpath and notes that we're extending a Spring Data repository interface, then creates a database proxy automatically with no additional code required to instantiate it. Just like that, the application has access to an `AircraftRepository` bean. Let's plug it in and put it to use.

Revisiting the `PlaneFinderPoller` class, I can now replace the lower-level references to and operations using `RedisOperations` and replace them with `AircraftRepository`.

First, I remove the `RedisOperations` member variable:

```
private final RedisOperations<String, Aircraft> redisOperations;
```

Then replace it with one for the `AircraftRepository` to autowire:

```
private final AircraftRepository repository;
```

Next, I replace the `RedisOperations` bean autowired via constructor injection with the `AircraftRepository` and the assignment within the constructor to the applicable member variable so that the constructor ends up like so:

```
public PlaneFinderPoller(RedisConnectionFactory connectionFactory,
                AircraftRepository repository) {
    this.connectionFactory = connectionFactory;
    this.repository = repository;
}
```

The next step is to refactor the `pollPlanes()` method to replace template-based operations with repository-based ops.

Changing the last line of the first statement is a simple matter. Using a method reference further simplifies the lambda:

```
client.get()
        .retrieve()
        .bodyToFlux(Aircraft.class)
        .filter(plane -> !plane.getReg().isEmpty())
        .toStream()
        .forEach(repository::save);
```

And the second one reduces even more, again including use of a method reference:

```
repository.findAll().forEach(System.out::println);
```

The newly repository-enabled `PlaneFinderPoller` now consists of the following code:

```
import org.springframework.data.redis.connection.RedisConnectionFactory;
import org.springframework.scheduling.annotation.EnableScheduling;
import org.springframework.scheduling.annotation.Scheduled;
import org.springframework.stereotype.Component;
import org.springframework.web.reactive.function.client.WebClient;

@EnableScheduling
@Component
class PlaneFinderPoller {
    private WebClient client =
            WebClient.create("http://localhost:7634/aircraft");

    private final RedisConnectionFactory connectionFactory;
    private final AircraftRepository repository;

    PlaneFinderPoller(RedisConnectionFactory connectionFactory,
                      AircraftRepository repository) {
        this.connectionFactory = connectionFactory;
        this.repository = repository;
    }

    @Scheduled(fixedRate = 1000)
    private void pollPlanes() {
        connectionFactory.getConnection().serverCommands().flushDb();

        client.get()
                .retrieve()
                .bodyToFlux(Aircraft.class)
                .filter(plane -> !plane.getReg().isEmpty())
                .toStream()
                .forEach(repository::save);

        repository.findAll().forEach(System.out::println);
    }
}
```

With no further need of a bean implementing the `RedisOperations` interface, I can now delete its `@Bean` definition from the main application class, leaving `SburRedisAp plication`, as shown in the following code:

```
import org.springframework.boot.SpringApplication;
import org.springframework.boot.autoconfigure.SpringBootApplication;

@SpringBootApplication
public class SburRedisApplication {

    public static void main(String[] args) {
        SpringApplication.run(SburRedisApplication.class, args);
    }

}
```

Only one small task and a very nice code reduction remain to fully enable Redis repository support in our application. I add the @RedisHash annotation to the Air craft entity to indicate that Aircraft is an aggregate root to be stored in a Redis hash, performing a function similar to what @Entity annotation does for JPA objects. I then remove the explicit accessors and mutators previously required for the Instant-typed member variables, as the converters in Spring Data's repository support handle complex type conversions with ease. The newly streamlined Aircraft class now looks like this:

```
import com.fasterxml.jackson.annotation.JsonIgnoreProperties;
import com.fasterxml.jackson.annotation.JsonProperty;
import lombok.AllArgsConstructor;
import lombok.Data;
import lombok.NoArgsConstructor;
import org.springframework.data.annotation.Id;
import org.springframework.data.redis.core.RedisHash;

import java.time.Instant;

@Data
@NoArgsConstructor
@AllArgsConstructor
@RedisHash
@JsonIgnoreProperties(ignoreUnknown = true)
public class Aircraft {
    @Id
    private Long id;
    private String callsign, squawk, reg, flightno, route, type, category;
    private int altitude, heading, speed;
    @JsonProperty("vert_rate")
    private int vertRate;
    @JsonProperty("selected_altitude")
    private int selectedAltitude;
    private double lat, lon, barometer;
    @JsonProperty("polar_distance")
    private double polarDistance;
    @JsonProperty("polar_bearing")
    private double polarBearing;
    @JsonProperty("is_adsb")
    private boolean isADSB;
    @JsonProperty("is_on_ground")
    private boolean isOnGround;
    @JsonProperty("last_seen_time")
    private Instant lastSeenTime;
    @JsonProperty("pos_update_time")
    private Instant posUpdateTime;
    @JsonProperty("bds40_seen_time")
    private Instant bds40SeenTime;
}
```

With the latest changes in place, restarting the service results in output indistinguishable from the template-based approach but with much less code and inherent ceremony required. An example of results follows, again edited for brevity and formatted for readability:

```
Aircraft(id=59, callsign=KAP20, squawk=4615, reg=N678JG, flightno=,
route=STL-IRK, type=C402, category=A1, altitude=3825, heading=0, speed=143,
vertRate=768, selectedAltitude=0, lat=38.881034, lon=-90.261475, barometer=0.0,
polarDistance=5.915421, polarBearing=222.434158, isADSB=true, isOnGround=false,
lastSeenTime=2020-11-27T18:47:31Z, posUpdateTime=2020-11-27T18:47:31Z,
bds40SeenTime=1970-01-01T00:00:00Z)

Aircraft(id=60, callsign=SWA442, squawk=5657, reg=N928WN, flightno=WN442,
route=CMH-DCA-BNA-STL-PHX-BUR-OAK, type=B737, category=A3, altitude=8250,
heading=322, speed=266, vertRate=-1344, selectedAltitude=0, lat=38.604034,
lon=-90.357593, barometer=0.0, polarDistance=22.602864, polarBearing=201.283,
isADSB=true, isOnGround=false, lastSeenTime=2020-11-27T18:47:25Z,
posUpdateTime=2020-11-27T18:47:24Z, bds40SeenTime=1970-01-01T00:00:00Z)

Aircraft(id=61, callsign=null, squawk=null, reg=N702QS, flightno=,
route=SNA-RIC, type=CL35, category=, altitude=43000, heading=90, speed=500,
vertRate=0, selectedAltitude=0, lat=39.587997, lon=-90.921299, barometer=0.0,
polarDistance=51.544552, polarBearing=316.694343, isADSB=true, isOnGround=false,
lastSeenTime=2020-11-27T18:47:19Z, posUpdateTime=2020-11-27T18:47:19Z,
bds40SeenTime=1970-01-01T00:00:00Z)
```

If you need direct access to the lower-level capabilities exposed by Spring Data templates, template-based database support is indispensable. But for nearly all common use cases, when Spring Data offers repository-based access for a target database, it's best to begin—and in all likelihood remain—there.

Creating a Repository-Based Service Using the Java Persistence API (JPA)

One of the Spring ecosystem's strengths is consistency: once you learn how to accomplish something, the same approach can be applied to drive successful outcomes with different components. Database access is a case in point.

Spring Boot and Spring Data provide repository support for a number of different databases: JPA-compliant databases, numerous NoSQL datastores of varying types, and in-memory and/or persistent stores. Spring smooths the bumps a developer runs into when transitioning between databases, whether for a single application or throughout a vast system of them.

To demonstrate some of the flexible options at your disposal when creating data-aware Spring Boot applications, I highlight a few different approaches supported by Spring Boot in each of the following sections, while relying on Boot (and Spring Data) to streamline the database portion of the different, but similar, services. First up is JPA, and for this example I use Lombok throughout to reduce code and increase readability.

Initializing the Project

Once again we return to the Spring Initializr. This time, I choose the following options:

- Maven project
- Java
- Current production version of Spring Boot
- Packaging: Jar
- Java: 11

And for dependencies:

- Spring Reactive Web (`spring-boot-starter-webflux`)
- Spring Data JPA (`spring-boot-starter-data-jpa`)
- MySQL Driver (`mysql-connector-java`)
- Lombok (`lombok`)

Next, I generate the project and save it locally, unzip it, and open it in the IDE.

 As with the earlier Redis project and most other examples in this chapter, each data-aware service must be able to access a running database. Please refer to this book's associated code repositories for Docker scripts to create and run suitable containerized database engines.

Developing the JPA (MySQL) Service

Considering both Chapter 4's example built using JPA and the H2 database and the previous Redis repository-based example, the JPA-based service using MariaDB/MySQL clearly demonstrates the way in which Spring's consistency amplifies developer productivity.

Defining the domain class

As with all of this chapter's projects, I create an `Aircraft` domain class to serve as the primary (data) focus. Each different project will have slight variations around a common theme pointed out along the way. Here is the JPA-centric `Aircraft` domain class structure:

```
import com.fasterxml.jackson.annotation.JsonProperty;
import lombok.AllArgsConstructor;
import lombok.Data;
```

```
import lombok.NoArgsConstructor;

import javax.persistence.Entity;
import javax.persistence.GeneratedValue;
import javax.persistence.Id;
import java.time.Instant;

@Entity
@Data
@NoArgsConstructor
@AllArgsConstructor
public class Aircraft {
    @Id
    @GeneratedValue
    private Long id;

    private String callsign, squawk, reg, flightno, route, type, category;

    private int altitude, heading, speed;
    @JsonProperty("vert_rate")
    private int vertRate;
    @JsonProperty("selected_altitude")
    private int selectedAltitude;

    private double lat, lon, barometer;
    @JsonProperty("polar_distance")
    private double polarDistance;
    @JsonProperty("polar_bearing")
    private double polarBearing;

    @JsonProperty("is_adsb")
    private boolean isADSB;
    @JsonProperty("is_on_ground")
    private boolean isOnGround;

    @JsonProperty("last_seen_time")
    private Instant lastSeenTime;
    @JsonProperty("pos_update_time")
    private Instant posUpdateTime;
    @JsonProperty("bds40_seen_time")
    private Instant bds40SeenTime;
}
```

There are a few particulars of note with regard to this version of Aircraft versus prior versions and those to come.

First, the @Entity, @Id, and @GeneratedValue annotations are all imported from the javax.persistence package. You may remember that in the Redis version (and some others), @Id comes from org.springframework.data.annotation.

Class-level annotations closely parallel those used in the example using Redis repository support, with the replacement of @RedisHash with a JPA @Entity annotation. To revisit the other (unchanged) annotations shown, please refer to the aforementioned earlier section.

Field-level annotations are also similar, with the addition of `@GeneratedValue`. As its name implies, `@GeneratedValue` indicates that the identifier will be generated by the underlying database engine. The developer can—if desired or necessary—provide additional guidance for key generation, but for our purposes, the annotation itself is sufficient.

As with Spring Data's repository support for Redis, there is no need for explicit accessors/mutators for the member variables of type `Instant`, leaving (once again) a very svelte `Aircraft` domain class.

Creating the repository interface

Next, I define the required repository interface, extending Spring Data's `CrudReposi tory` and providing the type of object to store and its key: `Aircraft` and `Long`, in this case:

```
public interface AircraftRepository extends CrudRepository<Aircraft, Long> {}
```

 Both Redis and JPA databases function well with unique key values/identifiers of type `Long`, so this is identical to the one defined in the earlier Redis example.

Bringing it all together

Now to create the `PlaneFinder` polling component and configure it for database access.

Polling PlaneFinder. Once again I create a Spring Boot `@Component` class to poll for current position data and handle the resultant `Aircraft` records it receives.

Like the earlier example, I create a `WebClient` object and assign it to a member variable, pointing it to the destination endpoint exposed by the `PlaneFinder` service on port 7634.

As you should expect from a sibling repository implementation, the code is quite similar to the Redis repository endstate. I demonstrate a couple of differences in approach for this example.

Rather than manually creating a constructor via which to receive the autowired `Air craftRepository` bean, I instruct Lombok—via its compile-time code generator—to provide a constructor with any required member variables. Lombok determines which arguments are required via two annotations: `@RequiredArgsConstructor` on the class and `@NonNull` on the member variable(s) designated as requiring initialization. By annotating the `AircraftRepository` member variable as an `@NonNull` property, Lombok creates a constructor with an `AircraftRepository` as a parameter; Spring Boot then dutifully autowires the existing repository bean for use within the `PlaneFinderPoller` bean.

 The wisdom of deleting all stored entries in a database each time a poll is conducted depends heavily on requirements, polling frequency, and storage mechanism involved. For example, the costs involved in clearing an in-memory database before each poll is quite different from deleting all records in a cloud-hosted database's table. Frequent polling also increases associated costs. Alternatives exist; please choose wisely.

To revisit the details of the remaining code in `PlaneFinderPoller`, please review the corresponding section under Redis repository support. Refactored to take full advantage of Spring Data JPA support, the complete code for `PlaneFinderPoller` is shown in the following listing:

```java
import lombok.NonNull;
import lombok.RequiredArgsConstructor;
import org.springframework.scheduling.annotation.EnableScheduling;
import org.springframework.scheduling.annotation.Scheduled;
import org.springframework.stereotype.Component;
import org.springframework.web.reactive.function.client.WebClient;

@EnableScheduling
@Component
@RequiredArgsConstructor
class PlaneFinderPoller {
    @NonNull
    private final AircraftRepository repository;
    private WebClient client =
            WebClient.create("http://localhost:7634/aircraft");

    @Scheduled(fixedRate = 1000)
    private void pollPlanes() {
        repository.deleteAll();

        client.get()
                .retrieve()
                .bodyToFlux(Aircraft.class)
                .filter(plane -> !plane.getReg().isEmpty())
                .toStream()
                .forEach(repository::save);

        repository.findAll().forEach(System.out::println);
    }
}
```

Connecting to MariaDB/MySQL. Spring Boot autoconfigures the application's environment using all information available at runtime; that's one of the key enablers of its unrivaled flexibility. Since there are many JPA-compliant databases supported by Spring Boot and Spring Data, we need to provide a few key bits of information for Boot to use to seamlessly connect to the database of our choosing for this particular application. For this service running in my environment, these properties include:

```
spring.datasource.platform=mysql
spring.datasource.url=jdbc:mysql://${MYSQL_HOST:localhost}:3306/mark
spring.datasource.username=mark
spring.datasource.password=sbux
```

 Both the database name and the database username are "mark" in the example above. Replace datasource, username, and password values with those specific to your environment.

The results

With the PlaneFinder service still running on my machine, I start the *sbur-jpa* service to obtain, store and retrieve (in MariaDB), and display the results of each polling of PlaneFinder. An example of the results follows, edited for brevity and formatted for readability:

```
Aircraft(id=106, callsign=null, squawk=null, reg=N7816B, flightno=WN2117,
route=SJC-STL-BWI-FLL, type=B737, category=, altitude=4400, heading=87,
speed=233, vertRate=2048, selectedAltitude=15008, lat=0.0, lon=0.0,
barometer=1017.6, polarDistance=0.0, polarBearing=0.0, isADSB=false,
isOnGround=false, lastSeenTime=2020-11-27T18:59:10Z,
posUpdateTime=2020-11-27T18:59:17Z, bds40SeenTime=2020-11-27T18:59:10Z)

Aircraft(id=107, callsign=null, squawk=null, reg=N963WN, flightno=WN851,
route=LAS-DAL-STL-CMH, type=B737, category=, altitude=27200, heading=80,
speed=429, vertRate=2112, selectedAltitude=0, lat=0.0, lon=0.0, barometer=0.0,
polarDistance=0.0, polarBearing=0.0, isADSB=false, isOnGround=false,
lastSeenTime=2020-11-27T18:58:45Z, posUpdateTime=2020-11-27T18:59:17Z,
bds40SeenTime=2020-11-27T18:59:17Z)

Aircraft(id=108, callsign=null, squawk=null, reg=N8563Z, flightno=WN1386,
route=DEN-IAD, type=B738, category=, altitude=39000, heading=94, speed=500,
vertRate=0, selectedAltitude=39008, lat=0.0, lon=0.0, barometer=1013.6,
polarDistance=0.0, polarBearing=0.0, isADSB=false, isOnGround=false,
lastSeenTime=2020-11-27T18:59:10Z, posUpdateTime=2020-11-27T18:59:17Z,
bds40SeenTime=2020-11-27T18:59:10Z)
```

The service works as expected to poll, capture, and display aircraft positions.

Loading Data

This chapter's focus thus far has been how to interact with a database when data flows into the application. What happens if data exists—sample, test, or actual seed data—that must be persisted?

Spring Boot has a few different mechanisms to initialize and populate a database. I cover what I consider to be the two most useful approaches here:

- Using Data Definition Language (DDL) and Data Manipulation Language (DML) scripts to initialize and populate
- Allowing Boot (via Hibernate) to automatically create the table structure from defined @Entity class(es) and populating via a repository bean

Each approach to data definition and population has its pros and cons.

API- or database-specific scripts

Spring Boot checks the usual root classpath locations for files that fit the following naming format:

- *schema.sql*
- *data.sql*
- *schema-${platform}.sql*
- *data-${platform}.sql*

The last two filenames are matched to the developer-assigned application property `spring.datasource.platform`. Valid values include `h2`, `mysql`, `postgresql`, and other Spring Data JPA databases, and using a combination of the `spring.data source.platform` property and related `.sql` files enables a developer to fully leverage syntax specific to that particular database.

Creating and populating with scripts.   To leverage scripts to create and populate a MariaDB/MySQL database in the most straightforward way, I create two files under the `resources` directory of the *sbur-jpa* project: *schema-mysql.sql* and *data-mysql.sql*.

To create the `aircraft` table schema, I add the following DDL to *schema-mysql.sql*:

```
DROP TABLE IF EXISTS aircraft;
CREATE TABLE aircraft (id BIGINT not null primary key, callsign VARCHAR(7),
squawk VARCHAR(4), reg VARCHAR(6), flightno VARCHAR(10), route VARCHAR(25),
type VARCHAR(4), category VARCHAR(2),
altitude INT, heading INT, speed INT, vert_rate INT, selected_altitude INT,
lat DOUBLE, lon DOUBLE, barometer DOUBLE,
polar_distance DOUBLE, polar_bearing DOUBLE,
isadsb BOOLEAN, is_on_ground BOOLEAN,
last_seen_time TIMESTAMP, pos_update_time TIMESTAMP, bds40seen_time TIMESTAMP);
```

To populate the `aircraft` table with a single sample row, I add the following DML to *data-mysql.sql*:

```
INSERT INTO aircraft (id, callsign, squawk, reg, flightno, route, type,
category, altitude, heading, speed, vert_rate, selected_altitude, lat, lon,
```

```
barometer, polar_distance, polar_bearing, isadsb, is_on_ground,
last_seen_time, pos_update_time, bds40seen_time)
VALUES (81, 'AAL608', '1451', 'N754UW', 'AA608', 'IND-PHX', 'A319', 'A3', 36000,
255, 423, 0, 36000, 39.150284, -90.684795, 1012.8, 26.575562, 295.501994,
true, false, '2020-11-27 21:29:35', '2020-11-27 21:29:34',
'2020-11-27 21:29:27');
```

By default, Boot automatically creates table structures from any classes annotated with @Entity. It's simple to override this behavior with the following property settings, shown here from the app's *application.properties* file:

```
spring.datasource.initialization-mode=always
spring.jpa.hibernate.ddl-auto=none
```

Setting spring.datasource.initialization-mode to "always" indicates that the app is expecting to use an external (nonembedded) database and should initialize it each time the application executes. Setting spring.jpa.hibernate.ddl-auto to "none" disables Spring Boot's automatic table creation from @Entity classes.

To verify that the preceding scripts are being used to create and populate the air craft table, I visit the PlaneFinderPoller class and do the following:

- Comment out the repository.deleteAll(); statement in pollPlanes(). This is necessary to avoid deleting the record added via *data-mysql.sql*.

- Comment out the client.get()... statement, also in pollPlanes(). This results in no additional records being retrieved and created from polling the external PlaneFinder service for easier verification.

Restarting the *sbur-jpa* service now results in the following output (id fields may differ), edited for brevity and formatted for clarity:

```
Aircraft(id=81, callsign=AAL608, squawk=1451, reg=N754UW, flightno=AA608,
route=IND-PHX, type=A319, category=A3, altitude=36000, heading=255, speed=423,
vertRate=0, selectedAltitude=36000, lat=39.150284, lon=-90.684795,
barometer=1012.8, polarDistance=26.575562, polarBearing=295.501994, isADSB=true,
isOnGround=false, lastSeenTime=2020-11-27T21:29:35Z,
posUpdateTime=2020-11-27T21:29:34Z, bds40SeenTime=2020-11-27T21:29:27Z)
```

 The only record saved is the one specified in *data-mysql.sql*.

Like all approaches to anything, there are pros and cons to this method of table creation and population. Upsides include:

- The ability to directly use SQL scripts, both DDL and DML, leveraging existing scripts and/or SQL expertise

- Access to SQL syntax specific to the chosen database

Downsides aren't particularly serious but should be recognized:

- Using SQL files is obviously specific to SQL-supporting relational databases.
- Scripts can rely on SQL syntax for a particular database, which can require editing if the choice of underlying database changes.
- Some (two) application properties must be set to override default Boot behavior.

Populating the database using the application's repository

There is another way, one that I find particularly powerful and more flexible: using Boot's default behavior to create the table structures (if they don't already exist) and the application's repository support to populate sample data.

To restore Spring Boot's default behavior of creating the `aircraft` table from the `Aircraft` JPA `@Entity` class, I comment out the two properties just added to *application.properties*:

```
#spring.datasource.initialization-mode=always
#spring.jpa.hibernate.ddl-auto=none
```

With these properties no longer being defined, Spring Boot will not search for and execute *data-mysql.sql* or other data initialization scripts.

Next, I create a class with a purpose-descriptive name like `DataLoader`. I add class-level annotations of `@Component` (so Spring creates a `DataLoader` bean) and `@AllArgs Constructor` (so Lombok creates a constructor with a parameter for each member variable). I then add a single member variable to hold the `AircraftRepository` bean Spring Boot will autowire for me via constructor injection:

```
private final AircraftRepository repository;
```

And a method called `loadData()` to both clear and populate the `aircraft` table:

```
@PostConstruct
private void loadData() {
    repository.deleteAll();

    repository.save(new Aircraft(81L,
            "AAL608", "1451", "N754UW", "AA608", "IND-PHX", "A319", "A3",
            36000, 255, 423, 0, 36000,
            39.150284, -90.684795, 1012.8, 26.575562, 295.501994,
            true, false,
            Instant.parse("2020-11-27T21:29:35Z"),
            Instant.parse("2020-11-27T21:29:34Z"),
            Instant.parse("2020-11-27T21:29:27Z")));
}
```

And that's it. Really. Restarting the the the *sbur-jpa* service now results in the output that follows (id fields may differ), edited for brevity and formatted for clarity:

```
Aircraft(id=110, callsign=AAL608, squawk=1451, reg=N754UW, flightno=AA608,
route=IND-PHX, type=A319, category=A3, altitude=36000, heading=255, speed=423,
vertRate=0, selectedAltitude=36000, lat=39.150284, lon=-90.684795,
barometer=1012.8, polarDistance=26.575562, polarBearing=295.501994, isADSB=true,
isOnGround=false, lastSeenTime=2020-11-27T21:29:35Z,
posUpdateTime=2020-11-27T21:29:34Z, bds40SeenTime=2020-11-27T21:29:27Z)
```

 The only record saved is the one defined in the previous Data Loader class, with one small difference: since the id field is generated by the database (as specified in the Aircraft domain class specification), the provided id value is replaced by the database engine when the record is saved.

Advantages of this approach are significant:

- Fully database independent.
- Any code/annotations specific to a particular database are already within the app simply to support db access.
- Easy to disable by simply commenting out the @Component annotation on the DataLoader class.

Other mechanisms

These are two powerful and widely used options for database initialization and population, but there are other options, including using Hibernate support for an *import.sql* file (similar to the JPA approach introduced earlier), using external imports, and using FlywayDB, among others. Exploring the numerous other options is out of scope for this book and is left as an optional exercise for the reader.

Creating a Repository-Based Service Using a NoSQL Document Database

As mentioned earlier, there are several ways to further enhance developer productivity when creating applications using Spring Boot. One of these is to increase code conciseness by using Kotlin as the foundational app language.

An exhaustive exploration of the Kotlin language is well beyond the scope of this book, and there are other books that fulfill that role. Fortunately, though, while Kotlin definitely differs from Java in numerous meaningful ways, it is similar enough to pose no great hardship in adapting to its idioms with a few well-placed explanations when things diverge from the "Java way." I'll endeavor to provide those explanations as I proceed; for background or additional information, please refer to Kotlin-specific tomes.

For this example, I use MongoDB. Perhaps the best-known document datastore, MongoDB is widely used and wildly popular for good reason: it works well and generally makes life easier for developers to store, manipulate, and retrieve data in all of its varied (and sometimes messy) forms. The team at MongoDB also constantly strives to improve their feature set, security, and APIs: MongoDB was one of the first databases to offer reactive database drivers, leading the industry in taking nonblocking access all the way down to the database level.

Initializing the Project

As you might expect, we return to the Spring Initializr to get started. For this project, I choose the following options (also shown in Figure 6-1)—somewhat of a departure from prior visits:

- Gradle project
- Kotlin
- Current production version of Spring Boot
- Packaging: Jar
- Java: 11

And for dependencies:

- Spring Reactive Web (`spring-boot-starter-webflux`)
- Spring Data MongoDB (`spring-boot-starter-data-mongodb`)
- Embedded MongoDB Database (`de.flapdoodle.embed.mongo`)

Next, I generate the project and save it locally, unzip it, and open it in the IDE.

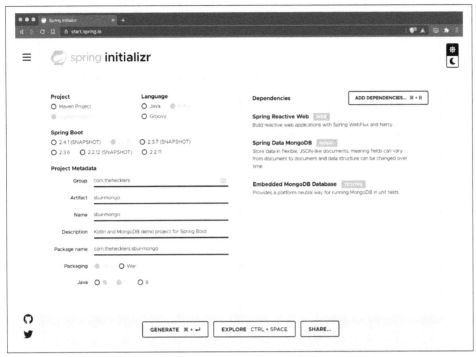

Figure 6-1. Using the Spring Boot Initializr to create a Kotlin application

A couple of things of particular note about the options selected: First, I chose Gradle for this project's build system for good reason—simply choosing to use Gradle with Kotlin in a Spring Boot project results in the Gradle build file using the Kotlin DSL, which is supported by the Gradle team on equal footing with the Groovy DSL. Note that the resultant build file is *build.gradle.kts*—the .kts extension indicates it is a Kotlin script—rather than the Groovy-based *build.gradle* file you may be accustomed to seeing. Maven works perfectly well as a build system for Spring Boot + Kotlin applications too, but being an XML-based declarative build system, it doesn't directly use Kotlin or any other language.

Second, I took advantage of the presence of a Spring Boot Starter for an embedded MongoDB database for this application. Because an embedded MongoDB instance is meant solely for testing, I advise against using it in a production setting; that said, it's a wonderful option for demonstrating how Spring Boot and Spring Data work with MongoDB, and from the developer's perspective, it matches locally deployed database capabilities without the additional steps of installing and/or running a containerized instance of MongoDB. The only adjustment necessary to use the embedded database from (nontest) code is to change a single line in *build.gradle.kts* from this:

```
testImplementation("de.flapdoodle.embed:de.flapdoodle.embed.mongo")
```

to this:

```
implementation("de.flapdoodle.embed:de.flapdoodle.embed.mongo")
```

And with that, we're ready to create our service.

Developing the MongoDB Service

As with previous examples, the MongoDB-based service offers a very consistent approach and experience, even when using Kotlin instead of Java as the language foundation.

Defining the domain class

For this project I create a Kotlin `Aircraft` domain class to serve as the primary (data) focus. Here is the new `Aircraft` domain class structure with a few observations following:

```kotlin
import com.fasterxml.jackson.annotation.JsonIgnoreProperties
import com.fasterxml.jackson.annotation.JsonProperty
import org.springframework.data.annotation.Id
import org.springframework.data.mongodb.core.mapping.Document
import java.time.Instant

@Document
@JsonIgnoreProperties(ignoreUnknown = true)
data class Aircraft(
    @Id val id: String,
    val callsign: String? = "",
    val squawk: String? = "",
    val reg: String? = "",
    val flightno: String? = "",
    val route: String? = "",
    val type: String? = "",
    val category: String? = "",
    val altitude: Int? = 0,
    val heading: Int? = 0,
    val speed: Int? = 0,
    @JsonProperty("vert_rate") val vertRate: Int? = 0,
    @JsonProperty("selected_altitude")
    val selectedAltitude: Int? = 0,
    val lat: Double? = 0.0,
    val lon: Double? = 0.0,
    val barometer: Double? = 0.0,
    @JsonProperty("polar_distance")
    val polarDistance: Double? = 0.0,
    @JsonProperty("polar_bearing")
    val polarBearing: Double? = 0.0,
    @JsonProperty("is_adsb")
    val isADSB: Boolean? = false,
    @JsonProperty("is_on_ground")
    val isOnGround: Boolean? = false,
    @JsonProperty("last_seen_time")
    val lastSeenTime: Instant? = Instant.ofEpochSecond(0),
```

```
@JsonProperty("pos_update_time")
val posUpdateTime: Instant? = Instant.ofEpochSecond(0),
@JsonProperty("bds40_seen_time")
val bds40SeenTime: Instant? = Instant.ofEpochSecond(0)
)
```

The first thing to note is that there are no curly braces to be seen; put succinctly, this class has no body. If you're new to Kotlin, this may seem a bit unusual, but in cases where there is nothing to place in a class (or interface) body, curly braces add no value. As such, Kotlin doesn't require them.

The second interesting thing is the many assignments shown between parentheses immediately after the classname. What purpose do these serve?

A Kotlin class's primary constructor is often shown this way: in the class header, immediately following the classname. Here is an example of the full, formal format:

```
class Aircraft constructor(<parameter1>,<parameter2>,...,<parametern>)
```

As is often the case in Kotlin, if a pattern is clearly identifiable and repeats consistently, it can be condensed. Removing the `constructor` keyword before the parameter list leads to no confusion with any other language construct, so it is optional.

Within the constructor are parameters. By placing a `var` (for repeatedly assignable mutable variables) or `val` (for single-assignment values equivalent to Java's `final` variables) before each parameter, it also becomes a property. A Kotlin property is roughly equivalent in function to a Java member variable, its accessor, and (if declared with `var`) its mutator combined.

The values with types containing a question mark (?), e.g., `Double?`, indicate that the constructor parameter may be omitted. If so, that parameter is assigned the default value shown after the equals sign (=).

Kotlin method (including constructor) parameters and properties can also include annotations, just like their Java counterparts. `@Id` and `@JsonProperty` perform the same functions that they did in earlier Java examples.

Regarding class-level annotations, `@Document` indicates to MongoDB that each object of type `Aircraft` will be stored as a document within the database. As before, `@Jso nIgnoreProperties(ignoreUnknown = true)` simply builds a bit of flexibility into the *sbur-mongo* service; if at some point additional fields are added to the data feed produced by the upstream `PlaneFinder` service, they will simply be ignored and *sbur_mongo* will continue to run without issue.

The final point of note is the word `data` that precedes the class definition. It's a frequent pattern to create domain classes that serve primarily as data buckets to be manipulated and/or passed between processes. It's such a common pattern in fact that the capability to create so-called data classes manifests itself in several ways; as one example, @Data has been a feature of Lombok for years.

Kotlin rolled this capability into the language itself and added the data keyword to signal that a data class automatically derives the following from all properties declared in the class's primary constructor:

- equals() and hashCode() functions (Java has methods; Kotlin has functions)
- toString()
- componentN() functions, one for each property in the order in which they were declared
- copy() function

Kotlin data classes have certain requirements and limitations, but they are reasonable and minimal. For details, please refer to the Kotlin documentation for data classes (*https://kotlinlang.org/docs/reference/data-classes.html#data-classes*).

 One other change of interest is the type of each aircraft position's id field/property. In Redis and JPA, it was a Long; but MongoDB uses a String for its unique document identifier. This is of no real consequence, only something to be aware of.

Creating the repository interface

Next, I define the required repository interface, extending Spring Data's CrudReposi tory and providing the type of object to store and its unique identifier: Aircraft and String, as mentioned earlier:

```
interface AircraftRepository: CrudRepository<Aircraft, String>
```

There are two things of interest in this concise interface definition:

1. With no actual interface body, no curly braces are required in Kotlin. If your IDE added them when you created this interface, you can safely remove them.

2. Kotlin uses the colon (:) contextually to indicate a val or var type, or in this case, to indicate that a class or interface extends or implements another. In this particular instance, I define an interface AircraftRepository, and it extends the Cru dRepository interface.

There is a MongoRepository interface that extends both PagingAnd SortingRepository (which extends CrudRepository) and Query ByExampleExecutor that can be used instead of CrudRepository, as I do here. But unless the additional capabilities are required, it is a good practice and habit to write to the highest-level interface that satisfies all requirements. In this case, CrudRepository is sufficient for current needs.

Bringing it all together

The next step is to create the component that periodically polls the PlaneFinder service.

Polling PlaneFinder. Similar to earlier examples, I create a Spring Boot component class PlaneFinderPoller to poll for current position data and handle any Aircraft records received, as shown here:

```
import org.springframework.scheduling.annotation.EnableScheduling
import org.springframework.scheduling.annotation.Scheduled
import org.springframework.stereotype.Component
import org.springframework.web.reactive.function.client.WebClient
import org.springframework.web.reactive.function.client.bodyToFlux

@Component
@EnableScheduling
class PlaneFinderPoller(private val repository: AircraftRepository) {
    private val client =
        WebClient.create("http://localhost:7634/aircraft")

    @Scheduled(fixedRate = 1000)
    private fun pollPlanes() {
        repository.deleteAll()

        client.get()
            .retrieve()
            .bodyToFlux<Aircraft>()
            .filter { !it.reg.isNullOrEmpty() }
            .toStream()
            .forEach { repository.save(it) }

        println("--- All aircraft ---")
        repository.findAll().forEach { println(it) }
    }
}
```

I create the primary constructor in the header with an AircraftRepository parameter. Spring Boot automatically autowires the existing AircraftRepository bean into the PlaneFinderPoller component for use, and I mark it as a private val to ensure the following:

- It isn't assignable later.

- It isn't exposed externally as a property from the `PlaneFinderPoller` bean, as the repository is already accessible throughout the application.

Next, I create a `WebClient` object and assign it to a property, pointing it to the destination endpoint exposed by the `PlaneFinder` service on port 7634.

I annotate the class with `@Component` to have Spring Boot create a component (bean) upon application startup and `@EnableScheduling` to enable periodic polling via an annotated function to follow.

And finally, I create a function to delete all existing `Aircraft` data, poll the `Plane Finder` endpoint via the `WebClient` client property, convert and store the retrieved aircraft positions in MongoDB, and display them. The `@Scheduled(fixedRate = 1000)` results in the polling function being executed once every 1,000 ms (once per second).

There are three more interesting things to note in the `pollPlanes()` function, and both regard Kotlin's lambdas.

First is that if a lambda is the final parameter of a function, parentheses can be omitted, as they add nothing to clarity or meaning. If a function has only a single parameter of a lambda, this fits the criteria as well, of course. This results in fewer symbols to sift through in sometimes busy lines of code.

Second is that if a lambda itself has a single parameter, a developer can still explicitly specify it but isn't required to do so. Kotlin implicitly recognizes and refers to a sole lambda parameter as `it`, which further streamlines lambdas, as demonstrated by this lambda parameter to `forEach()`:

```
forEach { repository.save(it) }
```

Finally, the function `isNullOrEmpty()` that operates on a `CharSequence` provides a very nice all-in-one capability for String evaluation. This function performs both a null check (first), then if the value is determined to be non-null, it checks to see if it has zero length, i.e., is empty. There are many times that a developer can process properties only if they contain actual values, and this single function performs both validations in one step. If a value exists in the `Aircraft`'s registration property `reg`, that incoming aircraft position report is passed along; aircraft position reports with missing registration values are filtered out.

All remaining position reports are streamed to the repository to be saved, then we query the repository for all persisted documents and display the results.

The results

With the `PlaneFinder` service running on my machine, I start the *sbur-mongo* service to obtain, store and retrieve (in an embedded MongoDB instance), and display the results of each polling of `PlaneFinder`. An example of the results follows, edited for brevity and formatted for readability:

```
Aircraft(id=95, callsign=N88846, squawk=4710, reg=N88846, flightno=, route=,
type=P46T, category=A1, altitude=18000, heading=234, speed=238, vertRate=-64,
selectedAltitude=0, lat=39.157288, lon=-90.844992, barometer=0.0,
polarDistance=33.5716, polarBearing=290.454061, isADSB=true, isOnGround=false,
lastSeenTime=2020-11-27T20:16:57Z, posUpdateTime=2020-11-27T20:16:57Z,
bds40SeenTime=1970-01-01T00:00:00Z)

Aircraft(id=96, callsign=MVJ710, squawk=1750, reg=N710MV, flightno=,
route=IAD-TEX, type=GLF4, category=A2, altitude=18050, heading=66, speed=362,
vertRate=2432, selectedAltitude=23008, lat=38.627655, lon=-90.008897,
barometer=0.0, polarDistance=20.976944, polarBearing=158.35465, isADSB=true,
isOnGround=false, lastSeenTime=2020-11-27T20:16:57Z,
posUpdateTime=2020-11-27T20:16:57Z, bds40SeenTime=2020-11-27T20:16:56Z)

Aircraft(id=97, callsign=SWA1121, squawk=6225, reg=N8654B, flightno=WN1121,
route=MDW-DAL-PHX, type=B738, category=A3, altitude=40000, heading=236,
speed=398, vertRate=0, selectedAltitude=40000, lat=39.58548, lon=-90.049259,
barometer=1013.6, polarDistance=38.411587, polarBearing=8.70042, isADSB=true,
isOnGround=false, lastSeenTime=2020-11-27T20:16:57Z,
posUpdateTime=2020-11-27T20:16:55Z, bds40SeenTime=2020-11-27T20:16:54Z)
```

As expected, the service polls, captures, and displays aircraft positions without issue using Spring Boot, Kotlin, and MongoDB to make it nearly effortless.

Creating a Repository-Based Service Using a NoSQL Graph Database

Graph databases bring a different approach to data, in particular how it's interrelated. There are a few graph databases on the market, but for all intents and purposes, the segment leader is Neo4j.

While graph theory and graph database design is far afield of the scope of this book, demonstrating how best to work with a graph database using Spring Boot and Spring Data falls squarely within its purview. This section shows you how to easily connect to and work with data using Spring Data Neo4j in your Spring Boot application.

Initializing the Project

Once more we return to the Spring Initializr. This time, I choose the following options:

- Gradle project

- Java
- Current production version of Spring Boot
- Packaging: Jar
- Java: 11

And for dependencies:

- Spring Reactive Web (`spring-boot-starter-webflux`)
- Spring Data Neo4j (`spring-boot-starter-data-neo4j`)

Next, I generate the project and save it locally, unzip it, and open it in the IDE.

I chose Gradle for this project's build system solely to demonstrate that when creating a Spring Boot Java application using Gradle, the generated *build.gradle* file uses the Groovy DSL, but Maven is a valid option as well.

 As with most other examples in this chapter, I have a Neo4j database instance running in a locally hosted container, ready to respond to this application.

And with that, we're ready to create our service.

Developing the Neo4j Service

As with previous examples, Spring Boot and Spring Data make the experience of working with Neo4j databases highly consistent with using other types of underlying datastores. The full power of a graph datastore is available and easily accessible from Spring Boot applications, but ramp-up is drastically reduced.

Defining the domain class

Once more I begin by defining the `Aircraft` domain. Without Lombok as a dependency, I create it with the usual extensive list of constructors, accessors, mutators, and supporting methods:

```
import com.fasterxml.jackson.annotation.JsonIgnoreProperties;
import com.fasterxml.jackson.annotation.JsonProperty;
import org.springframework.data.neo4j.core.schema.GeneratedValue;
import org.springframework.data.neo4j.core.schema.Id;
import org.springframework.data.neo4j.core.schema.Node;

@Node
@JsonIgnoreProperties(ignoreUnknown = true)
public class Aircraft {
    @Id
```

```java
@GeneratedValue
private Long neoId;

private Long id;
private String callsign, squawk, reg, flightno, route, type, category;

private int altitude, heading, speed;
@JsonProperty("vert_rate")
private int vertRate;
@JsonProperty("selected_altitude")
private int selectedAltitude;

private double lat, lon, barometer;
@JsonProperty("polar_distance")
private double polarDistance;
@JsonProperty("polar_bearing")
private double polarBearing;

@JsonProperty("is_adsb")
private boolean isADSB;
@JsonProperty("is_on_ground")
private boolean isOnGround;

@JsonProperty("last_seen_time")
private Instant lastSeenTime;
@JsonProperty("pos_update_time")
private Instant posUpdateTime;
@JsonProperty("bds40_seen_time")
private Instant bds40SeenTime;

public Aircraft() {
}

public Aircraft(Long id,
                String callsign, String squawk, String reg, String flightno,
                String route, String type, String category,
                int altitude, int heading, int speed,
                int vertRate, int selectedAltitude,
                double lat, double lon, double barometer,
                double polarDistance, double polarBearing,
                boolean isADSB, boolean isOnGround,
                Instant lastSeenTime,
                Instant posUpdateTime,
                Instant bds40SeenTime) {
    this.id = id;
    this.callsign = callsign;
    this.squawk = squawk;
    this.reg = reg;
    this.flightno = flightno;
    this.route = route;
    this.type = type;
    this.category = category;
    this.altitude = altitude;
    this.heading = heading;
    this.speed = speed;
    this.vertRate = vertRate;
```

```java
        this.selectedAltitude = selectedAltitude;
        this.lat = lat;
        this.lon = lon;
        this.barometer = barometer;
        this.polarDistance = polarDistance;
        this.polarBearing = polarBearing;
        this.isADSB = isADSB;
        this.isOnGround = isOnGround;
        this.lastSeenTime = lastSeenTime;
        this.posUpdateTime = posUpdateTime;
        this.bds40SeenTime = bds40SeenTime;
    }

    public Long getNeoId() {
        return neoId;
    }

    public void setNeoId(Long neoId) {
        this.neoId = neoId;
    }

    public Long getId() {
        return id;
    }

    public void setId(Long id) {
        this.id = id;
    }

    public String getCallsign() {
        return callsign;
    }

    public void setCallsign(String callsign) {
        this.callsign = callsign;
    }

    public String getSquawk() {
        return squawk;
    }

    public void setSquawk(String squawk) {
        this.squawk = squawk;
    }

    public String getReg() {
        return reg;
    }

    public void setReg(String reg) {
        this.reg = reg;
    }

    public String getFlightno() {
        return flightno;
    }
```

```java
public void setFlightno(String flightno) {
    this.flightno = flightno;
}

public String getRoute() {
    return route;
}

public void setRoute(String route) {
    this.route = route;
}

public String getType() {
    return type;
}

public void setType(String type) {
    this.type = type;
}

public String getCategory() {
    return category;
}

public void setCategory(String category) {
    this.category = category;
}

public int getAltitude() {
    return altitude;
}

public void setAltitude(int altitude) {
    this.altitude = altitude;
}

public int getHeading() {
    return heading;
}

public void setHeading(int heading) {
    this.heading = heading;
}

public int getSpeed() {
    return speed;
}

public void setSpeed(int speed) {
    this.speed = speed;
}

public int getVertRate() {
    return vertRate;
}
```

```java
    public void setVertRate(int vertRate) {
        this.vertRate = vertRate;
    }

    public int getSelectedAltitude() {
        return selectedAltitude;
    }

    public void setSelectedAltitude(int selectedAltitude) {
        this.selectedAltitude = selectedAltitude;
    }

    public double getLat() {
        return lat;
    }

    public void setLat(double lat) {
        this.lat = lat;
    }

    public double getLon() {
        return lon;
    }

    public void setLon(double lon) {
        this.lon = lon;
    }

    public double getBarometer() {
        return barometer;
    }

    public void setBarometer(double barometer) {
        this.barometer = barometer;
    }

    public double getPolarDistance() {
        return polarDistance;
    }

    public void setPolarDistance(double polarDistance) {
        this.polarDistance = polarDistance;
    }

    public double getPolarBearing() {
        return polarBearing;
    }

    public void setPolarBearing(double polarBearing) {
        this.polarBearing = polarBearing;
    }

    public boolean isADSB() {
        return isADSB;
    }
```

```java
public void setADSB(boolean ADSB) {
    isADSB = ADSB;
}

public boolean isOnGround() {
    return isOnGround;
}

public void setOnGround(boolean onGround) {
    isOnGround = onGround;
}

public Instant getLastSeenTime() {
    return lastSeenTime;
}

public void setLastSeenTime(Instant lastSeenTime) {
    this.lastSeenTime = lastSeenTime;
}

public Instant getPosUpdateTime() {
    return posUpdateTime;
}

public void setPosUpdateTime(Instant posUpdateTime) {
    this.posUpdateTime = posUpdateTime;
}

public Instant getBds40SeenTime() {
    return bds40SeenTime;
}

public void setBds40SeenTime(Instant bds40SeenTime) {
    this.bds40SeenTime = bds40SeenTime;
}

@Override
public boolean equals(Object o) {
    if (this == o) return true;
    if (o == null || getClass() != o.getClass()) return false;
    Aircraft aircraft = (Aircraft) o;
    return altitude == aircraft.altitude &&
            heading == aircraft.heading &&
            speed == aircraft.speed &&
            vertRate == aircraft.vertRate &&
            selectedAltitude == aircraft.selectedAltitude &&
            Double.compare(aircraft.lat, lat) == 0 &&
            Double.compare(aircraft.lon, lon) == 0 &&
            Double.compare(aircraft.barometer, barometer) == 0 &&
            Double.compare(aircraft.polarDistance, polarDistance) == 0 &&
            Double.compare(aircraft.polarBearing, polarBearing) == 0 &&
            isADSB == aircraft.isADSB &&
            isOnGround == aircraft.isOnGround &&
            Objects.equals(neoId, aircraft.neoId) &&
            Objects.equals(id, aircraft.id) &&
```

```
                Objects.equals(callsign, aircraft.callsign) &&
                Objects.equals(squawk, aircraft.squawk) &&
                Objects.equals(reg, aircraft.reg) &&
                Objects.equals(flightno, aircraft.flightno) &&
                Objects.equals(route, aircraft.route) &&
                Objects.equals(type, aircraft.type) &&
                Objects.equals(category, aircraft.category) &&
                Objects.equals(lastSeenTime, aircraft.lastSeenTime) &&
                Objects.equals(posUpdateTime, aircraft.posUpdateTime) &&
                Objects.equals(bds40SeenTime, aircraft.bds40SeenTime);
    }

    @Override
    public int hashCode() {
        return Objects.hash(neoId, id, callsign, squawk, reg, flightno, route,
                type, category, altitude, heading, speed, vertRate,
                selectedAltitude,  lat, lon, barometer, polarDistance,
                polarBearing, isADSB, isOnGround, lastSeenTime, posUpdateTime,
                bds40SeenTime);
    }

    @Override
    public String toString() {
        return "Aircraft{" +
                "neoId=" + neoId +
                ", id=" + id +
                ", callsign='" + callsign + '\'' +
                ", squawk='" + squawk + '\'' +
                ", reg='" + reg + '\'' +
                ", flightno='" + flightno + '\'' +
                ", route='" + route + '\'' +
                ", type='" + type + '\'' +
                ", category='" + category + '\'' +
                ", altitude=" + altitude +
                ", heading=" + heading +
                ", speed=" + speed +
                ", vertRate=" + vertRate +
                ", selectedAltitude=" + selectedAltitude +
                ", lat=" + lat +
                ", lon=" + lon +
                ", barometer=" + barometer +
                ", polarDistance=" + polarDistance +
                ", polarBearing=" + polarBearing +
                ", isADSB=" + isADSB +
                ", isOnGround=" + isOnGround +
                ", lastSeenTime=" + lastSeenTime +
                ", posUpdateTime=" + posUpdateTime +
                ", bds40SeenTime=" + bds40SeenTime +
                '}';
    }
}
```

Java code can indeed be verbose. To be fair this isn't a huge problem in cases like domain classes, because while accessors and mutators take up a significant amount of space, they can be generated by IDEs and typically don't involve much maintenance due to their long-term stability. That said, it *is* a lot of boilerplate code, which is why many developers use solutions like Lombok or Kotlin—even if only creating domain classes in Kotlin for Java applications.

 Neo requires a database-generated unique identifier, even if entities being persisted contain a unique identifier already. To satisfy this requirement, I add a `neoId` parameter/member variable and annotate it with `@Id` and `GeneratedValue` so Neo4j correctly associates this member variable with the value it generates internally.

Next, I add two class-level annotations:

`@Node`:: To designate each instance of this `record` as an instance of the Neo4j node `Aircraft @JsonIgnoreProperties(ignoreUnknown = true)`:: To ignore new fields that might be added to feed from the `PlaneFinder` service endpoint

Note that like `@Id` and `@GeneratedValue`, the `@Node` annotation is from the `org.springframework.data.neo4j.core.schema` package for Spring Data Neo4j-based applications.

With that, the domain for our service is defined.

Creating the repository interface

For this application I again define the required repository interface, extending Spring Data's `CrudRepository` and providing the type of object to store and its key: `Aircraft` and `Long`, in this case:

```
public interface AircraftRepository extends CrudRepository<Aircraft, Long> {}
```

 Similar to the earlier MongoDB-based project, there is a `Neo4jRepository` interface that extends `PagingAndSortingRepository` (which extends `CrudRepository`) that can used instead of `CrudRepository`; however, since `CrudRepository` is the highest-level interface that satisfies all requirements, I use it as the basis for `AircraftRepository`.

Bringing it all together

Now to create the component to poll `PlaneFinder` and configure it to access the Neo4j database.

Polling PlaneFinder. Once more I create a Spring Boot `@Component` class to poll for current aircraft positions and handle `Aircraft` records received.

Like other Java-based projects in this chapter, I create a WebClient object and assign it to a member variable, pointing it to the destination endpoint exposed by the Plane Finder service on port 7634.

Without Lombok as a dependency, I create a constructor via which to receive the autowired AircraftRepository bean.

As shown in the following full listing of the PlaneFinderPoller class, the poll Planes() method looks nearly identical to other examples, owing to the abstractions brought to bear by repository support. To revisit any other details of the remaining code in PlaneFinderPoller, please review the corresponding section under earlier sections:

```
import org.springframework.scheduling.annotation.EnableScheduling;
import org.springframework.scheduling.annotation.Scheduled;
import org.springframework.stereotype.Component;
import org.springframework.web.reactive.function.client.WebClient;

@EnableScheduling
@Component
public class PlaneFinderPoller {
    private WebClient client =
            WebClient.create("http://localhost:7634/aircraft");
    private final AircraftRepository repository;

    public PlaneFinderPoller(AircraftRepository repository) {
        this.repository = repository;
    }

    @Scheduled(fixedRate = 1000)
    private void pollPlanes() {
        repository.deleteAll();

        client.get()
                .retrieve()
                .bodyToFlux(Aircraft.class)
                .filter(plane -> !plane.getReg().isEmpty())
                .toStream()
                .forEach(repository::save);

        System.out.println("--- All aircraft ---");
        repository.findAll().forEach(System.out::println);
    }
}
```

Connecting to Neo4j.   As with the earlier MariaDB/MySQL example, we need to provide a few key bits of information for Boot to use to seamlessly connect to a Neo4j database. For this service running in my environment, these properties include:

```
spring.neo4j.authentication.username=neo4j
spring.neo4j.authentication.password=mkheck
```

Replace username and password values shown with those specific to your environment.

The results

With the `PlaneFinder` service running on my machine, I start the *sbur-neo* service to obtain, store and retrieve, and display the results of each polling of `PlaneFinder` using Neo4j as the datastore of choice. An example of the results follows, edited for brevity and formatted for readability:

```
Aircraft(neoId=64, id=223, callsign='GJS4401', squawk='1355', reg='N542GJ',
flightno='UA4401', route='LIT-ORD', type='CRJ7', category='A2', altitude=37000,
heading=24, speed=476, vertRate=128, selectedAltitude=36992, lat=39.463961,
lon=-90.549927, barometer=1012.8, polarDistance=35.299257,
polarBearing=329.354686, isADSB=true, isOnGround=false,
lastSeenTime=2020-11-27T20:42:54Z, posUpdateTime=2020-11-27T20:42:53Z,
bds40SeenTime=2020-11-27T20:42:51Z)

Aircraft(neoId=65, id=224, callsign='N8680B', squawk='1200', reg='N8680B',
flightno='', route='', type='C172', category='A1', altitude=3100, heading=114,
speed=97, vertRate=64, selectedAltitude=0, lat=38.923955, lon=-90.195618,
barometer=0.0, polarDistance=1.986086, polarBearing=208.977102, isADSB=true,
isOnGround=false, lastSeenTime=2020-11-27T20:42:54Z,
posUpdateTime=2020-11-27T20:42:54Z, bds40SeenTime=null)

Aircraft(neoId=66, id=225, callsign='AAL1087', squawk='1712', reg='N181UW',
flightno='AA1087', route='CLT-STL-CLT', type='A321', category='A3',
altitude=7850, heading=278, speed=278, vertRate=-320, selectedAltitude=4992,
lat=38.801559, lon=-90.226474, barometer=0.0, polarDistance=9.385111,
polarBearing=194.034005, isADSB=true, isOnGround=false,
lastSeenTime=2020-11-27T20:42:54Z, posUpdateTime=2020-11-27T20:42:53Z,
bds40SeenTime=2020-11-27T20:42:53Z)
```

The service is fast and efficient, using Spring Boot and Neo4j to retrieve, capture, and display aircraft positions as they're reported.

Code Checkout Checkup

For complete chapter code, please check out branch *chapter6end* from the code repository.

Summary

Data can be a complex topic with innumerable variables and constraints, including data structures, relationships, applicable standards, providers and mechanisms, and more. Yet without data in some form, most applications provide little or no value.

As something that forms the foundation of nearly all application value, "data" has attracted a great deal of innovation from database providers and platform vendors. In many cases, though, complexity remains, and developers have to tame that complexity to unlock the value.

Spring Data's stated mission is "to provide a familiar and consistent, Spring-based programming model for data access while still retaining the special traits of the underlying data store." Regardless of database engine or platform, Spring Data's goal is to make the developer's use of data as simple and as powerful as humanly possible.

This chapter demonstrated how to streamline data storage and retrieval using various database options and the Spring Data projects and facilities that enable their use in the most powerful ways possible: via Spring Boot.

In the next chapter, I'll show how to create imperative applications using Spring MVC's REST interactions, messaging platforms, and other communications mechanisms, as well as provide an introduction to templating language support. While this chapter's focus was from the application downward, Chapter 7 focuses on the application outward.

Creating Applications Using Spring MVC

This chapter demonstrates how to create Spring Boot applications using Spring MVC with REST interactions, messaging platforms, and other communications mechanisms and provides an introduction to templating language support. Although I introduced interservice interactions as part of last chapter's dive into Spring Boot's many options for handling data, this chapter shifts the primary focus from the application itself to the outside world: its interactions with other applications and/or services and with end users.

Code Checkout Checkup

Please check out branch *chapter7begin* from the code repository to begin.

Spring MVC: What Does It Mean?

Like many other things in technology, the term *Spring MVC* is somewhat overloaded. When someone refers to Spring MVC, they could mean any of the following:

- Implementing (in some manner) the Model-View-Controller pattern in a Spring application
- Creating an application specifically using Spring MVC component concepts like the Model interface, @Controller classes, and view technologies
- Developing blocking/nonreactive applications using Spring

Depending on context, Spring MVC can be considered both an approach and an implementation. It can also be used within or without Spring Boot. Generic application of the MVC pattern using Spring and Spring MVC use outside of Spring Boot both fall outside the scope of this book. I'll focus specifically on the final two concepts previously listed using Spring Boot to implement them.

End User Interactions Using Template Engines

While Spring Boot applications handle a lot of heavy-lifting chores on the backend, Boot also supports direct end-user interactions as well. Although long-established standards like Java Server Pages (JSP) are still supported by Boot for legacy applications, most current applications either leverage more powerful view technologies supported by still-evolving and -maintained template engines or shift frontend development to a combination of HTML and JavaScript. It's even possible to mix the two options successfully and play to each one's strengths.

Spring Boot works well with HTML and JavaScript frontends, as I demonstrate later in this chapter. For now, let's take a closer look at template engines.

Template engines provide a way for a so-called server-side application to generate the final pages that will be displayed and executed in the end user's browser. These view technologies differ in approaches but generally provide the following:

- A template language and/or collection of tags that define inputs used by the template engine to produce the expected outcome
- A view resolver that determines the view/template to use to fulfill a requested resource

Among other lesser-used options, Spring Boot supports view technologies such as Thymeleaf (*https://www.thymeleaf.org*), FreeMarker (*https://freemarker.apache.org*), Groovy Markup (*http://groovy-lang.org/templating.html*), and Mustache (*https://mustache.github.io*). Thymeleaf is perhaps the most widely used of these for several reasons and provides excellent support for both Spring MVC and Spring WebFlux applications.

Thymeleaf uses natural templates: files that incorporate code elements but that can be opened and viewed directly (and correctly) in any standard web browser. Being able to view the template files as HTML enables developers or designers to create and evolve Thymeleaf templates without any running server processes. Any code integrations that expect corresponding server-side elements are tagged as Thymeleaf-specific and simply don't display what isn't present.

Building on previous efforts, let's build a simple web application using Spring Boot, Spring MVC, and Thymeleaf to present to the end user an interface for querying PlaneFinder for current aircraft positions and displaying the results. Initially this will be a rudimentary proof of concept to be evolved in subsequent chapters.

Initializing the Project

To begin, we return to the Spring Initializr. From there, I choose the following options:

- Maven project
- Java
- Current production version of Spring Boot
- Packaging: Jar
- Java: 11

And for dependencies:

- Spring Web (`spring-boot-starter-web`)
- Spring Reactive Web (`spring-boot-starter-webflux`)
- Thymeleaf (`spring-boot-starter-thymeleaf`)
- Spring Data JPA (`spring-boot-starter-data-jpa`)
- H2 Database (`h2`)
- Lombok (`lombok`)

The next step is to generate the project and save it locally, unzip it, and open it in the IDE.

Developing the Aircraft Positions Application

Since this application is concerned only with the current state—aircraft positions at the moment the request is made, not historically—an in-memory database seems a reasonable choice. One could instead use an `Iterable` of some kind, of course, but Spring Boot's support for Spring Data repositories and the H2 database fulfill the current use case and position the application well for planned future expansion.

Defining the domain class

As with other projects interacting with `PlaneFinder`, I create an `Aircraft` domain class to serve as the primary (data) focus. Here is the `Aircraft` domain class structure for the `Aircraft Positions` application:

```
@Entity
@Data
@NoArgsConstructor
@AllArgsConstructor
public class Aircraft {
    @Id
```

```
            private Long id;
            private String callsign, squawk, reg, flightno, route, type, category;

            private int altitude, heading, speed;
            @JsonProperty("vert_rate")
            private int vertRate;
            @JsonProperty("selected_altitude")
            private int selectedAltitude;

            private double lat, lon, barometer;
            @JsonProperty("polar_distance")
            private double polarDistance;
            @JsonProperty("polar_bearing")
            private double polarBearing;

            @JsonProperty("is_adsb")
            private boolean isADSB;
            @JsonProperty("is_on_ground")
            private boolean isOnGround;

            @JsonProperty("last_seen_time")
            private Instant lastSeenTime;
            @JsonProperty("pos_update_time")
            private Instant posUpdateTime;
            @JsonProperty("bds40_seen_time")
            private Instant bds40SeenTime;
    }
```

This domain class is defined using JPA with H2 as the underlying JPA-compliant database and leveraging Lombok to create a data class with constructors having zero arguments and all arguments, one for every member variable.

Creating the repository interface

Next, I define the required repository interface, extending Spring Data's `CrudReposi tory` and providing the type of object to store and its key: `Aircraft` and `Long`, in this case:

```
public interface AircraftRepository extends CrudRepository<Aircraft, Long> {}
```

Working with Model and Controller

I've defined the data behind the model with the `Aircraft` domain class; now it's time to incorporate it into the `Model` and expose it via a `Controller`.

As discussed in Chapter 3, `@RestController` is a convenience notation that combines `@Controller` with `@ResponseBody` into a single descriptive annotation, returning a formatted response as JavaScript Object Notation (JSON) or as other data-oriented format. This results in the Object/Iterable return value of a method being the *entire body* of the response to a web request, instead of being returned as a part of the

Model. An @RestController enables the creation of an API, a specialized, but very common, use case.

The goal now is to create an application that also includes a user interface, and @Controller enables that. Within an @Controller class, each method annotated with @RequestMapping or one of its specialized aliases like @GetMapping will return a String value that corresponds to the name of a template file minus its extension. For example, Thymeleaf files have the *.html* file extension, so if an @Controller class's @GetMapping method returns the String "myfavoritepage", the Thymeleaf template engine will use the *myfavoritepage.html* template to create and return the generated page to the user's browser.

 View technology templates are placed under the project's *src/main/resources/templates* directory by default; the template engine will look here for them unless overridden via application properties or programmatic means.

Returning to the controller, I create a class PositionController as follows:

```
@RequiredArgsConstructor
@Controller
public class PositionController {
    @NonNull
    private final AircraftRepository repository;
    private WebClient client =
            WebClient.create("http://localhost:7634/aircraft");

    @GetMapping("/aircraft")
    public String getCurrentAircraftPositions(Model model) {
        repository.deleteAll();

        client.get()
                .retrieve()
                .bodyToFlux(Aircraft.class)
                .filter(plane -> !plane.getReg().isEmpty())
                .toStream()
                .forEach(repository::save);

        model.addAttribute("currentPositions", repository.findAll());
        return "positions";
    }
}
```

This controller looks very similar to previous iterations but with a few key differences. First, of course, is the @Controller annotation previously discussed instead of @RestController. Second is that the getCurrentAircraftPositions() method has an automatically autowired parameter: Model model. This parameter is the Model bean that is leveraged by the template engine to provide access to the application's components—their data and operations—once we add those components to the Model as an attribute. And third is the method's return type of String instead of a class type and the actual return statement with the name of a template (sans *.html* extension).

 In a complex domain/application, I prefer to separate concerns a bit more by creating distinct @Service and @Controller classes. In this example, there is a single method making a single repository access, so I've placed all functionality to populate the underlying data, populate the Model, and hand it off to the appropriate View within the Controller.

Creating the requisite View files

As a basic foundation for this and future chapters, I create one plain HTML file and one template file.

Since I want to display a plain HTML page to all visitors, and since this page requires no template support, I place *index.html* directly in the project's *src/main/resources/static* directory:

```
<!DOCTYPE html>
<html lang="en">
<head>
    <meta charset="UTF-8">
    <title>Retrieve Aircraft Position Report</title>
</head>
<body>
    <p><a href="/aircraft">Click here</a>
        to retrieve current aircraft positions in range of receiver.</p>
</body>
</html>
```

Notes About index.html

By default, a Spring Boot application will look for static pages in the classpath under *static* and *public* directories. To properly place them there during build, place them within one of those two directories under *src/main/resources* within the project.

Of particular interest to this application is the href hyperlink "/aircraft". This link matches the @GetMapping annotation for the PositionController getCurrentAir craftPositions() method and points to the endpoint exposed by it, another example of the internal integration by Spring Boot across various components within the application. Clicking *Click here* from the page displayed by the running application will execute getCurrentAircraftPositions(), which will return "positions", prompting the ViewResolver to generate and return the next page based on the template *positions.html*.

As a final note, if an *index.html* file is located in one of the searched classpath directories, Spring Boot will automatically load it for the user when the application's *host:port* address is accessed from a browser or other user agent with no configuration required from the developer.

For the dynamic content, I create a template file, adding an XML namespace for Thymeleaf tags to the otherwise plain HTML file and then using those tags as content injection guidance for the Thymeleaf template engine, as shown in the following *positions.html* file. To designate this as a template file for processing by the engine, I place it in the *src/main/resources/templates* project directory:

```
<!DOCTYPE HTML>
<html lang="en" xmlns:th="http://www.thymeleaf.org">
<head>
    <title>Position Report</title>
    <meta http-equiv="Content-Type" content="text/html; charset=UTF-8"/>
</head>
<body>
<div class="positionlist" th:unless="${#lists.isEmpty(currentPositions)}">

    <h2>Current Aircraft Positions</h2>

    <table>
        <thead>
        <tr>
            <th>Call Sign</th>
            <th>Squawk</th>
            <th>AC Reg</th>
            <th>Flight #</th>
            <th>Route</th>
            <th>AC Type</th>
            <th>Altitude</th>
            <th>Heading</th>
            <th>Speed</th>
            <th>Vert Rate</th>
            <th>Latitude</th>
            <th>Longitude</th>
            <th>Last Seen</th>
            <th></th>
        </tr>
        </thead>
        <tbody>
        <tr th:each="ac : ${currentPositions}">
            <td th:text="${ac.callsign}"></td>
            <td th:text="${ac.squawk}"></td>
            <td th:text="${ac.reg}"></td>
            <td th:text="${ac.flightno}"></td>
            <td th:text="${ac.route}"></td>
            <td th:text="${ac.type}"></td>
            <td th:text="${ac.altitude}"></td>
            <td th:text="${ac.heading}"></td>
            <td th:text="${ac.speed}"></td>
```

```
                <td th:text="${ac.vertRate}"></td>
                <td th:text="${ac.lat}"></td>
                <td th:text="${ac.lon}"></td>
                <td th:text="${ac.lastSeenTime}"></td>
            </tr>
            </tbody>
        </table>
    </div>
    </body>
    </html>
```

For the aircraft position report page, I reduce the information displayed to a select few elements of particular importance and interest. There are a few items of note in the *positions.html* Thymeleaf template:

First, as mentioned earlier, I add the Thymeleaf tags to the XML namespace with the *th* prefix with the following line:

```
<html lang="en" xmlns:th="http://www.thymeleaf.org">
```

When defining the `division` that will display the current aircraft positions, I direct that the positionList division should be shown only if data is present; if the `currentPo sitions` element within the `Model` is empty, simply omit the entire division:

```
<div class="positionlist" th:unless="${#lists.isEmpty(currentPositions)}">
```

Finally, I define a table using standard HTML table tags for the table itself and the header row and its contents. For the table body, I use Thymeleaf's `each` to iterate through all `currentPositions` and populate each row's columns using the Thymeleaf's `text` tag and referencing each position object's properties via the "${object.property}" variable expression syntax. With that, the application is ready for testing.

The results

With the `PlaneFinder` service running, I execute the `Aircraft Positions` application from the IDE. Once it has successfully started, I open a browser tab and enter `localhost:8080` in the address bar and hit enter. Figure 7-1 shows the resultant page.

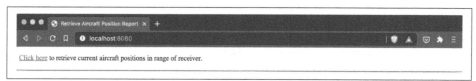

Figure 7-1. The Aircraft Positions application (very simple) landing page

From here, I click the *Click here* link to proceed to the Aircraft Position Report page, as shown in Figure 7-1.

Current Aircraft Positions

Call Sign	Squawk	AC Reg	Flight #	Route	AC Type	Altitude	Heading	Speed	Vert Rate	Latitude	Longitude	Last Seen
EJA428	1646	N428QS		BTR-DAL	E55P	41000	189	390	0	38.661075	-90.03479	2020-07-31T21:40:55Z
AAL2913	1146	N737US	AA2913	ORD-STL-ORD	A319	23300	23	423	1408	39.470851	-90.549988	2020-07-31T21:40:24Z
UPS2910	6752	N281UP	5X2910	SDF-ONT	MD11	35975	279	460	64	38.906662	-90.872338	2020-07-31T21:40:42Z
N630CC	6255	N630CC			C550	35975	226	290	-128	38.653564	-90.222712	2020-07-31T21:40:55Z
	0570	N355PU	AA1202	DFW-IND	B738	37000	86	489	64	38.830765	-90.39097	2020-07-31T21:40:55Z
		N583UW	AA1659	CLT-SFO	A321	35975	272	417	-64	39.129856	-89.766663	2020-07-31T21:40:55Z

Figure 7-2. The Aircraft Position Report Page

Refreshing the page will requery `PlaneFinder` and update the report with current data on demand.

A refreshing flourish

Being able to request a listing of aircraft currently in the area along with their exact positions is a useful thing. But having to manually refresh the page could also become quite tedious and result in missing data of great interest, if one is so disposed. To add a timed refresh function to the Aircraft Position Report template, simply add a Java-Script function to the page body similar to the following, specifying the page refresh rate in milliseconds:

```
<script type="text/javascript">
    window.onload = setupRefresh;

    function setupRefresh() {
        setTimeout("refreshPage();", 5000); // refresh rate in milliseconds
    }

    function refreshPage() {
        window.location = location.href;
    }
</script>
```

The Thymeleaf template engine passes this code into the generated page untouched, and the user's browser executes the script at the designated refresh rate. It isn't the most elegant solution, but for simple use cases, it does the job.

Passing Messages

When use cases are a bit more demanding, more sophisticated solutions may be required. The preceding code does provide dynamic updates reflecting the latest available position data, but among other potential concerns are that periodic requests for updated data can be somewhat chatty. If several clients are requesting and receiving updates constantly, network traffic can be substantial.

In order to fulfill more complex use cases while simultaneously addressing network demands, it's helpful to shift perspectives: from a pull model to a push model, or some combination of the two.

 This section and the next explore two different and incremental steps toward a push model, culminating in an *entirely* push-based model from the PlaneFinder service outward. Use cases will indicate (or dictate) conditions that may favor one of these approaches or something else entirely. I continue to explore and demonstrate additional alternatives in subsequent chapters, so stay tuned.

Messaging platforms were made to efficiently accept, route, and deliver messages between applications. Examples include RabbitMQ (*https://www.rabbitmq.com*) and Apache Kafka (*https://kafka.apache.org*) and numerous other offerings, both open source and commercial. Spring Boot and the Spring ecosystem provide a few different options for leveraging message pipelines, but my hands-down favorite is Spring Cloud Stream.

Spring Cloud Stream elevates the level of abstraction for developers while still providing access to supported platforms' unique attributes via application properties, beans, and direct configuration. Binders form the connection between streaming platform drivers and Spring Cloud Stream (SCSt), allowing developers to maintain focus on the key tasks—sending, routing, and receiving messages—which don't differ in concept regardless of the underlying plumbing.

Powering Up PlaneFinder

The first order of business is to refactor the PlaneFinder service to use Spring Cloud Stream to publish messages for consumption by the Aircraft Positions (and any other applicable) application.

Required dependencies

I add the following dependencies to PlaneFinder's *pom.xml* Maven build file:

```
<dependency>
    <groupId>org.springframework.boot</groupId>
    <artifactId>spring-boot-starter-amqp</artifactId>
</dependency>
<dependency>
    <groupId>org.springframework.cloud</groupId>
    <artifactId>spring-cloud-stream</artifactId>
</dependency>
<dependency>
    <groupId>org.springframework.cloud</groupId>
    <artifactId>spring-cloud-stream-binder-kafka</artifactId>
</dependency>
```

```
<dependency>
    <groupId>org.springframework.cloud</groupId>
    <artifactId>spring-cloud-stream-binder-rabbit</artifactId>
</dependency>
<dependency>
    <groupId>org.springframework.kafka</groupId>
    <artifactId>spring-kafka</artifactId>
</dependency>
```

The first thing to note is actually the second dependency listed: `spring-cloud-stream`. This is the code dependency for Spring Cloud Stream, but it can't do the job alone. As mentioned, SCSt uses binders to enable its powerful abstraction to work with various streaming platforms' drivers seamlessly. There is even a helpful reminder on the Spring Cloud Stream entry accessible from the Spring Initializr to that effect:

> Framework for building highly scalable event-driven microservices connected with shared messaging systems (requires a binder, e.g., Apache Kafka, RabbitMQ, or Solace PubSub+)

For Spring Cloud Stream to work with a messaging platform, it requires a messaging platform driver and the binder that works with it. In the preceding example, I include a binder+driver combination for RabbitMQ *and* for Apache Kafka.

 If only one binder+driver combination is included—for RabbitMQ, for example—Spring Boot's autoconfiguration can unambiguously determine that your application should support communication with RabbitMQ instance(s) and associated exchanges and queues and create the appropriate supporting beans with no additional effort required on the developer's part. Including more than one set of binders+drivers requires us to specify which one to use, but it also allows us to dynamically switch among all included platforms at runtime, with no change to the tested and deployed application. This is an extremely powerful and useful capability.

Two more additions to the *pom.xml* file are necessary. First is to indicate the project-level version of Spring Cloud to use by adding this line to the `<properties></properties>` section:

```
<spring-cloud.version>2020.0.0-M5</spring-cloud.version>
```

Second is to provide guidance on the Spring Cloud Bill of Materials (BOM), from which the build system can determine versions for any Spring Cloud components—in this case, Spring Cloud Stream—that are used in this project:

```
<dependencyManagement>
    <dependencies>
        <dependency>
            <groupId>org.springframework.cloud</groupId>
```

```
        <artifactId>spring-cloud-dependencies</artifactId>
        <version>${spring-cloud.version}</version>
        <type>pom</type>
        <scope>import</scope>
      </dependency>
    </dependencies>
  </dependencyManagement>
```

 Versions of Spring component projects are updated frequently. An easy way to determine correct, synchronized versions tested with the current version of Spring Boot is to use the Spring Initializr. Selecting the desired dependencies and clicking the button to *"Explore CTRL+SPACE"* displays the build file with the appropriate elements and versions.

After refreshing the project's dependencies, it's on to the code.

Supplying aircraft positions

Due to PlaneFinder 's existing structure and Spring Cloud Stream's clean, functional approach, only one small class is required to publish current aircraft positions to RabbitMQ for consumption by other applications:

```
@AllArgsConstructor
@Configuration
public class PositionReporter {
    private final PlaneFinderService pfService;

    @Bean
    Supplier<Iterable<Aircraft>> reportPositions() {
        return () -> {
            try {
                return pfService.getAircraft();
            } catch (IOException e) {
                e.printStackTrace();
            }
            return List.of();
        };
    }
}
```

A Few Thoughts on Application Design

First, technically speaking, only the `reportPositions()` bean creation method is required, not the entire `PositionReporter` class. Since the main application class is annotated with `@SpringBootApplication`, a meta-annotation that incorporates `@Configuration` within, one could simply place `reportPositions()` within the main application class, `PlanefinderApplication`. My preference is to place `@Bean` methods within relevant `@Configuration` classes, especially in cases where numerous beans are created.

Second, Spring Cloud Stream's annotation-driven legacy API is still fully supported, but in this book I focus exclusively on the newer functional API. Spring Cloud Stream builds on the clean lines of Spring Cloud Function, which builds on *standard Java concepts/interfaces*: `Supplier<T>`, `Function<T, R>`, and `Consumer<T>`. This removes from SCSt the slightly leaky abstraction of Spring Integration concepts and supplants it with core language constructs; it also enables some new capabilities, as you might imagine.

Briefly stated, applications can either supply messages (`Supplier<T>`), transform messages (`Function<T, R>`) from one kind of thing to another, or consume messages (`Consumer<T>`). Any supported streaming platform can supply the connecting pipelines.

Platforms currently supported by Spring Cloud Stream include the following:

- RabbitMQ
- Apache Kafka
- Kafka Streams
- Amazon Kinesis
- Google Pub/Sub (partner maintained)
- Solace PubSub+ (partner maintained)
- Azure Event Hubs (partner maintained)
- Apache RocketMQ (partner maintained)

Since each poll by `PlaneFinder` of the upstream radio device produces a listing of positions of aircraft currently within range, the `PlaneFinder` service creates a message consisting of 1+ aircraft in an `Iterable<Aircraft>` by calling the `PlaneFinder Service getAircraft()` method. An opinion—that a `Supplier` is called once per second by default (overridable via application property)—and some required/ optional application properties inform Spring Boot's autoconfiguration and set things in motion.

Application properties

Only one property is required, although others are helpful. Here are the contents of the updated `PlaneFinder` 's *application.properties* file:

```
server.port=7634

spring.cloud.stream.bindings.reportPositions-out-0.destination=aircraftpositions
spring.cloud.stream.bindings.reportPositions-out-0.binder=rabbit
```

The `server.port` remains from the first version and indicates the application should listen on port 7634.

Spring Cloud Stream's functional API relies on minimal property configuration when necessary (as a baseline) to enable its functionality. A `Supplier` has only output channels, as it produces only messages. A `Consumer` has only input channels, as it consumes only messages. A `Function` has both input and output channels, which are necessary due to its use in transforming one thing to another.

Each binding uses the interface (`Supplier`, `Function`, or `Consumer`) bean method's name for the channel name, along with `in` or `out` and a channel number from 0 to 7. Once concatenated in the form `<method>-<in|out>-n`, binding properties can be defined for the channel.

The only property required for this use case is `destination`, and even that is for convenience. Specifying the `destination` name results in RabbitMQ creating an exchange named `aircraftpositions` (in this example).

Since I included binders and drivers for both RabbitMQ and Kafka in the project dependencies, I must specify which binder the application should use. For this example, I choose `rabbit`.

With all required and desired application properties defined, `PlaneFinder` is ready to publish current aircraft positions each second to RabbitMQ for consumption by any applications desiring to do so.

Extending the Aircraft Positions Application

Converting `Aircraft Positions` to consume messages from a RabbitMQ pipeline using Spring Cloud Stream is similarly straightforward. Only a few changes to the workings behind the scenes are necessary to replace frequent HTTP requests with a message-driven architecture.

Required dependencies

Just as with `PlaneFinder`, I add the following dependencies to the `Aircraft Positions` application's *pom.xml*:

```
<dependency>
    <groupId>org.springframework.boot</groupId>
    <artifactId>spring-boot-starter-amqp</artifactId>
</dependency>
<dependency>
    <groupId>org.springframework.cloud</groupId>
    <artifactId>spring-cloud-stream</artifactId>
</dependency>
<dependency>
    <groupId>org.springframework.cloud</groupId>
    <artifactId>spring-cloud-stream-binder-kafka</artifactId>
</dependency>
<dependency>
    <groupId>org.springframework.cloud</groupId>
    <artifactId>spring-cloud-stream-binder-rabbit</artifactId>
</dependency>
<dependency>
    <groupId>org.springframework.kafka</groupId>
    <artifactId>spring-kafka</artifactId>
</dependency>
```

As previously mentioned, I include binders and drivers for both RabbitMQ and Kafka for planned future use, but only the RabbitMQ set—spring-boot-starter-amqp and spring-cloud-stream-binder-rabbit—are required for the current use case in order for Spring Cloud Stream (spring-cloud-stream) to use RabbitMQ.

I also add the two additional required entries to *pom.xml*. First, this goes into the <properties></properties> section, with the java.version:

```
<spring-cloud.version>2020.0.0-M5</spring-cloud.version>
```

Second is the Spring Cloud BOM information:

```
<dependencyManagement>
    <dependencies>
        <dependency>
            <groupId>org.springframework.cloud</groupId>
            <artifactId>spring-cloud-dependencies</artifactId>
            <version>${spring-cloud.version}</version>
            <type>pom</type>
            <scope>import</scope>
        </dependency>
    </dependencies>
</dependencyManagement>
```

A quick refresh of the project's dependencies and we're on to the next step.

Consuming aircraft positions

In order to retrieve and store messages listing current aircraft positions, only one small additional class is required:

```
@AllArgsConstructor
@Configuration
public class PositionRetriever {
    private final AircraftRepository repo;

    @Bean
    Consumer<List<Aircraft>> retrieveAircraftPositions() {
        return acList -> {
            repo.deleteAll();

            repo.saveAll(acList);

            repo.findAll().forEach(System.out::println);
        };
    }
}
```

Like its `PositionReporter` counterpart in `PlaneFinder`, the `PositionRetriever` class is an `@Configuration` class in which I define a bean for use with Spring Cloud Stream: in this case, a `Consumer` of messages, each consisting of a `List` of one or more `Aircraft`. With each incoming message, the `Consumer` bean deletes all positions in the (in-memory) datastore, saves all incoming positions, and then prints all stored positions to the console for verification. Note that the last statement printing all positions to the console is optional; it's included only for confirmation as I develop the app.

Application properties

In order to provide the application the few remaining bits of information necessary to connect to the incoming stream of messages, I add the following entries to the *application.properties* file:

```
spring.cloud.stream.bindings.retrieveAircraftPositions-in-0.destination=
    aircraftpositions
spring.cloud.stream.bindings.retrieveAircraftPositions-in-0.group=
    aircraftpositions
spring.cloud.stream.bindings.retrieveAircraftPositions-in-0.binder=
    rabbit
```

As with `PlaneFinder`, the channel is defined by concatenating the following, separated by a hyphen (-):

- The bean name, in this case, a `Consumer<T>` bean

- `in`, since consumers only consume and thus have only input(s)

- A number between 0 and 7 inclusive, supporting up to eight inputs

The `destination` and `binder` properties match those of `PlaneFinder` because the `Air craft Positions` application must point to the same destination as input that `Plane`

Finder used as output and because to do so, both must be using the same messaging platform—in this case, RabbitMQ. The group property is new, though.

For any kind of Consumer (including the receiving portion of a Function<T, R>), one can specify a group, but it isn't required; in fact, including or omitting group forms a starting point for a particular routing pattern.

If a message-consuming application doesn't specify a group, the RabbitMQ binder creates a randomized unique name and assigns it, and the consumer, to an auto-delete queue within the RabbitMQ instance or cluster. This results in each generated queue being serviced by one—and only one—consumer. Why is this important?

Whenever a message arrives at a RabbitMQ exchange, a copy is routed automatically to all queues assigned to that exchange by default. If an exchange has multiple queues, the same message is sent to every queue in what's referred to as a *fan-out pattern*, a useful capability when each message must be delivered to numerous destinations to satisfy various requirements.

If an application specifies a consumer group to which it belongs, that group name is used to name the underlying queue within RabbitMQ. When multiple applications specify the same group property and thus connect to the same queue, together those applications fulfill the competing consumer pattern in which each message arriving in the designated queue is processed by only one of the consumers. This allows the number of consumers to scale to accommodate varying volumes of messages.

 It is also possible to employ partitioning and routing keys for even finer-grained and flexible routing options, if needed.

Specifying the group property for this application enables scaling, should multiple instances be needed to keep pace with the flow of arriving messages.

Contacting the Controller

Since the Consumer bean automatically checks for and processes messages automatically, the PositionController class and its getCurrentAircraftPositions() method become dramatically leaner.

All references to WebClient can be removed, since getting a list of current positions is now only a matter of retrieving the current contents of the repository. The stream-lined class now looks like this:

```
@RequiredArgsConstructor
@Controller
public class PositionController {
```

```
    @NonNull
    private final AircraftRepository repository;

    @GetMapping("/aircraft")
    public String getCurrentAircraftPositions(Model model) {
        model.addAttribute("currentPositions", repository.findAll());
        return "positions";
    }
}
```

With that, all changes to both message-producer (the `PlaneFinder` app) and message-consumer (the `Aircraft Positions` app) are now complete.

In order to use any external messaging platform, said platform must be running and accessible to the applications. I run a local instance of RabbitMQ using Docker; scripts for quick creation and startup/shutdown are provided in this book's associated repositories.

The results

After verifying that RabbitMQ is accessible, it's time to start the applications and verify everything works as expected.

Although it isn't a requirement to do so, I prefer to start the message-consuming application first so it's ready and waiting for messages to arrive. In this case, that means executing `Aircraft Positions` from my IDE.

Next, I start up the new and improved `PlaneFinder` application. This initiates the flow of messages to the `Aircraft Positions` application, as shown in the `Aircraft Positions` app's console. That's gratifying, but we can follow this path of success all the way to the end user as well.

Returning to the browser and accessing *localhost:8080*, we're presented with the landing page once again, and opting to *Click here*, are taken to the Positions Report. As before, the Positions Report is refreshed automatically and displays current aircraft positions; now however, those positions are pushed independently from `PlaneFinder` behind the scenes to the `Aircraft Positions` application, without first receiving an HTTP request for them, which brings the architecture one step closer to a fully event-driven system.

Creating Conversations with WebSocket

In its first iteration, the distributed system we created to query and display current aircraft positions was entirely pull-based. A user requested (or re-requested with a refresh) the latest positions from the browser, which passed the request to the `Air`

---

craft Positions application, which in turn relayed the request to the PlaneFinder application. Responses then were returned from one to the next, to the next. The last chapter segment replaced the midsection of our distributed system with an event-driven architecture. Now whenever PlaneFinder retrieves positions from the upstream radio device, it pushes those positions to a streaming platform pipeline and the Aircraft Positions app consumes them. The last mile (or kilometer, if you prefer) is still pull-based, however; updates must be requested via browser refresh, either manually or automatically.

Standard request-response semantics work brilliantly for numerous use cases, but they largely lack the ability for the responding "server" side to, independent of any request, initiate a transmission to the requestor. There are various workarounds and clever ways to satisfy this use case—each of which has its own pros and cons, and some of the best of which I discuss in subsequent chapters—but one of the more versatile options is WebSocket.

What Is WebSocket?

In a nutshell, WebSocket is a full-duplex communications protocol that connects two systems over a single TCP connection. Once a WebSocket connection is established, either party can initiate a transmission to the other, and the designated server application can maintain numerous client connections, enabling low-overhead broadcast and chat types of systems. WebSocket connections are forged from standard HTTP connections using the HTTP upgrade header, and once the handshake is complete, the protocol used for the connection shifts from HTTP to WebSocket.

WebSocket was standardized by the IETF in 2011, and by now every major browser and programming language supports it. Compared to HTTP requests and responses, WebSocket is extremely low overhead; transmissions don't have to identify themselves and the terms of their communication with each transmission, thus reducing WebSocket framing to a few bytes. With its full-duplex capabilities, the ability of a server to handle a multiple of the number of open connections other options can support, and its low overhead, WebSocket is a useful tool for developers to have in their toolbox.

Refactoring the Aircraft Positions Application

Although I refer to the Aircraft Positions application as a single unit, the *aircraft-positions* project comprises both the backend Spring Boot+Java application and the frontend HTML+JavaScript functionality. During development, both portions execute in a single environment, usually the developer's machine. While they are built, tested, and deployed as a single unit to production settings as well, execution in production settings is divided as follows:

- Backend Spring+Java code is run in the cloud, including the template engine (if applicable) that generates final webpages to deliver to the end user.

- Frontend HTML+JavaScript—static and/or generated content—is displayed and run in the end user's browser, wherever that browser may be located.

In this section, I leave existing functionality intact and add the ability to the system to automatically display aircraft positions as they are reported via a live feed. With a WebSocket connection in place between frontend and backend applications, the backend app is free to push updates to the end user's browser and update the display automatically, with no need to trigger a page refresh.

Additional dependencies

To add WebSocket capabilities to the Aircraft Positions application, I need add only a single dependency to its *pom.xml*:

```
<dependency>
        <groupId>org.springframework.boot</groupId>
        <artifactId>spring-boot-starter-websocket</artifactId>
</dependency>
```

A quick refresh of the project's dependencies and we're on to the next step.

Handling WebSocket connections and messages

Spring offers a couple of different approaches for configuring and using WebSocket, but I recommend following the clean lines of a direct implementation based on the WebSocketHandler interface. Owing to the frequency of requirements for exchanging text-based, i.e., nonbinary, information, there is even a TextWebSocketHandler class. I build on that here:

```
@RequiredArgsConstructor
@Component
public class WebSocketHandler extends TextWebSocketHandler {
    private final List<WebSocketSession> sessionList = new ArrayList<>();
    @NonNull
    private final AircraftRepository repository;

    public List<WebSocketSession> getSessionList() {
        return sessionList;
    }

    @Override
    public void afterConnectionEstablished(WebSocketSession session)
            throws Exception {
        sessionList.add(session);
        System.out.println("Connection established from " + session.toString() +
            " @ " + Instant.now().toString());
    }
```

```
    @Override
    protected void handleTextMessage(WebSocketSession session,
            TextMessage message) throws Exception {
        try {
            System.out.println("Message received: '" +
                message + "', from " + session.toString());

            for (WebSocketSession sessionInList : sessionList) {
                if (sessionInList != session) {
                    sessionInList.sendMessage(message);
                    System.out.println("--> Sending message '"
                        + message + "' to " + sessionInList.toString());
                }
            }
        } catch (Exception e) {
                System.out.println("Exception handling message: " +
                e.getLocalizedMessage());
        }
    }

    @Override
    public void afterConnectionClosed(WebSocketSession session,
            CloseStatus status) throws Exception {
        sessionList.remove(session);
        System.out.println("Connection closed by " + session.toString() +
            " @ " + Instant.now().toString());
    }
}
```

The preceding code implements two of the `WebSocketHandler` interface's methods, `afterConnectionEstablished` and `afterConnectionClosed`, to maintain a `List` of active `WebSocketSession` and `log` connections and disconnections. I also implement `handleTextMessage`, broadcasting any incoming message to all other active sessions. This single class provides the WebSocket capability for the backend, ready to be activated when aircraft positions are received from `PlaneFinder` via RabbitMQ.

Broadcasting aircraft positions to WebSocket connections

In its previous iteration, the `PositionRetriever` class consumed aircraft position lists received via RabbitMQ messages and stored them in the in-memory H2 database. I build on that now by replacing the logging confirmation `System.out::println` call with a call to a new `sendPositions()` method, whose purpose is to use the newly added `@Autowired WebSocketHandler` bean to send the latest list of aircraft positions to all WebSocket-connected clients:

```
@AllArgsConstructor
@Configuration
public class PositionRetriever {
    private final AircraftRepository repository;
    private final WebSocketHandler handler;

    @Bean
```

```
        Consumer<List<Aircraft>> retrieveAircraftPositions() {
            return acList -> {
                repository.deleteAll();

                repository.saveAll(acList);

                sendPositions();
            };
        }

        private void sendPositions() {
            if (repository.count() > 0) {
                for (WebSocketSession sessionInList : handler.getSessionList()) {
                    try {
                        sessionInList.sendMessage(
                            new TextMessage(repository.findAll().toString())
                        );
                    } catch (IOException e) {
                        e.printStackTrace();
                    }
                }
            }
        }
    }
```

Now that we have WebSocket configured properly and have a way for the backend to broadcast aircraft positions to connected WebSocket clients as soon as a new position list is received, the next step is to provide a way for the backend application to listen for and accept connection requests. This is accomplished by registering the WebSocketHandler created earlier via the WebSocketConfigurer interface and annotating the new @Configuration class with @EnableWebSocket to direct the application to process WebSocket requests:

```
@Configuration
@EnableWebSocket
public class WebSocketConfig implements WebSocketConfigurer {
    private final WebSocketHandler handler;

    WebSocketConfig(WebSocketHandler handler) {
        this.handler = handler;
    }

    @Override
    public void registerWebSocketHandlers(WebSocketHandlerRegistry registry) {
        registry.addHandler(handler, "/ws");
    }
}
```

In the registerWebSocketHandlers(WebSocketHandlerRegistry registry) method, I tie the WebSocketHandler bean created earlier to the endpoint *ws://<hostname:hostport>/ws*. The application will listen on this endpoint for HTTP requests with WebSocket upgrade headers and act accordingly when one is received.

If HTTPS is enabled for your application, *wss://* (WebSocket Secure) would be used in place of *ws://*.

WebSocket in back, WebSocket in front

With the backend work done, it's time to collect the payoff in the frontend functionality.

To create a simple example of how WebSocket enables the backend app to push updates unprompted by the user and their browser, I create the following file with a single HTML division and label and a few lines of JavaScript and place it in the project's *src/main/resources/static* directory along with the existing *index.html*:

```
<!DOCTYPE html>
<html lang="en">
<head>
    <meta charset="UTF-8">
    <title>Aircraft Position Report (Live Updates)</title>
    <script>
        var socket = new WebSocket('ws://' + window.location.host + '/ws');

        socket.onopen = function () {
            console.log(
              'WebSocket connection is open for business, bienvenidos!');
        };

        socket.onmessage = function (message) {
            var text = "";
            var arrAC = message.data.split("Aircraft");
            var ac = "";

            for (i = 1; i < arrAC.length; i++) {
                ac = (arrAC[i].endsWith(", "))
                    ? arrAC[i].substring(0, arrAC[i].length - 2)
                    : arrAC[i]

                text += "Aircraft" + ac + "\n\n";
            }

            document.getElementById("positions").innerText = text;
        };

        socket.onclose = function () {
            console.log('WebSocket connection closed, hasta la próxima!');
        };
    </script>
</head>
<body>
```

```
<h1>Current Aircraft Positions</h1>
<div style="border-style: solid; border-width: 2px; margin-top: 15px;
        margin-bottom: 15px; margin-left: 15px; margin-right: 15px;">
    <label id="positions"></label>
</div>
</body>
</html>
```

As short as this page is, it could be shorter. The socket.onopen and socket.onclose
function definitions are logging functions that could be omitted, and socket.onmes
sage could almost certainly be refactored by someone with actual JavaScript chops
and the desire to do so. These are the key bits:

- The defined division and label in the HTML at bottom
- The socket variable that establishes and references a WebSocket connection
- The socket.onmessage function that parses the aircraft position list and assigns
  the reformatted output to the HTML "positions" label's innerText

Once we rebuild and execute the project, it is of course possible to simply access the
wspositions.html page directly from the browser. This is a poor way to create an application for actual users, though—providing no way to access a page and its functionality unless they know its location and enter it manually into the address bar—and it
does nothing to set the table for upcoming chapters' expansions to this example.

Keeping it simple for the time being, I add another line to the existing *index.html* to
allow the user to navigate to the *wspositions.html* WebSocket-driven page in addition
to the existing one:

```
<!DOCTYPE html>
<html lang="en">
<head>
    <meta charset="UTF-8">
    <title>Retrieve Aircraft Position Report</title>
</head>
<body>
    <p><a href="/aircraft">Click here</a> to retrieve current aircraft positions
        in range of receiver.</p>
    <p><a href="/wspositions.html">Click here</a> to retrieve a livestream of
        current aircraft positions in range of receiver.</p>
</body>
</html>
```

With frontend work now complete, it's time to test the WebSocket waters.

The results

From the IDE, I launch the Aircraft Positions application and PlaneFinder.
Opening a browser window, I access the frontend application at *localhost:8080*, as
shown in Figure 7-3.

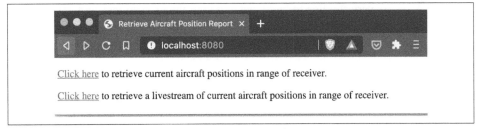

Figure 7-3. Aircraft Positions landing page, now with two options

From the still rather rudimentary landing page, choosing the second option—*Click here* to retrieve a livestream of current aircraft positions in range of receiver—produces the *wspositions.html* page and results similar to those shown in Figure 7-4.

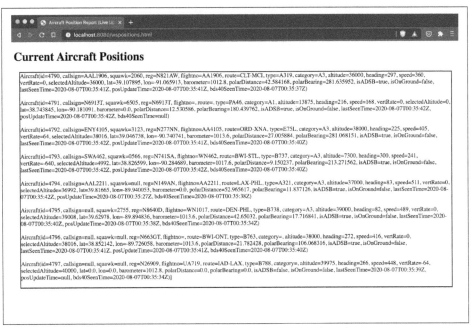

Figure 7-4. Aircraft Position report with live updates via WebSocket

It's a trivial exercise to convert the database record format shown with JSON, and just a bit more involved to dynamically populate a table with results received live from the backend application via WebSocket. Please refer to this book's code repositories for examples.

It's perfectly fine to build and run both the `PlaneFinder` and `Aircraft Positions` applications from the command line; while I do so on occasion, for most build/run cycles, I find it much faster to run (and debug) directly from within the IDE.

Summary

Nearly every application must interact with end users or other applications in some manner to provide real utility, and that requires useful and efficient means of interaction.

This chapter introduced view technologies—template languages/tags like Thymeleaf and engines that process them—and how Spring Boot uses them to create and deliver functionality to an end user's browser. Also introduced was how Spring Boot handles static content like standard HTML along with JavaScript that can be delivered directly without processing by template engines. The chapter's first project iteration showed examples of both with a Thymeleaf-driven application that retrieved and displayed aircraft positions within range at the time of the request, an entirely pull-based model.

The chapter next showed how to harness the power of messaging platforms from Spring Boot using Spring Cloud Stream and RabbitMQ. The `PlaneFinder` application was refactored to push a list of current aircraft positions, each time retrieved from the upstream device, and the `Aircraft Positions` app was modified to accept new aircraft position listings as they arrived via the RabbitMQ pipeline. This replaced the pull-based model between the two applications with a push-based one, making the backend functionality of the `Aircraft Positions` app event-driven. The front end functionality still required a refresh (either manual or hard-coded) to update results shown to the user.

Finally, implementing a WebSocket connection and handler code within backend and frontend components of the `Aircraft Positions` application enabled the Spring +Java backend app to push aircraft position updates *as they are received* via a RabbitMQ pipeline from `PlaneFinder`. Position updates are shown live in a simple HTML+JavaScript page and require no update requests be issued by the end user or their browser, showcasing WebSocket's bidirectional nature, lack of required request-response pattern (or workaround), and low communication overhead.

Code Checkout Checkup

For complete chapter code, please check out branch *chapter7end* from the code repository.

The next chapter introduces reactive programming and describes how Spring is leading the development and advancement of numerous tools and technologies that make it one of the best possible solutions for numerous use cases. More specifically, I'll demonstrate how to use Spring Boot and Project Reactor to drive database access, integrate reactive types with view technologies like Thymeleaf, and take interprocess communication to unexpected new levels.

## CHAPTER 8

Reactive Programming with Project Reactor and Spring WebFlux

This chapter introduces reactive programming, discusses its origins and reasons for being, and demonstrates how Spring is leading the development and advancement of numerous tools and technologies that make it one of the best possible solutions for numerous use cases. More specifically, I demonstrate how to use Spring Boot and Project Reactor to drive database access using SQL and NoSQL databases, integrate reactive types with view technologies like Thymeleaf, and take interprocess communication to unexpected new levels with RSocket.

Code Checkout Checkup

Please check out branch *chapter8begin* from the code repository to begin.

Introduction to Reactive Programming

While a full treatise on reactive programming could—and has, and will—consume an entire book, it's critical to understand why it's such an important concept in the first place.

In a typical service, a thread is created for each request to be handled. Each thread requires resources, and as such, the number of threads that an application can manage is limited. As a somewhat simplified example, if an app can service 200 threads, that application can accept requests from up to 200 discrete clients at once, but no more; any additional attempts to connect to the service must wait for a thread to become available.

Performance for the 200 connected clients may or may not be satisfactory, depending on a number of factors. What is uncontestable is that for the client application making concurrent request number 201 and up, response time may be dramatically worse due to blocking by the service while it waits for an available thread. This hard stop in scalability can go from nonissue to crisis without warning and with no simple solution, and workarounds like the traditional "throw more instances at the problem" introduce both pressure relief and new problems to solve. Reactive programming was created to address this scalability crisis.

The Reactive Manifesto (*https://www.reactivemanifesto.org*) states that reactive systems are:

- Responsive
- Resilient
- Elastic
- Message driven

In a nutshell, the four key points of reactive systems as listed combine to create (at the macro level) a maximally available, scalable, and performant system requiring the fewest resources possible to do the job effectively.

Speaking at a systems level, i.e., several applications/services working together to fulfill various use cases, we might notice that most of the challenges involve communication between applications: one app responding to another, app/service availability when requests arrive, the ability of a service to scale out or in to adjust to demand, one service notifying other interested services of updated/available information, etc. Addressing the potential pitfalls of interapplication interactions can go a long way toward mitigating and/or solving the scalability issues referenced earlier.

This very observation of communication being the greatest potential source of issues and consequently the greatest opportunity for their resolution led to the Reactive Streams initiative (*http://www.reactive-streams.org*). The Reactive Streams (RS) initiative focuses on the interactions among services—the Streams, if you will—and includes four key elements:

- The Application Programming Interface (API)
- The specification
- Examples for implementations
- The Technology Compatibility Kit (TCK)

The API consists of only four interfaces:

- `Publisher`: Creator of things

- **Subscriber**: Consumer of things

- **Subscription**: Contract between Publisher and Subscriber

- **Processor**: Incorporates both Subscriber and Publisher in order to receive, transform, and dispatch things

This lean simplicity is key, as is the fact that the API consists solely of *interfaces* and not *implementations*. This allows for various interoperable implementations across different platforms, languages, and programming models.

The textual specification details expected and/or required behavior for API implementations. For example:

```
If a Publisher fails it MUST signal an onError.
```

Examples for implementations are useful aids for implementors, providing reference code for use when creating a particular RS implementation.

Perhaps the most critical piece is the Technology Compatibility Kit. The TCK enables implementors to verify and demonstrate the level of compatibility—and any current shortcomings—with their RS implementation (or someone else's). Knowledge is power, and identifying anything that doesn't work in full compliance with the specification can speed resolution while providing a warning to current library consumers until the shortcoming is resolved.

Notes About Reactive Streams, Asynchronicity, and Backpressure

Reactive Streams build on a foundation of asynchronous communication and processing, as stated clearly in the purpose statement located in the very first paragraph of the Reactive Streams information site (*http://www.reactive-streams.org*):

> Reactive Streams is an initiative to provide a standard for asynchronous
> stream processing with nonblocking back pressure. This encompasses efforts
> aimed at runtime environments (JVM and JavaScript) as well as network
> protocols.

At the risk of oversimplification, it may help to think in this way of the various concepts and components that compose Reactive Streams:

Asynchronicity is achieved when the application doesn't stop the world while one thing takes place. As an example, when Service A requests information from Service B, Service A doesn't postpone processing all subsequent instructions until receiving a response, idling (and thus wasting) precious compute resources while awaiting its answer from B; instead, Service A continues with other tasks until notified that a response has arrived.

As opposed to synchronous processing, in which tasks are executed sequentially, each one beginning only after the prior task completes, asynchronous processing can involve starting a task, then jumping to another if the original task can be performed

---

in the background (or can await a notification of readiness/completion) and tasks can be performed concurrently. This enables fuller use of resources, since CPU time that would have been spent at idle or near-idle levels can be used for actual processing instead of just *waiting*. It also can—in some cases—improve performance.

Performance gains are not universal when adopting an asynchronous model of any kind. It's practically impossible to exceed the performance provided by a blocking, synchronous communication and processing model when only two services are interacting directly with only one exchange at a time. This is easily demonstrated: if Service B has only a single client, Service A, and Service A makes only a single request at a time and *blocks* all other activity, dedicating all resources to awaiting the response from Service B, this dedicated processing and connection results in the best possible performance for the two applications' interactions, all other circumstances being equal. This scenario and other similar ones are exceedingly rare, but they are possible.

Asynchronous processing adds minimal overhead due to implementation mechanisms like an event loop, in which a service "listens" for responses to pending requests. As a result, for scenarios involving very limited interapplication connections, performance may be slightly less than an exchange involving synchronous communications and processing. This outcome flips quickly as connections increase and thread exhaustion becomes a reality. Unlike with synchronous processing, resources aren't simply obligated and idled with asynchronous processing; they're repurposed and used, resulting in both increased resource utilization and application scalability.

Reactive Streams goes beyond asynchronous processing, adding nonblocking backpressure. This introduces flow control and robustness to interapplication communication.

Without backpressure, Service A can request information from Service B with no means of protecting against an overwhelming response. For example, if Service B returns one million objects/records, Service A dutifully tries to ingest all of them, likely buckling under the load. If Service A doesn't have sufficient compute and network resources to handle the staggering influx of information, the app can and will crash. At that point, asynchronicity isn't a factor, as app resources are wholly consumed trying (and failing) to keep up with the deluge. This is where backpressure demonstrates its value.

The concept of nonblocking backpressure simply means that Service A has a way to inform Service B of its capacity to handle response(s). Rather than just saying "give me everything," Service A requests a number of objects from Service B, processes them, and requests more when it is ready and able to process them. Originating in the field of fluid dynamics, the term *backpressure* represents a way of controlling flow from the point of origin by applying pressure back through the conduit against the supplier's flow of material(s). In Reactive Streams, backpressure provides Service A a way to manage the pace of incoming responses, setting and adjusting it in real time if circumstances change.

Although various workarounds have been created (with varying degrees of complexity, scope, and success) to implement means of backpressure within nonreactive systems, the declarative programming model favored by Reactive Streams makes the integration of asynchronicity and backpressure largely transparent and seamless to the developer.

Project Reactor

Although there are several available Reactive Streams implementations for the JVM, Project Reactor is among the most active, advanced, and performant. Reactor has been adopted by and provides the essential underpinnings for numerous mission-critical projects worldwide, including libraries, APIs, and applications developed and deployed by small organizations and global tech titans alike. Adding to this impressive momentum of development and adoption is the fact that Reactor provides the foundation for Spring's WebFlux reactive web capabilities, Spring Data's reactive database access for several open source and commercial databases, and interapplication communication, allowing for the creation of end-to-end reactive pipelines from top of stack to bottom and laterally as well. It's a 100% solution.

Why is this important?

From top of stack to bottom, from end user to lowest-tier computing resource, each interaction provides a potential sticking point. If interactions between the user's browser and the backend application are nonblocking but the app has to wait for a blocking interaction with the database, the result is a blocking system. The same goes with interapplication communication; if the user's browser communicates with backend Service A but Service A blocks waiting for a response from Service B, what has the user gained? Probably very little, and possibly nothing at all.

Developers usually can see the vast potential a switch to Reactive Streams offers them and their systems. A counterweight to that is the change in mindset that, combined with the relative newness of reactive (vs. imperative) programming constructs and tooling, can require adjustment and a bit more work from developers to harness, at least in the short term. This is still an easy decision to make as long as the effort required is clearly exceeded by the scalability benefits and the breadth and depth of Reactive Stream's application within overall systems. Having reactive pipelines throughout the entirety of a system's applications is a force multiplier on both counts.

Project Reactor's implementation of Reactive Streams is clean and simple, building on concepts with which Java and Spring developers are already well acquainted. Resembling Java 8+'s Stream API, Reactor is best utilized via declarative, chained operators, often with lambdas. Compared to more procedural, imperative code, it first feels somewhat different and then fairly elegant. Familiarity with `Stream` speeds the acclimatization and appreciation.

Reactor takes the concept of a Reactive Streams `Publisher` and specializes it, providing constructs similar to imperative Java in the process. Rather than using a common `Publisher` for everything in which a Reactive Stream—think of it as an on-demand, dynamic `Iterable`—is required, Project Reactor defines two types of `Publisher`:

`Mono::` emits 0 or 1 element `Flux::` emits 0 to *n* elements, a defined number or boundless

This aligns brilliantly with imperative constructs. For example, in standard Java, a method may return an object of type T or an `Iterable<T>`. Using Reactor, that same method would return a `Mono<T>` or a `Flux<T>`—one object or potentially many, or in the case of the reactive code, a `Publisher` of those objects.

Reactor also fits very naturally into Spring's opinions. Depending on the use case, converting from blocking to nonblocking code can be as simple as changing a project dependency and a few method return values as shown previously. This chapter's examples demonstrate how to do exactly that, along with extending outward—up, down, and laterally—to go from a single reactive application to a reactive system, including reactive database access, for maximum benefit.

Tomcat versus Netty

In the imperative world of Spring Boot, Tomcat is the default servlet engine used for web applications, although even at that level, developers have options like Jetty and Undertow that can be used as drop-in replacements. Tomcat makes a great deal of sense as a default, though, as it is established, proven, and performant, and Spring team developers have contributed (and still do contribute) to refining and evolving Tomcat's codebase. It's a superb servlet engine for Boot applications.

That said, numerous iterations of the servlet specification have been intrinsically synchronous with no async capabilities. Servlet 3.0 began to address this with asynchronous request processing but still only supported traditional blocking I/O. Version 3.1 of the spec added nonblocking I/O, making it suitable for asynchronous, and thus also reactive, applications.

Spring WebFlux is the name for Spring's reactive counterpart to Spring WebMVC (package name), usually referred to simply as Spring MVC. Spring WebFlux is built on Reactor and uses Netty as the default network engine, just as Spring MVC uses Tomcat to listen for and service requests. Netty is a proven and performant asynchronous engine, and Spring team developers also contribute to Netty to tightly integrate Reactor and keep Netty on the cutting edge of features and performance.

Just as with Tomcat, though, you have options. Any Servlet 3.1–compatible engine can be used with Spring WebFlux applications, should your mission or organization require it. Netty is the category leader for a reason, however, and for the vast majority of use cases, it is the best choice.

Reactive Data Access

As mentioned previously, the ultimate goal for ultimate scalability and optimal systemwide throughput is a fully end-to-end reactive implementation. At the lowest level, this rests on database access.

Years of effort have gone into designing databases in ways to minimize contention and system performance blockages. Even with this impressive work, there are areas that remain problematic in many database engines and drivers, among them means for performing operations without blocking the requesting application(s) and sophisticated flow control/backpressure mechanisms.

Paging constructs have been used to address both of these constraints, but they are imperfect solutions. Using an imperative model with paging typically requires a query to be issued for each page with a different range and/or constraints. This requires a new request and new response each time instead of the continuation that is possible with a `Flux`. An analogy is scooping up one cup of water at a time from a basin (imperative approach) versus simply turning on the tap to refill the cup. Rather than a "go get, bring back" imperative operation, the water is waiting to flow in the reactive scenario.

R2DBC with H2

In the existing version of PlaneFinder, I use the Java Persistence API (JPA) and the H2 database to store (in an in-memory instance of H2) aircraft positions retrieved from my local device that monitors in-range aircraft. JPA was built on an imperative specification and is thus inherently blocking. Seeing the need for a nonblocking reactive means of interacting with SQL databases, several industry leaders and luminaries joined forces to create and evolve the Reactive Relational Database Connectivity (R2DBC) project.

Like JPA, R2DBC is an open specification that can be used, along with the Service Provider Interface (SPI) it provides, by vendors or other interested parties to create drivers for relational databases and client libraries for downstream developers. Unlike JPA, R2DBC builds on Project Reactor's implementation of Reactive Streams and is fully reactive and nonblocking.

Updating PlaneFinder

As with most complex systems, we don't (currently) control all aspects and nodes of the entire distributed system. Also like most complex systems, the more completely a paradigm is embraced, the more can be gained from it. I start this "journey to reactive" as close to the point of origin of the communication chain as possible: in the PlaneFinder service.

Refactoring PlaneFinder to use Reactive Streams `Publisher` types, e.g., `Mono` and `Flux`, is the first step. I'll stay with the existing H2 database, but in order to "reactivate" it, I need to remove the JPA project dependency and replace it with R2DBC libraries. I update PlaneFinder's *pom.xml* Maven build file as follows:

```
<!--   Comment out or remove this   -->
<!--<dependency>-->
<!--   <groupId>org.springframework.boot</groupId>-->
<!--   <artifactId>spring-boot-starter-data-jpa</artifactId>-->
<!--</dependency>-->

<!--   Add this                -->
<dependency>
    <groupId>org.springframework.boot</groupId>
    <artifactId>spring-boot-starter-data-r2dbc</artifactId>
</dependency>

<!--   Add this too        -->
<dependency>
    <groupId>io.r2dbc</groupId>
    <artifactId>r2dbc-h2</artifactId>
    <scope>runtime</scope>
</dependency>
```

The `PlaneRepository` interface must be updated to extend the `ReactiveCrudRepository` interface instead of its blocking counterpart `CrudRepository`. This simple update is shown here:

```
public interface PlaneRepository
    extends ReactiveCrudRepository<Aircraft, String> {}
```

The change to `PlaneRepository` ripples outward, which leads naturally to the next stop, the `PlaneFinderService` class, where the `getAircraft()` method returns the result of `PlaneRepository::saveAll` when aircraft are found and of the `saveSamplePositions()` method otherwise. Replacing the value returned, a blocking `Iterable<Aircraft>`, with `Flux<Aircraft>` for the `getAircraft()` and `saveSamplePositions()` methods again correctly specifies the method return value.

```
public Flux<Aircraft> getAircraft() {
    ...
}

private Flux<Aircraft> saveSamplePositions() {
    ...
}
```

Since the `PlaneController` class's method `getCurrentAircraft()` calls `PlaneFinderService::getAircraft`, it now returns a `Flux<Aircraft>`. This necessitates a change to the signature for `PlaneController::getCurrentAircraft` as well:

```
public Flux<Aircraft> getCurrentAircraft() throws IOException {
    ...
}
```

Using H2 with JPA is a fairly mature affair; the specifications involved, along with the relevant APIs and libraries, have been under development for roughly a decade. R2DBC is a relatively recent development, and while support is expanding apace, a few features present in the Spring Data JPA's support for H2 have yet to be implemented. This doesn't pose much of an increased burden but is something to keep in mind when choosing to use a relational database—in this case, H2—reactively.

Currently, to use H2 with R2DBC, it is necessary to create and configure a `Connec tionFactoryInitializer` bean for use by the application. Configuration requires only two steps in reality:

- Setting the connection factory to the (already autoconfigured) `ConnectionFac tory` bean, injected as a parameter
- Configuring the database "populator" to execute one or more scripts to initialize or reinitialize the database as desired/required

Recall that when using Spring Data JPA with H2, an associated `@Entity` class is used to create a corresponding table within the H2 database. This step is completed manually when using H2 with R2DBC using a standard SQL DDL (Data Definition Language) script.

```
DROP TABLE IF EXISTS aircraft;

CREATE TABLE aircraft (id BIGINT auto_increment primary key,
callsign VARCHAR(7), squawk VARCHAR(4), reg VARCHAR(8), flightno VARCHAR(10),
route VARCHAR(30), type VARCHAR(4), category VARCHAR(2),
altitude INT, heading INT, speed INT, vert_rate INT, selected_altitude INT,
lat DOUBLE, lon DOUBLE, barometer DOUBLE, polar_distance DOUBLE,
polar_bearing DOUBLE, is_adsb BOOLEAN, is_on_ground BOOLEAN,
last_seen_time TIMESTAMP, pos_update_time TIMESTAMP, bds40_seen_time TIMESTAMP);
```

 This is an additional step, but it isn't without precedent. Many SQL databases require this step when used with Spring Data JPA as well; H2 was an exception to the rule.

Next up is the code for the `DbConxInit`, or Database Connection Initializer, class. The required bean-creation method is the first one—`initializer()`—that produces the needed `ConnectionFactoryInitializer` bean. The second method produces a `CommandLineRunner` bean that is executed once the class is configured. `CommandLineR unner` is a functional interface with a single abstract method, `run()`. As such, I provide a lambda as its implementation, populating (and then listing) the contents of the

PlaneRepository with a single Aircraft. Currently I have the @Bean annotation for the init() method commented out, so the method is never called, the CommandLineR unner bean is never produced, and the sample record is never stored:

```
import io.r2dbc.spi.ConnectionFactory;
import org.springframework.beans.factory.annotation.Qualifier;
import org.springframework.boot.CommandLineRunner;
import org.springframework.context.annotation.Bean;
import org.springframework.context.annotation.Configuration;
import org.springframework.core.io.ClassPathResource;
import org.springframework.r2dbc.connection.init.ConnectionFactoryInitializer;
import org.springframework.r2dbc.connection.init.ResourceDatabasePopulator;

@Configuration
public class DbConxInit {
    @Bean
    public ConnectionFactoryInitializer
            initializer(@Qualifier("connectionFactory")
            ConnectionFactory connectionFactory) {
        ConnectionFactoryInitializer initializer =
            new ConnectionFactoryInitializer();
        initializer.setConnectionFactory(connectionFactory);
        initializer.setDatabasePopulator(
            new ResourceDatabasePopulator(new ClassPathResource("schema.sql"))
        );
        return initializer;
    }

//   @Bean // Uncomment @Bean annotation to add sample data
    public CommandLineRunner init(PlaneRepository repo) {
        return args -> {
            repo.save(new Aircraft("SAL001", "N12345", "SAL001", "LJ",
                    30000, 30, 300,
                    38.7209228, -90.4107416))
                .thenMany(repo.findAll())
                    .subscribe(System.out::println);
        };
    }
}
```

The CommandLineRunner lambda merits some explanation.

The structure itself is a typical lambda of x -> { <code to execute here> }, but the code contained within has a couple of interesting Reactive Streams–specific features.

The first declared operation is repo::save, which saves the content provided—in this case, a new Aircraft object—and returns a Mono<Aircraft>. It's possible to simply subscribe() to this result and log/print it for verification. But a good habit to adopt is to save all desired sample data, then query the repository to produce all records. Doing so allows for full verification of the final state of the table at that point in time and should result in all records being displayed.

Recall, though, that reactive code doesn't block, so how can one be certain that all previous operations have completed prior to proceeding? In this case, how can we be sure all records are saved before trying to retrieve all records? Within Project Reactor there are operators that await the completion signal, then proceed with the next function in the chain. The `then()` operator waits for a `Mono` as input, then accepts another `Mono` to play going forward. The `thenMany()` operator shown in the previous example awaits the completion of any upstream `Publisher` and plays a new `Flux` going forward. In the `init` method that produces the `CommandLineRunner` bean, `repo.findAll()` produces a `Flux<Aircraft>`, filling the bill as expected.

Finally, I subscribe to the `Flux<Aircraft>` output from `repo.findAll()` and print the results to the console. It isn't necessary to log the results, and in fact a plain `subscribe()` fulfills the requirement to start the flow of data. But why is it necessary to subscribe?

With few exceptions, `Reactive Streams Publishers` are *cold publishers*, meaning they perform no work and consume no resources if they have no subscriber(s). This maximizes efficiency and thus scalability and makes perfect sense, but it also provides a common trap for those new to reactive programming. If you aren't returning a `Publisher` to calling code for subscription and use there, be sure to add a `subscribe()` to it to activate the `Publisher` or chain of operations that results in one.

Going Declarative

I often refer to nonreactive code as *blocking*, which makes sense in most cases, as code (with a few notable exceptions) executes sequentially; one line of code begins after the previous one finishes. Reactive code doesn't block, though—unless it calls blocking code, which I address in an upcoming chapter—and as a result, sequential lines of code don't provide any delineation between instructions whatsoever. This can be a bit jarring, especially for developers coming from a sequential execution background or who still work in one much or all of the time, which is most of us.

Most blocking code is imperative code, in which we specify *how* to do something. Using a *for* loop as an example, we do the following:

- Declare a variable and assign an initial value.
- Check against an outer boundary.
- Perform some instructions.
- Adjust the variable's value.
- Repeat the loop beginning with the value check.

While there are very useful declarative constructs in blocking code—perhaps the best-known and -loved is the Java Stream API—these declarative morsels add zest to the meal but together still compose a relatively small portion of it. Not so with reactive programming.

Because of the name Reactive Streams, you might form associations with Java's `Stream`. Although the two are not connected, the declarative approach used in `java.util.Stream` fits perfectly with Reactive Streams as well: declaring outcomes via a chain of functions that operate by passing output from one to the next as immutable results. This adds structure, both visually and logically, to reactive code.

Finally, some changes to the domain class `Aircraft` are required due to differences in JPA and R2DBC and their supporting H2 code. The `@Entity` notation used by JPA is no longer required, and the `@GeneratedValue` annotation for the primary key-associated member variable `id` is now similarly unnecessary. Removing both of these and their associated import statements are the only required changes when migrating from PlaneFinder from JPA to R2DBC using H2.

To accommodate the `CommandLineRunner` bean shown earlier (should sample data be desired) and its field-limited constructor call, I create an additional constructor in `Aircraft` to match. Note that this is required only if you wish to create an `Aircraft` instance without providing all parameters as required by the constructor Lombok based on the `@AllArgsConstructor` annotation. Note that I call the all-args constructor from this limited-args constructor:

```
public Aircraft(String callsign, String reg, String flightno, String type,
                int altitude, int heading, int speed,
                double lat, double lon) {

    this(null, callsign, "sqwk", reg, flightno, "route", type, "ct",
            altitude, heading, speed, 0, 0,
            lat, lon, 0D, 0D, 0D,
            false, true,
            Instant.now(), Instant.now(), Instant.now());
}
```

With that, it's time to verify our work.

After starting the PlaneFinder application from within the IDE, I return to HTTPie in a terminal window to test the updated code:

```
mheckler-a01 :: OReilly/code » http -b :7634/aircraft
[
    {
        "altitude": 37000,
        "barometer": 0.0,
        "bds40_seen_time": null,
        "callsign": "EDV5123",
        "category": "A3",
        "flightno": "DL5123",
        "heading": 131,
        "id": 1,
```

```json
        "is_adsb": true,
        "is_on_ground": false,
        "last_seen_time": "2020-09-19T21:40:56Z",
        "lat": 38.461505,
        "lon": -89.896606,
        "polar_bearing": 156.187542,
        "polar_distance": 32.208164,
        "pos_update_time": "2020-09-19T21:40:56Z",
        "reg": "N582CA",
        "route": "DSM-ATL",
        "selected_altitude": 0,
        "speed": 474,
        "squawk": "3644",
        "type": "CRJ9",
        "vert_rate": -64
    },
    {
        "altitude": 38000,
        "barometer": 0.0,
        "bds40_seen_time": null,
        "callsign": null,
        "category": "A4",
        "flightno": "FX3711",
        "heading": 260,
        "id": 2,
        "is_adsb": true,
        "is_on_ground": false,
        "last_seen_time": "2020-09-19T21:40:57Z",
        "lat": 39.348558,
        "lon": -90.330383,
        "polar_bearing": 342.006425,
        "polar_distance": 24.839372,
        "pos_update_time": "2020-09-19T21:39:50Z",
        "reg": "N924FD",
        "route": "IND-PHX",
        "selected_altitude": 0,
        "speed": 424,
        "squawk": null,
        "type": "B752",
        "vert_rate": 0
    },
    {
        "altitude": 35000,
        "barometer": 1012.8,
        "bds40_seen_time": "2020-09-19T21:41:11Z",
        "callsign": "JIA5304",
        "category": "A3",
        "flightno": "AA5304",
        "heading": 112,
        "id": 3,
        "is_adsb": true,
        "is_on_ground": false,
        "last_seen_time": "2020-09-19T21:41:12Z",
        "lat": 38.759811,
        "lon": -90.173632,
        "polar_bearing": 179.833023,
```

```
        "polar_distance": 11.568717,
        "pos_update_time": "2020-09-19T21:41:11Z",
        "reg": "N563NN",
        "route": "CLT-RAP-CLT",
        "selected_altitude": 35008,
        "speed": 521,
        "squawk": "6506",
        "type": "CRJ9",
        "vert_rate": 0
    }
]
```

Confirming that the refactored, reactive PlaneFinder works properly, we can now turn our attention to the Aircraft Positions application.

Updating the Aircraft Positions application

Currently the *aircraft-positions* project uses Spring Data JPA and H2, just as Plane-Finder did when it was a blocking application. While I could update Aircraft Positions to use R2DBC and H2 just as PlaneFinder now does, this required refactoring of the *aircraft-positions* project offers the perfect opportunity to explore other reactive database solutions.

MongoDB is often at the forefront of database innovation, and indeed it was one of the first database providers of any kind to develop fully reactive drivers for use with its namesake database. Developing applications using Spring Data and MongoDB is nearly frictionless, reflecting the maturity of its reactive streams support. For the reactive refactoring of Aircraft Positions, MongoDB is a natural choice.

Some changes to the build file, *pom.xml* in this case, are in order. First I remove the unnecessary dependencies for Spring MVC, Spring Data JPA, and H2:

- `spring-boot-starter-web`
- `spring-boot-starter-data-jpa`
- `h2`

Next I add the following dependencies for the reactive version going forward:

- `spring-boot-starter-data-mongodb-reactive`
- `de.flapdoodle.embed.mongo`
- `reactor-test`

`spring-boot-starter-webflux` was already a dependency due to `WebClient`, so it wasn't necessary to add it.

As in Chapter 6, I will make use of the embedded MongoDB for this example. Since the embedded MongoDB is typically used only for testing, it usually includes a scope of "test"; since I use this during application execution, I omit or remove that scoping qualifier from the build file. The updated Maven *pom.xml* dependencies look like this:

```
<dependencies>
    <dependency>
        <groupId>org.springframework.boot</groupId>
        <artifactId>spring-boot-starter-thymeleaf</artifactId>
    </dependency>
    <dependency>
        <groupId>org.springframework.boot</groupId>
        <artifactId>spring-boot-starter-data-mongodb-reactive</artifactId>
    </dependency>
    <dependency>
        <groupId>org.springframework.boot</groupId>
        <artifactId>spring-boot-starter-webflux</artifactId>
    </dependency>

    <dependency>
        <groupId>org.projectlombok</groupId>
        <artifactId>lombok</artifactId>
        <optional>true</optional>
    </dependency>
    <dependency>
        <groupId>org.springframework.boot</groupId>
        <artifactId>spring-boot-starter-test</artifactId>
        <scope>test</scope>
        <exclusions>
            <exclusion>
                <groupId>org.junit.vintage</groupId>
                <artifactId>junit-vintage-engine</artifactId>
            </exclusion>
        </exclusions>
    </dependency>
    <dependency>
        <groupId>de.flapdoodle.embed</groupId>
        <artifactId>de.flapdoodle.embed.mongo</artifactId>
    </dependency>
    <dependency>
        <groupId>io.projectreactor</groupId>
        <artifactId>reactor-test</artifactId>
        <scope>test</scope>
    </dependency>
</dependencies>
```

A quick refresh to the dependencies either via command line or the IDE and we're ready to refactor.

I begin again with the very simple change to the `AircraftRepository` interface, changing it to extend `ReactiveCrudRepository` instead of the blocking `CrudReposi tory`:

```
public interface AircraftRepository extends ReactiveCrudRepository<Aircraft, Long> {}
```

Updating the `PositionController` class is a fairly small chore, since `WebClient` already converses using Reactive Streams `Publisher` types. I define a local variable `Flux<Aircraft> aircraftFlux`, then chain the requisite declarative operations to clear the repository of previously retrieved aircraft positions, retrieve new positions, convert them to instances of the `Aircraft` class, filter out positions without a listed aircraft registration number, and save them to the embedded MongoDB repository. I then add the `aircraftFlux` variable to the `Model` for use in the user-facing web UI and return the name of the Thymeleaf template for rendering:

```
@RequiredArgsConstructor
@Controller
public class PositionController {
    @NonNull
    private final AircraftRepository repository;
    private WebClient client
        = WebClient.create("http://localhost:7634/aircraft");

    @GetMapping("/aircraft")
    public String getCurrentAircraftPositions(Model model) {
        Flux<Aircraft> aircraftFlux = repository.deleteAll()
                .thenMany(client.get()
                        .retrieve()
                        .bodyToFlux(Aircraft.class)
                        .filter(plane -> !plane.getReg().isEmpty())
                        .flatMap(repository::save));

        model.addAttribute("currentPositions", aircraftFlux);
        return "positions";
    }
}
```

Finally, a few small changes are required for the domain class `Aircraft` itself. The class-level `@Entity` annotation is JPA-specific; the corresponding annotation used by MongoDB is `@Document`, indicating that instances of a class are to be stored as documents within the database. Additionally, the `@Id` annotation used previously referenced `javax.persistence.Id`, which disappears without the JPA dependency. Replacing `import javax.persistence.Id;` with `import org.springframe work.data.annotation.Id;` retains the table identifier context for use with MongoDB. The class file in its entirety is shown for reference:

```
import com.fasterxml.jackson.annotation.JsonProperty;
import lombok.AllArgsConstructor;
import lombok.Data;
import lombok.NoArgsConstructor;
import org.springframework.data.annotation.Id;
```

```
import org.springframework.data.mongodb.core.mapping.Document;

import java.time.Instant;

@Document
@Data
@NoArgsConstructor
@AllArgsConstructor
public class Aircraft {
    @Id
    private Long id;
    private String callsign, squawk, reg, flightno, route, type, category;

    private int altitude, heading, speed;
    @JsonProperty("vert_rate")
    private int vertRate;
    @JsonProperty("selected_altitude")
    private int selectedAltitude;

    private double lat, lon, barometer;
    @JsonProperty("polar_distance")
    private double polarDistance;
    @JsonProperty("polar_bearing")
    private double polarBearing;

    @JsonProperty("is_adsb")
    private boolean isADSB;
    @JsonProperty("is_on_ground")
    private boolean isOnGround;

    @JsonProperty("last_seen_time")
    private Instant lastSeenTime;
    @JsonProperty("pos_update_time")
    private Instant posUpdateTime;
    @JsonProperty("bds40_seen_time")
    private Instant bds40SeenTime;
}
```

Running both the PlaneFinder and Aircraft Positions applications, I return to a browser tab and type *http://localhost:8080* into the address bar and load it, resulting in the page shown in Figure 8-1.

Figure 8-1. The Aircraft Positions application landing page, index.html

Clicking on the *Click here* link loads the `Aircraft Positions` report page, as shown in Figure 8-2.

Current Aircraft Positions

Call Sign	Squawk	AC Reg	Flight #	Route	AC Type	Altitude	Heading	Speed	Vert Rate	Latitude	Longitude	Last Seen
N1826Q	1200	N1826Q			C177	4200	257	138	-128	39.081482	-90.281704	2020-09-20T19:30:29Z
		N156AN	AA686	PHL-PHX	A321	34025	261	417	0	39.045456	-89.98167	2020-09-20T19:31:01Z
		N373DX	DL976	ATL-STL-ATL	A321	7500	129	275	3136	38.634796	-90.170288	2020-09-20T19:30:28Z
LXJ357	1373	N357FX		FTW-DAL	E55P	43000	222	386	0	38.943554	-90.389221	2020-09-20T19:31:01Z
		N369DN	DL1878	MSP-TPA-MSP	A321	38000	331	428	0	38.801523	-89.782776	2020-09-20T19:31:01Z
EJA509		N509QS		BZN-HPN	C68A	40000	298	384	0	39.095673	-90.035049	2020-09-20T19:30:58Z

Figure 8-2. The Aircraft Positions report page

With each periodic refresh, the page will requery PlaneFinder and update the report with current data on demand as before, with one very key difference: the multiple aircraft positions that are supplied to the *positions.html* Thymeleaf template for display are no longer a fully formed, blocking `List` but rather a Reactive Streams `Publisher`, specifically of type `Flux`. The next section addresses this further, but for now, it's important to realize that this content negotiation/accommodation occurs with no effort required from the developer.

Reactive Thymeleaf

As mentioned in Chapter 7, the vast majority of frontend web applications are now being developed using HTML and JavaScript. This doesn't alter the existence of a number of production applications that use view technologies/templating to fulfill their objectives; neither does it imply that said technologies don't continue to satisfy a range of requirements simply and effectively. This being the case, it's important for template engines and languages to adapt to circumstances in which Reactive Streams are also brought to bear on a problem.

Thymeleaf approaches RS support at three different levels, allowing developers to settle on the one that best fits their requirements. As mentioned earlier, it's possible to convert backend processing to leverage Reactive Streams and let Reactor feed Thymeleaf values supplied by a `Publisher`—like a `Mono` or `Flux`—instead of `Object<T>` and `Iterable<T>`. This doesn't result in a reactive frontend, but if the concern is primarily conversion of backend logic to use Reactive Streams to eliminate blocking and implement flow control among services, this is a frictionless on-ramp to deploying a supporting user-facing application with the least possible effort.

Thymeleaf also supports chunked and data-driven modes in support of Spring WebFlux, both involving the use of Server Sent Events and some JavaScript code to accomplish the feed of data to the browser. While both of these modalities are entirely valid, the increased amount of JavaScript required to achieve the desired outcome may tip the scales away from templating+HTML+JavaScript and toward 100% HTML +JavaScript frontend logic. This decision is heavily dependent on requirements, of course, and should be left to the developer(s) tasked with creating and supporting said functionality.

In the preceding section, I demonstrated how to migrate the backend functionality to RS constructs and how Spring Boot uses Reactor+Thymeleaf to maintain functionality in the front end, helping ease conversions of blocking systems of applications while minimizing downtime. This is sufficient to satisfy the current use case, allowing us to examine ways to further improve backend functionality before returning (in an upcoming chapter) to expanding frontend capabilities.

RSocket for Fully Reactive Interprocess Communication

Already in this chapter I've laid the groundwork for interprocess communication using Reactive Streams between separate applications. While the distributed system created does indeed use reactive constructs, the system has yet to reach its potential. Crossing the network boundary using higher-level HTTP-based transports imposes limitations due to the request-response model, and even upgrading to WebSocket alone doesn't address all of them. RSocket was created to eliminate interprocess communication shortfalls flexibly and powerfully.

What Is RSocket?

The result of a collaboration among several industry leaders and cutting-edge innovators, RSocket is a blazing-fast binary protocol that can be used over TCP, WebSocket, and Aeron transport mechanisms. RSocket supports four asynchronous interaction models:

- Request-response
- Request-stream
- Fire & forget
- Request channel (bidirectional stream)

RSocket builds on the reactive streams paradigm and Project Reactor, enabling fully interconnected systems of applications while providing mechanisms that increase flexibility and resilience. Once a connection is made between two apps/services, distinctions of client versus server disappear and the two are effectively peers. Any of the four interaction models can be initiated by either party and accommodate all use cases:

- A 1:1 interaction in which one party issues a request and receives a response from the other party

- A 1:N interaction in which one party issues a request and receives a stream of responses from the other party

- A 1:0 interaction in which one party issues a request

- A fully bidirectional channel in which both parties can send requests, responses, or data streams of any kind unbidden

As you can see, RSocket is incredibly flexible. Being a binary protocol with a performance focus, it is also fast. On top of that, RSocket is resilient, making it possible for a dropped connection to be reestablished and communications to automatically resume where they left off. And since RSocket is built on Reactor, developers who use RSocket can truly consider separate applications as a fully integrated system, since the network boundary no longer imposes any limitations on flow control.

Spring Boot, with its legendary autoconfiguration, arguably provides the fastest, most developer-friendly way for Java and Kotlin developers to use RSocket.

Putting RSocket to Work

Currently both the PlaneFinder and Aircraft Positions applications use HTTP-based transports to communicate. Converting both Spring Boot apps to use RSocket is the obvious next step forward.

Migrating PlaneFinder to RSocket

First, I add the RSocket dependency to the PlaneFinder build file:

```
<dependency>
    <groupId>org.springframework.boot</groupId>
    <artifactId>spring-boot-starter-rsocket</artifactId>
</dependency>
```

After a quick Maven re-import, it's off to refactor the code.

For the time being, I'll leave the existing endpoint of */aircraft* intact and add an RSocket endpoint to `PlaneController`. In order to place both REST endpoints and RSocket endpoints in the same class, I decouple the functionality built into the `@Rest Controller` annotation into its component parts: `@Controller` and `@ResponseBody`.

Replacing the class-level `@RestController` annotation with `@Controller` means that for any REST endpoints from which we wish to return objects directly as JSON—such as the existing */aircraft* endpoint associated with the `getCurrentAircraft()` method—it is necessary to add `@ResponseBody` to the method. The advantage to this seeming step back is that RSocket endpoints can then be defined in the same `@Con`

troller class as REST endpoints, keeping points of ingress and egress for Plane-
Finder in one, and only one, location:

```
import org.springframework.messaging.handler.annotation.MessageMapping;
import org.springframework.stereotype.Controller;
import org.springframework.web.bind.annotation.GetMapping;
import org.springframework.web.bind.annotation.ResponseBody;
import reactor.core.publisher.Flux;

import java.io.IOException;
import java.time.Duration;

@Controller
public class PlaneController {
    private final PlaneFinderService pfService;

    public PlaneController(PlaneFinderService pfService) {
        this.pfService = pfService;
    }

    @ResponseBody
    @GetMapping("/aircraft")
    public Flux<Aircraft> getCurrentAircraft() throws IOException {
        return pfService.getAircraft();
    }

    @MessageMapping("acstream")
    public Flux<Aircraft> getCurrentACStream() throws IOException {
        return pfService.getAircraft().concatWith(
                Flux.interval(Duration.ofSeconds(1))
                        .flatMap(l -> pfService.getAircraft()));
    }
}
```

To create a repeating stream of aircraft positions sent initially and at subsequent one-
second intervals, I create the getCurrentACStream() method and annotate it as an
RSocket endpoint with @MessageMapping. Note that since RSocket mappings don't
build upon a root path as HTTP addresses/endpoints do, no forward slash (/) is
required in the mapping.

With the endpoint and servicing method defined, the next step is to designate a port
for RSocket to listen for connection requests. I do so in PlaneFinder's
application.properties file, adding a property value for spring.rsocket.server.port
to the existing one for the HTTP-based server.port:

```
server.port=7634
spring.rsocket.server.port=7635
```

The presence of this single RSocket server port assignment is sufficient for Spring
Boot to configure the containing application as an RSocket server, creating all necessary beans and performing all of the requisite configuration. Recall that while one of
the two applications involved in an RSocket connection must act initially as a server,

once the connection is established the distinction between client (the app that initiates a connection) and server (the app that listens for a connection) evaporates.

With those few changes, PlaneFinder is now RSocket ready. Simply start the application to ready it for connection requests.

Migrating Aircraft Positions to RSocket

Once again, the first step in adding RSocket is to add the RSocket dependency to the build file—in this case, for the Aircraft Positions application:

```
<dependency>
    <groupId>org.springframework.boot</groupId>
    <artifactId>spring-boot-starter-rsocket</artifactId>
</dependency>
```

Don't forget to re-import and thus activate changes with Maven for the project prior to continuing. Now, on to the code.

Similarly to how I did with PlaneFinder, I refactor the `PositionController` class to create a single point for all ingress/egress. Replacing the class-level `@RestController` annotation with `@Controller` allows for the inclusion of RSocket endpoints along with the HTTP-based (but template-driven, in this case) endpoint that activates the *positions.html* Thymeleaf template.

To enable Aircraft Positions to act as an RSocket client, I create an `RSocketRequester` by autowiring via constructor injection an `RSocketRequester.Builder` bean. The `RSocketRequester.Builder` bean is automatically created by Spring Boot as a result of adding the RSocket dependency to the project. Within the constructor, I use the builder to create a TCP connection (in this case) to PlaneFinder's RSocket server via the builder's `tcp()` method.

 Since I need to inject a bean (`RSocketRequester.Builder`) used to create an instance of a different object (`RSocketRequester`), I must create a constructor. Since I now have a constructor, I removed the class-level `@RequiredArgsConstructor` and member variable-level `@NonNull` Lombok annotations and simply add `AircraftReposi` `tory` to the constructor I wrote as well. Either way, Spring Boot autowires the bean, and it is assigned to the `repository` member variable.

To verify the RSocket connection is working properly and data is flowing, I create an HTTP-based endpoint */acstream*, specify it will return a stream of Server Sent Events (SSE) as a result, and with the `@ResponseBody` annotation indicate that the response will comprise JSON-formatted objects directly. Using the `RSocketRequester` member variable initialized in the constructor, I specify the `route` to match the RSocket endpoint defined in PlaneFinder, send some `data` (optional; I don't pass any useful data in this particular request), and retrieve the `Flux` of `Aircraft` returned from Plane-Finder:

```
import org.springframework.http.MediaType;
import org.springframework.messaging.rsocket.RSocketRequester;
import org.springframework.stereotype.Controller;
import org.springframework.ui.Model;
import org.springframework.web.bind.annotation.GetMapping;
import org.springframework.web.bind.annotation.ResponseBody;
import org.springframework.web.reactive.function.client.WebClient;
import reactor.core.publisher.Flux;

@Controller
public class PositionController {
    private final AircraftRepository repository;
    private final RSocketRequester requester;
    private WebClient client =
            WebClient.create("http://localhost:7634/aircraft");

    public PositionController(AircraftRepository repository,
                              RSocketRequester.Builder builder) {
        this.repository = repository;
        this.requester = builder.tcp("localhost", 7635);
    }

    // HTTP endpoint, HTTP requester (previously created)
    @GetMapping("/aircraft")
    public String getCurrentAircraftPositions(Model model) {
        Flux<Aircraft> aircraftFlux = repository.deleteAll()
                .thenMany(client.get()
                        .retrieve()
                        .bodyToFlux(Aircraft.class)
                        .filter(plane -> !plane.getReg().isEmpty())
                        .flatMap(repository::save));

        model.addAttribute("currentPositions", aircraftFlux);
        return "positions";
    }

    // HTTP endpoint, RSocket client endpoint
    @ResponseBody
    @GetMapping(value = "/acstream",
            produces = MediaType.TEXT_EVENT_STREAM_VALUE)
    public Flux<Aircraft> getCurrentACPositionsStream() {
        return requester.route("acstream")
                .data("Requesting aircraft positions")
                .retrieveFlux(Aircraft.class);
    }
}
```

To verify the RSocket connection is viable and PlaneFinder is feeding data to the Aircraft Positions application, I start Aircraft Positions and return to the terminal and HTTPie, adding the *-S* flag to the command to process the data as a stream, as it arrives, rather than wait for a response body completion. An example of the results follows, edited for brevity:

```
mheckler-a01 :: ~ » http -S :8080/acstream
HTTP/1.1 200 OK
Content-Type: text/event-stream;charset=UTF-8
transfer-encoding: chunked
```

```
data:{"id":1,"callsign":"RPA3427","squawk":"0526","reg":"N723YX","flightno":
"UA3427","route":"IAD-MCI","type":"E75L","category":"A3","altitude":36000,
"heading":290,"speed":403,"lat":39.183929,"lon":-90.72259,"barometer":0.0,
"vert_rate":64,"selected_altitude":0,"polar_distance":29.06486,
"polar_bearing":297.519943,"is_adsb":true,"is_on_ground":false,
"last_seen_time":"2020-09-20T23:58:51Z",
"pos_update_time":"2020-09-20T23:58:49Z","bds40_seen_time":null}

data:{"id":2,"callsign":"EDG76","squawk":"3354","reg":"N776RB","flightno":"",
"route":"TEB-VNY","type":"GLF5","category":"A3","altitude":43000,"heading":256,
"speed":419,"lat":38.884918,"lon":-90.363026,"barometer":0.0,"vert_rate":64,
"selected_altitude":0,"polar_distance":9.699159,"polar_bearing":244.237695,
"is_adsb":true,"is_on_ground":false,"last_seen_time":"2020-09-20T23:59:22Z",
"pos_update_time":"2020-09-20T23:59:14Z","bds40_seen_time":null}

data:{"id":3,"callsign":"EJM604","squawk":"3144","reg":"N604SD","flightno":"",
"route":"ENW-HOU","type":"C56X","category":"A2","altitude":38000,"heading":201,
"speed":387,"lat":38.627464,"lon":-90.01416,"barometer":0.0,"vert_rate":-64,
"selected_altitude":0,"polar_distance":20.898095,"polar_bearing":158.9935,
"is_adsb":true,"is_on_ground":false,"last_seen_time":"2020-09-20T23:59:19Z",
"pos_update_time":"2020-09-20T23:59:19Z","bds40_seen_time":null}
```

This confirms that data is flowing from PlaneFinder to Aircraft Positions via Reactive Streams over an RSocket connection using the *request-stream* model. All systems go.

Code Checkout Checkup

For complete chapter code, please check out branch *chapter8end* from the code repository.

Summary

Reactive programming gives developers a way to make better use of resources, and in an increasingly distributed world of interconnected systems, the master key to scalability involves extending scaling mechanisms beyond application boundaries and into the communication channels. The Reactive Streams initiative, and in particular Project Reactor, serves as a powerful, performant, and flexible foundation for maximizing system-wide scalability.

In this chapter, I introduced reactive programming and demonstrated how Spring is leading the development and advancement of numerous tools and technologies. I explained blocking and nonblocking communication and the engines that provide those capabilities, e.g., Tomcat, Netty, and others.

Next, I demonstrated how to enable reactive database access to SQL and NoSQL databases by refactoring the PlaneFinder and Aircraft Positions applications to use Spring WebFlux/Project Reactor. Reactive Relational Database Connectivity (R2DBC) provides a reactive replacement for the Java Persistence API (JPA) and works with several SQL databases; MongoDB and other NoSQL databases provide drop-in reactive drivers that work seamlessly with Spring Data and Spring Boot.

This chapter also discussed options for frontend integration of reactive types and demonstrated how Thymeleaf provides a limited migration path if your applications are still using generated view technologies. Additional options will be considered in future chapters.

Finally, I demonstrated how to take interprocess communication to unexpected new levels with RSocket. Doing so via Spring Boot's RSocket support and autoconfiguration provides the fast path to performance, scalability, resilience, and developer productivity.

In the next chapter, I'll dig into testing: how Spring Boot enables better, faster, and easier testing practices, how to create effective unit tests, and how to hone and focus testing to speed the build-and-test cycle.

## CHAPTER 9

Testing Spring Boot Applications for Increased Production Readiness

This chapter discusses and demonstrates core aspects of testing Spring Boot applications. While the subject of testing has numerous facets, I focus upon the fundamental elements of testing Spring Boot applications that dramatically improve the production readiness of each application. Topics include unit testing, holistic application testing using `@SpringBootTest`, how to write effective unit tests using JUnit, and using Spring Boot testing slices to isolate test subjects and streamline testing.

Code Checkout Checkup

Please check out branch *chapter9begin* from the code repository to begin.

Unit Testing

Unit testing serves as a precursor to other types of application testing for good reason: unit testing enables a developer to find and fix bugs at the earliest possible stages of the develop+deploy cycle and as a result, to fix them at the lowest possible cost.

Simply put, *unit testing* involves validating a defined unit of code isolated to the maximum possible and sensible extent. A test's number of outcomes increases exponentially with size and complexity; reducing the amount of functionality within each unit test makes each one more manageable, thus increasing the likelihood that all likely and/or possible outcomes are considered.

Only once unit testing is implemented successfully and sufficiently should integration testing, UI/UX testing, and so on be added to the mix. Fortunately Spring Boot incorporates features to simplify and streamline unit testing and includes those capabilities in every project built using the Spring Initializr by default, making it easy for developers to get started quickly and "do the right thing".

Introducing @SpringBootTest

So far I've primarily focused on the code under *src/main/java* in projects created using the Spring Initializr, beginning with the main application class. In every Initializr-spawned Spring Boot application, however, there is a corresponding *src/test/java* directory structure with a single pre-created (but as yet empty) test.

Named to correspond with the main application class as well — for example, if the main app class is named `MyApplication`, the main test class will be `MyApplicationTest` — this default 1:1 correlation helps with both organization and consistency. Within the test class, the Initializr creates a single test method, empty to provide a clean start and so that development begins with a clean build. You can add more test methods, or more typically create additional test classes to parallel other application classes and create 1+ test methods within each.

Normally I would encourage Test Driven Development (TDD) in which tests are written first and code is written to (and only to) make tests pass. Since I firmly believe key aspects of Spring Boot are important to understand prior to the introduction of how Boot handles testing, I trust the reader will indulge my delay in introducing this chapter's material until foundational topics were addressed.

With that in mind, let's return to the Aircraft Positions application and write some tests.

Notes about Test Coverage

There are many persuasive arguments for every level of unit testing, from minimal to 100% test coverage. I consider myself a pragmatist, balanced on recognizing that too little is, well, too little; and acknowledging the falsity of the idea that "if some is good, more must be better".

Everything has a cost. With too few tests the cost usually becomes apparent rather quickly: errors or edge cases slip through to production and often cause considerable headaches and unfortunate financial impacts. But writing tests for every accessor and mutator or for every element of exposed library/framework code can add burdensome costs to a project as well, often for very little (or zero) gain. Of course accessors and mutators can change, and of course underlying code can introduce bugs; but how often has that happened within your projects?

For this book and in my usual practice, I adopt a "test enough" mindset, purposely writing tests only for so-called interesting behavior. I generally do not write tests for

---

domain classes, straightforward accessors/mutators, well-established Spring code, or anything else that would seem already to be very stable or (nearly?) foolproof, with a few notable exceptions which I explain at the time; see the earlier comment about interesting behavior. Note also that this assessment should be challenged and revisited in real projects, as software is not static and constantly evolves.

Only you and your organization can determine your risk profile and exposure.

In order to demonstrate the broadest swath of testing features enabled by Spring Boot in the clearest and most concise manner, I return to the JPA version of AircraftPositions and use it as the foundation for this chapter's focus on testing. There are a few other testing-related topics that offer variations on a theme, complementary to this chapter's content without being represented within its project; these related topics will be covered in an upcoming chapter.

Important Unit Tests for the Aircraft Positions Application

Within AircraftPositions there is currently only one class with what might be considered interesting behavior. `PositionController` exposes an API to provide current aircraft positions to the end user directly or via web interface and within that API may perform actions including:

- Fetching current aircraft positions from PlaneFinder
- Storing the positions in a local database
- Retrieving the positions from the local database
- Returning current positions directly or by adding them to the document `Model` for a web page

Ignoring for the moment the fact that this functionality interacts with an external service, it also touches every layer of the application stack from user interface to data storage and retrieval. Recalling that a good testing approach should isolate and test small, cohesive bits of functionality, it's clear that an iterative approach to testing is in order, moving stepwise from the current state of code and no tests toward an eventual endstate of optimized application organization and testing. In this way, it accurately reflects typical production-targeted projects.

 Since applications in use are never really *done*, neither is testing. As an application's code evolves, tests must also be reviewed and potentially revised, removed, or added to maintain testing effectiveness.

I begin by creating a test class that parallels the `PositionController` class. The mechanism for creating a test class differs between IDEs, and of course it's possible to manually create one as well. Since I primarily use IntelliJ IDEA for development, I use the `CMD+N` keyboard shortcut or click the right mouse button and then "Generate" to open the Generate menu, then select the "Test…" option to create a test class. IntelliJ then presents the popup shown in Figure 9-1.

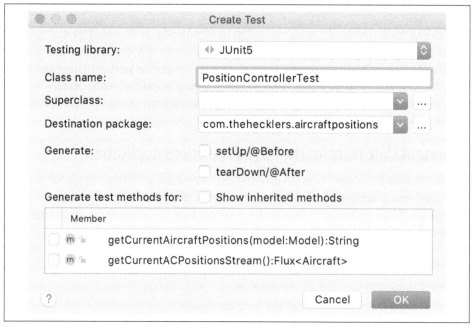

Figure 9-1. Create Test popup initiated from PositionController Class

From the *Create Test* popup, I keep the default "Testing library" option setting of JUnit 5. Since Spring Boot version 2.2 became generally available (GA), JUnit version 5 has been the default for Spring Boot application unit tests. Many other options are supported — including JUnit 3 and 4, Spock, and TestNG among others — but JUnit 5 with its Jupiter engine is a powerful option that offers several capabilities:

- Better testing of Kotlin code (compared to previous versions)
- More efficient once-only instantiation/configuration/cleanup of a test class for all contained tests, using `@BeforeAll` and `@AfterAll` method annotations
- Support for both JUnit 4 and 5 tests (unless JUnit 4 is specifically excluded from dependencies)

JUnit 5's Jupiter engine is the default, with the vintage engine provided for backward compatibility with JUnit 4 unit tests.

I keep the suggested class name of `PositionControllerTest`, check the boxes to generate `setup/@Before` and `tearDown/@After` methods, and check the box to generate a test method for the `getCurrentAircraftPositions()` method as shown in Figure 9-2.

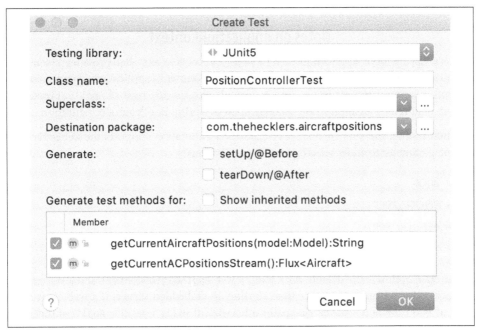

Figure 9-2. Create Test popup with Desired Options Selected

Once I click the OK button, IntelliJ creates the `PositionControllerTest` class with the chosen methods and opens it in the IDE, as shown here:

```
import org.junit.jupiter.api.AfterEach;
import org.junit.jupiter.api.BeforeEach;
import org.junit.jupiter.api.Test;

class PositionControllerTest {

    @BeforeEach
    void setUp() {
    }

    @AfterEach
    void tearDown() {
    }

    @Test
    void getCurrentAircraftPositions() {
    }
}
```

To get a running start on building a test suite after-the-fact, I begin by simply repro-ducing to the extent possible the existing operation of the `PositionController` method `getCurrentAircraftPositions()` within the same (literal) context it already successfully runs: the Spring Boot `ApplicationContext`.

Notes on ApplicationContext

Every Spring Boot application has an `ApplicationContext` that provides essential context — managing interactions with the environment, application components/beans, passing messages, etc. — and by default, the specific type of `ApplicationCon` text required by an application is determined by Spring Boot's autoconfiguration.

When testing, the `@SpringBootTest` class-level annotation supports the `webEnviron` ment parameter to allow selecting one of four options:

- `MOCK`
- `RANDOM_PORT`
- `DEFINED_PORT`
- `NONE`

The `MOCK` option is the default. `MOCK` loads a web `ApplicationContext` and leverages a mock web environment (rather than starting an embedded server) if a web environ-ment is on the application's classpath; otherwise, it loads a regular `ApplicationCon` text with no web capabilities. `@SpringBootTest(webEnvironment = SpringBootTest.WebEnvironment.MOCK)` or just `@SpringBootTest` is often accompa-nied by `@AutoConfigureMockMVC` or `@AutoConfigureWebTestClient` to facilitate mock-based testing of web-based APIs using the corresponding mechanisms.

The `RANDOM_PORT` option loads a web `ApplicationContext` and starts an embedded server to provide an actual web environment exposed on a random available port. `DEFINED_PORT` does the same with one exception: it listens on the port defined in the application's *application.properties* or *application.yml/yaml* file. If no port is defined in those locations, the default port of 8080 is used.

Choosing `NONE` results in the creation of an `ApplicationContext` with no web envi-ronment at all, mock or actual. No embedded server is started.

I begin by adding the `@SpringBootTest` annotation at the class level. Since the initial goal is to reproduce as closely as possible the behavior present when the application executes, I specify the option to start an embedded server and have it listen on a random port. To test the web API, I plan to use the `WebTestClient`, which is similar to the `WebClient` used in the application but with a focus on testing:

```
@SpringBootTest(webEnvironment = SpringBootTest.WebEnvironment.RANDOM_PORT)
@AutoConfigureWebTestClient
```

With only one unit test so far and no setup/teardown yet required, I turn attention to the test method for `getCurrentAircraftPositions()`:

```
@Test
void getCurrentAircraftPositions(@Autowired WebTestClient client) {
    assert client.get()
            .uri("/aircraft")
            .exchange()
            .expectStatus().isOk()
            .expectBody(Iterable.class)
            .returnResult()
            .getResponseBody()
            .iterator()
            .hasNext();
}
```

The first thing of note is that I autowire a `WebTestClient` bean for use within the method. This minimal effort on my part is all that is required to inject a `WebTest Client` bean from the `ApplicationContext`, due to the `@AutoConfigureWebTest Client` annotation I placed at the class level instructing Spring Boot to create and automatically configure a `WebTestClient`.

The single statement that is the entirety of the `@Test` method is an assertion that evaluates the expression that immediately follows. For the first iteration of this test, I use Java's `assert` to verify that final result of the chain of operations on the client is a `boolean` true value, thus resulting in a passing test.

The expression itself uses the injected `WebTestClient` bean, issuing a `GET` on the local endpoint */aircraft* serviced by the `PositionController`'s `getCurrentAircraftPosi tions()` method. Once the request/response exchange takes place, the HTTP status code is checked for a response of "OK" (200), the response body is verified to contain an `Iterable`, and the response is retrieved. Since the response consists of an `Itera ble`, I use an `Iterator` to determine if there is at least one value contained within the `Iterable`. If so, the test passes.

There are at least a couple small compromises in the current test. First, the test as currently written will fail if the external service that supplies aircraft positions (PlaneFinder) is unavailable, even if all code being tested in AircraftPositions is correct. This means that the test is not testing only the functionality it targets, but much more. Second, the extent of the test is somewhat limited since I test only that an Iterable is returned with 1+ element(s) and perform no examination of the element(s) themselves. This means that returning one element of any kind in an Iterable, or valid element(s) with invalid values, will result in a passing test. I'll remedy all of these shortcomings in iterations to follow.

Executing the test provides results similar to those shown in Figure 9-3, indicating that the test passed.

Figure 9-3. First test passed

This is a good start, but even this single test can be improved significantly. Let's clean up this test before further expanding our unit testing mandate.

Refactoring for Better Testing

In the vast majority of cases, loading an entire ApplicationContext with embedded server and all capabilities present in the application to run a handful of tests is overkill. As mentioned before, unit tests should be focused and to the extent possible, self-contained. The smaller the surface area and fewer the external dependencies, the more targeted the tests can be. This laserlike focus offers several benefits, including fewer overlooked scenarios/outcomes, greater potential specificity and rigor in testing, more readable and thus understandable tests, and no less importantly speed.

I mentioned earlier that it's counterproductive to write low- and no-value tests, although what that means is dependent upon context. One thing that can discourage developers from adding useful tests, however, is the amount of time it can take to execute the test suite. Once a certain threshold is reached — and such boundary is also context dependent — a developer may hesitate to add to the already significant time burden required to get a clean build. Fortunately Spring Boot has several means to simultaneously increase test quality and decrease test execution times.

If no calls using `WebClient` or `WebTestClient` were required to fulfill the demands of AircraftPosition's API, the next logical step would likely be to remove the `webEnviron ment` parameter within the class-level `@SpringBootTest` annotation. This would result in a basic `ApplicationContext` being loaded for the `PositionControllerTest` class's tests using a `MOCK` web environment, reducing the footprint and load time required. Since `WebClient` is a key part of the API and thus `WebTestClient` becomes the best way to test it, I instead replace the `@SpringBootTest` and `@AutoConfigureWebTest Client` class-level annotations with `@WebFluxTest` to streamline the `ApplicationCon text` while autoconfiguring and providing access to the `WebTestClient`:

```
@WebFluxTest({PositionController.class})
```

One other thing of note with the `@WebFluxTest` annotation: among other things, it can accept a parameter of `controllers` pointing to an array of `@Controller` bean types to be instantiated for use by the annotated test class. The actual `controllers = ` portion can be omitted, as I have, leaving only the array of `@Controller` classes — in this case only the one, `PositionController`.

Revisiting the code to isolate behavior

As mentioned earlier, the code for `PositionController` does several things, including making multiple database calls and directly using `WebClient` to access an external service. In order to better isolate the API from underlying actions so mocking becomes more granular and thus both easier and clearer, I refactor `PositionControl ler` to remove direct definition and use of a `WebClient` and move the entirety of the `getCurrentAircraftPositions()` method's logic to a `PositionRetriever` class, which is then injected into and used by `PositionController`:

```
import lombok.AllArgsConstructor;
import org.springframework.web.bind.annotation.GetMapping;
import org.springframework.web.bind.annotation.RestController;

@AllArgsConstructor
@RestController
public class PositionController {
    private final PositionRetriever retriever;

    @GetMapping("/aircraft")
    public Iterable<Aircraft> getCurrentAircraftPositions() {
```

```
        return retriever.retrieveAircraftPositions();
    }
}
```

The first mock-ready version of `PositionRetriever` largely consists of the code that had previously been in `PositionController`. The primary goal for this step is to facilitate mocking of the `retrieveAircraftPositions()` method; by removing this logic from the `getCurrentAircraftPositions()` method in `PositionController`, an upstream call can be mocked instead of the web API, thus enabling testing of the `PositionController`:

```
import lombok.AllArgsConstructor;
import org.springframework.stereotype.Component;
import org.springframework.web.reactive.function.client.WebClient;

@AllArgsConstructor
@Component
public class PositionRetriever {
    private final AircraftRepository repository;
    private final WebClient client =
            WebClient.create("http://localhost:7634");

    Iterable<Aircraft> retrieveAircraftPositions() {
        repository.deleteAll();

        client.get()
                .uri("/aircraft")
                .retrieve()
                .bodyToFlux(Aircraft.class)
                .filter(ac -> !ac.getReg().isEmpty())
                .toStream()
                .forEach(repository::save);

        return repository.findAll();
    }
}
```

With these changes to the code, the existing testing can be revised to isolate the Aircraft Positions application's functionality from external services and focus specifically upon the web API by mocking other components/functionality accessed by the web API, thus streamlining and speeding test execution.

Refining the test

Since the focus is on testing the web API, the more logic that isn't an actual web interaction that can be mocked, the better. `PositionController::getCurrentAircraftPositions` now calls on `PositionRetriever` to provide it with current aircraft positions upon request, so `PositionRetriever` is the first component to mock. Mockito's `@Mock Bean` annotation — Mockito is included automatically with the Spring Boot testing dependency — replaces the `PositionRetriever` bean that normally would be created on application startup with a mocked stand-in, which is then automatically injected:

```
@MockBean
private PositionRetriever retriever;
```

 Mock beans are automatically reset after each test method is executed.

I then turn my attention to the method that provides aircraft positions, `PositionRetriever::retrieveAircraftPositions`. Since I now inject a `PositionRetriever` mock for testing instead of the real thing, I must provide an implementation for the `retrieveAircraftPositions()` method so that it responds in a predictable and testable manner when it is called by the `PositionController`.

I create a couple aircraft positions to use as sample data for tests within the `PositionControllerTest` class, declaring the `Aircraft` variables at the class level and assigning representative values to them within the `setUp()` method:

```
private Aircraft ac1, ac2;

@BeforeEach
void setUp(ApplicationContext context) {
    // Spring Airlines flight 001 en route, flying STL to SFO,
    //    at 30000' currently over Kansas City
    ac1 = new Aircraft(1L, "SAL001", "sqwk", "N12345", "SAL001",
            "STL-SFO", "LJ", "ct",
            30000, 280, 440, 0, 0,
            39.2979849, -94.71921, 0D, 0D, 0D,
            true, false,
            Instant.now(), Instant.now(), Instant.now());

    // Spring Airlines flight 002 en route, flying SFO to STL,
    //    at 40000' currently over Denver
    ac2 = new Aircraft(2L, "SAL002", "sqwk", "N54321", "SAL002",
            "SFO-STL", "LJ", "ct",
            40000, 65, 440, 0, 0,
            39.8560963, -104.6759263, 0D, 0D, 0D,
            true, false,
            Instant.now(), Instant.now(), Instant.now());
}
```

 The number of aircraft positions retrieved in actual operation of the applications under development is nearly always more than one, often significantly more. Bearing that in mind, a sample data set used in testing should *at a minimum* return a number of positions of two. Edge cases involving zero, one, or very large numbers of positions should be considered for additional tests in subsequent iterations for similar production applications.

Now, back to the `retrieveAircraftPositions()` method. Mockito's `when...thenRe turn` combination returns a specified response when a specified condition is met. With sample data now defined, I can provide both the condition and the response to return to calls to `PositionRetriever::retrieveAircraftPositions`:

```
@BeforeEach
void setUp(ApplicationContext context) {
    // Aircraft variable assignments omitted for brevity

    ...

    Mockito.when(retriever.retrieveAircraftPositions())
        .thenReturn(List.of(ac1, ac2));
}
```

With the relevant method mocked, it's time to return attention to the unit test located in `PositionControllerTest::getCurrentAircraftPositions`.

Since I've instructed the test instance to load the `PositionController` bean with the class-level annotation `@WebFluxTest(controllers = {PositionControl ler.class})` and have created a mock `PositionRetriever` bean and defined its behavior, I can now refactor the portion of the test that retrieves positions with some certainty of what will be returned:

```
@Test
void getCurrentAircraftPositions(@Autowired WebTestClient client) {
    final Iterable<Aircraft> acPositions = client.get()
            .uri("/aircraft")
            .exchange()
            .expectStatus().isOk()
            .expectBodyList(Aircraft.class)
            .returnResult()
            .getResponseBody();

    // Still need to compare with expected results
}
```

The chain of operators shown should retrieve a `List<Aircraft>` consisting of `ac1` and `ac2`. In order to confirm the correct results, I need to compare `acPositions` — the actual outcome — with that expected outcome. One way of doing so is with a simple comparison such as this:

```
assertEquals(List.of(ac1, ac2), acPositions);
```

This works correctly and the test will pass. I could also have taken things a bit further in this intermediate step by comparing the actual results with results obtained via a mocked call to `AircraftRepository`. Adding the following bits of code to the class, the `setUp()` method, and the `getCurrentAircraftPositions()` test method produces similar (passing) test results:

```
@MockBean
private AircraftRepository repository;
```

```
@BeforeEach
void setUp(ApplicationContext context) {
    // Existing setUp code omitted for brevity

    ...

    Mockito.when(repository.findAll()).thenReturn(List.of(ac1, ac2));
}

@Test
void getCurrentAircraftPositions(@Autowired WebTestClient client) {
    // client.get chain of operations omitted for brevity

    ...

    assertEquals(repository.findAll(), acPositions);
}
```

 This variant also results in a passing test, but it somewhat contradicts the principle of focused testing, since I now mix the concepts of testing the repository with testing the web API. Since it doesn't actually use the CrudRepository::findAll method but simply mocks it, the value of testing it doesn't add any discernible value, either. However, you may encounter tests of this nature at some point, so I thought it worthwhile to show and discuss.

The current working version of PlaneControllerTest should now look like this:

```
import org.junit.jupiter.api.BeforeEach;
import org.junit.jupiter.api.Test;
import org.mockito.Mockito;
import org.springframework.beans.factory.annotation.Autowired;
import org.springframework.boot.test.autoconfigure.web.reactive.WebFluxTest;
import org.springframework.boot.test.mock.mockito.MockBean;
import org.springframework.context.ApplicationContext;
import org.springframework.test.web.reactive.server.WebTestClient;

import java.time.Instant;
import java.util.List;

import static org.junit.jupiter.api.Assertions.assertEquals;

@WebFluxTest(controllers = {PositionController.class})
class PositionControllerTest {
    @MockBean
    private PositionRetriever retriever;

    private Aircraft ac1, ac2;

    @BeforeEach
    void setUp(ApplicationContext context) {
        // Spring Airlines flight 001 en route, flying STL to SFO,
```

```
//    at 30000' currently over Kansas City
ac1 = new Aircraft(1L, "SAL001", "sqwk", "N12345", "SAL001",
        "STL-SFO", "LJ", "ct",
        30000, 280, 440, 0, 0,
        39.2979849, -94.71921, 0D, 0D, 0D,
        true, false,
        Instant.now(), Instant.now(), Instant.now());

// Spring Airlines flight 002 en route, flying SFO to STL,
//    at 40000' currently over Denver
ac2 = new Aircraft(2L, "SAL002", "sqwk", "N54321", "SAL002",
        "SFO-STL", "LJ", "ct",
        40000, 65, 440, 0, 0,
        39.8560963, -104.6759263, 0D, 0D, 0D,
        true, false,
        Instant.now(), Instant.now(), Instant.now());

Mockito.when(retriever.retrieveAircraftPositions())
        .thenReturn(List.of(ac1, ac2));
}

@Test
void getCurrentAircraftPositions(@Autowired WebTestClient client) {
    final Iterable<Aircraft> acPositions = client.get()
            .uri("/aircraft")
            .exchange()
            .expectStatus().isOk()
            .expectBodyList(Aircraft.class)
            .returnResult()
            .getResponseBody();

    assertEquals(List.of(ac1, ac2), acPositions);
}
}
```

Running it once again produces a passing test, with results similar to those shown in Figure 9-4.

Figure 9-4. New, improved test for AircraftRepository::getCurrentAircraftPositions

As the web API required to meet application/user requirements expands, unit tests should be specified first (before creating the actual code to fulfill those requirements) to ensure correct outcomes.

Testing Slices

I've already mentioned a few times the importance of focused testing, and Spring has another mechanism that helps developers accomplish that quickly and painlessly: test slices.

Several annotations are built into Spring Boot's testing dependency `spring-boot-starter-test` that automatically configure these slices of functionality. All of these test slice annotations work in similar fashion, loading an `ApplicationContext` and select components that make sense for the specified slice. Examples include:

- `@JsonTest`
- `@WebMvcTest`
- `@WebFluxText` (previously introduced)
- `@DataJpaTest`
- `@JdbcTest`
- `@DataJdbcTest`
- `@JooqTest`
- `@DataMongoTest`
- `@DataNeo4jTest`
- `@DataRedisTest`
- `@DataLdapTest`
- `@RestClientTest`
- `@AutoConfigureRestDocs`
- `@WebServiceClientTest`

During an earlier section leveraging `@WebFluxTest` to exercise and validate the web API, I mentioned testing datastore interactions and excluded doing so from the test, since it was focused on testing web interactions. To better demonstrate data testing and how test slices facilitate targeting specific functionality, I explore that next.

Since the current iteration of Aircraft Positions uses JPA and H2 to store and retrieve current positions, `@DataJpaTest` is a perfect fit. I begin by creating a new class for testing using IntelliJ IDEA, opening the `AircraftRepository` class and using the same approach to create a test class as before: CMD+N, "Test…", leaving JUnit5 as the "Testing Library" and other default values in place, and selecting *setUp/@Before* and *tearDown/@After* options as shown in Figure 9-5.

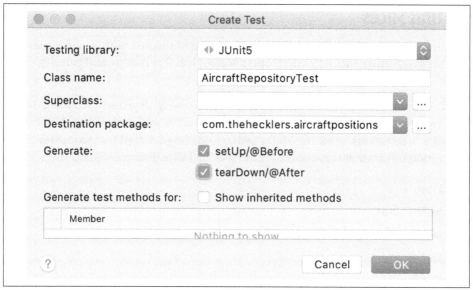

Figure 9-5. Create Test popup for AircraftRepository

 No methods are shown because Spring Data `Repository` beans provide common methods to Spring Boot applications via auto-configuration. I will add test methods to exercise these as an example next, and if you create custom repository methods, these can (and should be) tested as well.

Clicking the OK button generates the test class `AircraftRepositoryTest`:

```
import org.junit.jupiter.api.AfterEach;
import org.junit.jupiter.api.BeforeEach;

class AircraftRepositoryTest {

    @BeforeEach
    void setUp() {
    }

    @AfterEach
    void tearDown() {
    }
}
```

The first order of business is, of course, to add the test slice annotation `@DataJpaTest` to the `AircraftRepositoryTest` class:

```
@DataJpaTest
class AircraftRepositoryTest {

    ...

}
```

As a result of adding this single annotation, upon execution the test will scan for @Entity classes and configure Spring Data JPA repositories — in the Aircraft Positions application, Aircraft and AircraftRepository respectively. If an embedded database is in the classpath (as H2 is here), the test engine will configure it as well. Typical @Component annotated classes are not scanned for bean creation.

In order to test actual repository operations, the repository mustn't be mocked; and since the @DataJpaTest annotation loads and configures an AircraftRepository bean, there is no need to mock it anyway. I inject the repository bean using @Auto wire and just as in the PositionController test earlier, declare Aircraft variables to ultimately serve as test data:

```
@Autowired
private AircraftRepository repository;

private Aircraft ac1, ac2;
```

To setup the proper environment for the tests that will exist within this AircraftRepo sitoryTest class, I create two Aircraft objects, assign each to one of the declared member variables, and then save them to the repository within the setUp() method using Repository::saveAll.

```
@BeforeEach
void setUp() {
    // Spring Airlines flight 001 en route, flying STL to SFO,
    // at 30000' currently over Kansas City
    ac1 = new Aircraft(1L, "SAL001", "sqwk", "N12345", "SAL001",
            "STL-SFO", "LJ", "ct",
            30000, 280, 440, 0, 0,
            39.2979849, -94.71921, 0D, 0D, 0D,
            true, false,
            Instant.now(), Instant.now(), Instant.now());

    // Spring Airlines flight 002 en route, flying SFO to STL,
    // at 40000' currently over Denver
    ac2 = new Aircraft(2L, "SAL002", "sqwk", "N54321", "SAL002",
            "SFO-STL", "LJ", "ct",
            40000, 65, 440, 0, 0,
            39.8560963, -104.6759263, 0D, 0D, 0D,
            true, false,
            Instant.now(), Instant.now(), Instant.now());

    repository.saveAll(List.of(ac1, ac2));
}
```

Next, I create a test method to verify that what is returned as a result of executing a findAll() on the AircraftRepository bean is exactly what should be returned: an Iterable<Aircraft> containing the two aircraft positions saved in the test's setUp() method:

```
@Test
void testFindAll() {
    assertEquals(List.of(ac1, ac2), repository.findAll());
}
```

 List extends Collection which in turn extends Iterable.

Running this test provides a passing result that looks something like that shown in Figure 9-6.

Figure 9-6. Test results for findAll()

Similarly, I create a test for the AircraftRepository method to find a particular record by its ID field, findById(). Since there should be two records stored due to the Repository::saveAll method called in the test class's setUp(), I query for both and verify the results against expected values.

```
@Test
void testFindById() {
    assertEquals(Optional.of(ac1), repository.findById(ac1.getId()));
    assertEquals(Optional.of(ac2), repository.findById(ac2.getId()));
}
```

Running the testFindById() test yields a passing as well, as shown in Figure 9-7.

Figure 9-7. Test results for findById()

Testing the Tests

When a test passes, most developers assume that their code has been validated. But a passing test can be indicative of one of two possible things:

- The code works
- The test doesn't

As such, I strongly encourage *breaking the test* whenever possible to verify that the test actually is doing what it is supposed to do.

What do I mean by that?

The easiest example is to provide incorrect expected results. If the test suddenly breaks, examine the failure. If it failed in the expected manner, restore the correct functionality and verify the test once again works. However, if the test still passes after providing what should have been failing criteria, correct the test and re-verify. Once it breaks as expected, restore the correct expected results and run once more to confirm that the test is testing the right things in the right way.

Note that this is not an unusual occurrence, and it's far more gratifying to find bad tests when writing them than when troubleshooting and trying to determine how something slipped through testing to fail in production.

Finally, a bit of cleanup is in order once all tests have run. To the `tearDown()` method I add a single statement to delete all records in the `AircraftRepository`:

```
@AfterEach
void tearDown() {
    repository.deleteAll();
}
```

Note that it really isn't necessary in this case to erase all records from the repository, since it's an in-memory instance of the H2 database that is reinitialized before each test. This is however representative of the type of operation that would typically be placed in a test class's `tearDown()` method.

Executing all tests within `AircraftRepositoryTest` produces passing results similar to those shown in Figure 9-8.

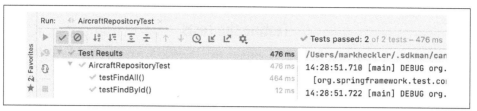

Figure 9-8. Test results for all tests in AircraftRepositoryTest

---

Test Times: The Need for Speed

As mentioned early in this chapter, reducing the scope of each test, along with the number of beans the test engine must load into the `ApplicationContext` to perform each test, improves the speed and fidelity of each test. Fewer unknowns mean a more comprehensive test suite, and faster tests mean that the test suite can do more in less time, working harder to save you headaches down the line.

As a quick measure of time savings seen so far, the initial version of `PositionControl lerTest` took 998ms — almost a full second — to load the full `ApplicationContext`, execute the test, and shut down. Doing a bit of refactoring to code and tests improved the application's modularity and honed the focus of the pertinent test, simultaneously reducing test execution time to 230ms — now less than 1/4 of a second. Saving more than 3/4 of a second every time a test is run adds up, and multiplied across several tests and several builds it makes a significant and welcome contribution to development velocity.

Testing is never complete for an application that is still evolving. For the functionality currently present in Aircraft Positions, however, the tests written in this chapter provide a good starting point for code validation and continued expansion as functionality is added to the application.

Code Checkout Checkup

For complete chapter code, please check out branch *chapter9end* from the code repository.

Summary

This chapter discussed and demonstrated core aspects of testing Spring Boot applications, focusing on the fundamental aspects of testing Spring Boot applications that most improve the production readiness of each application. Topics covered included unit testing, holistic application testing using `@SpringBootTest`, how to write effective unit tests using JUnit, and using Spring Boot testing slices to isolate test subjects and streamline testing.

The next chapter explores security concepts like Authentication and Authorization. I then demonstrate how to implement forms-based authentication for self-contained applications and for the most demanding requirements, how to leverage OpenID Connect and OAuth2 for maximum security and flexibility, all using Spring Security.

## CHAPTER 10

Securing Your Spring Boot Application

Understanding the concepts of authentication and authorization are critical to building secure applications, providing the foundations for user verification and access control. Spring Security combines options for authentication and authorization with other mechanisms like the HTTP Firewall, filter chains, extensive use of IETF and the World Wide Web Consortium (W3C) standards and options for exchanges, and more to help lock down applications. Adopting a secure out-of-the-box mindset, Spring Security leverages Boot's powerful autoconfiguration to evaluate developer inputs and available dependencies to deliver maximal security for Spring Boot applications with minimal effort.

This chapter introduces and explains core aspects of security and how they apply to applications. I demonstrate multiple ways to incorporate Spring Security into Spring Boot apps to strengthen an application's security posture, closing dangerous gaps in coverage and reducing attack surface area.

Code Checkout Checkup

Please check out branch *chapter10begin* from the code repository to begin.

Authentication and Authorization

Often used together, the terms *authentication* and *authorization* are related but separate concerns.

authentication

An act, process, or method of showing something (such as an identity, a piece of art, or a financial transaction) to be real, true, or genuine; the act or process of authenticating something.

authorization

1: the act of *authorizing* 2: an instrument that authorizes: SANCTION

The first definition for *authorization* points to *authorizing* for more information:

authorize

1: to endorse, empower, justify, or permit by or as if by some recognized or proper authority (such as custom, evidence, personal right, or regulating power) a custom authorized by time 2: to invest especially with legal authority: EMPOWER 3: archaic: JUSTIFY

The definition for *authorize* in turn points to *justify* for more information.

While somewhat interesting, these definitions aren't very clear. Sometimes the dictionary definitions can be less helpful than we might like. My own definitions follow.

authentication

Proving that someone is who they claim to be

authorization

Verifying that someone has access to a particular resource or operation

Authentication

Simply put, *authentication* is proving that someone (or something) is who (or what, in the case of a device, application, or service) they claim to be.

The concept of authentication has several concrete examples in the physical world. If you've ever had to show a form of ID like an employee badge, driver's license, or passport to prove your identity, you have been authenticated. Demonstrating that one is who one claims to be is a procedure to which we've all grown accustomed in a variety of situations, and the conceptual differences between authentication at the physical level and to an application are insignificant.

Authentication typically involves one or more of the following:

- Something you are
- Something you know
- Something you have

These three *factors* can be used individually or combined to compose Multi-Factor Authentication (MFA).

The manner in which authentication occurs in the physical and virtual worlds is of course different. Rather than a human being eyeing a photo ID and comparing it to your current physical appearance as often happens in the physical world, authenticating to an application often involves typing a password, inserting a security key, or providing biometric data (iris scan, fingerprint, etc.) that can be more easily evaluated by software than is currently feasible with a comparison of physical appearance with a photo. Nevertheless, a comparison of stored data with provided data is performed in both cases, and a match provides a positive authentication.

Authorization

Once a person is authenticated, they have the possibility of gaining access to resources available and/or operations permitted to one or more individuals.

In this context, an individual may (and most likely is) a human being, but the same concept and access considerations apply to applications, services, devices, and more, depending on context.

Once an individual's identity is proven, that individual gains some general level of access to an application. From there, the now-authenticated application user can request access to something. The application then must somehow determine if the user is allowed, i.e., *authorized*, to access that resource. If so, access is granted to the user; if not, the user is notified that their lack of *authority* has resulted in their request being rejected.

Spring Security in a Nutshell

In addition to providing solid options for authentication and authorization, Spring Security provides several other mechanisms to help developers lock down their Spring Boot applications. Thanks to autoconfiguration, Spring Boot applications enable each applicable Spring Security feature with an eye toward maximum possible security with the information provided, or even owing to the lack of more specific guidance. Security capabilities can of course be adjusted or relaxed by developers as necessary to accommodate their organizations' specific requirements.

Spring Security's capabilities are far too numerous to detail exhaustively in this chapter, but there are three key features I consider essential to understanding the Spring

Security model and its foundations. They are the HTTP Firewall, security filter chains, and Spring Security's extensive use of IETF and W3C standards and options for requests and corresponding responses.

The HTTP Firewall

While exact numbers are difficult to obtain, many security compromises begin with a request using a malformed URI and a system's unexpected response to it. This is really an application's first line of defense, and as such, it is the problem that should be solved prior to considering further efforts to secure one's application(s).

Since version 5.0, Spring Security has included a built-in HTTP Firewall that scrutinizes all inbound requests for problematic formatting. If there are any problems with a request, such as bad header values or incorrect formatting, the request is discarded. Unless overridden by the developer, the default implementation used is the aptly named `StrictHttpFirewall`, quickly closing the first and potentially easiest gap to exploit within an application's security profile.

Security Filter Chains

Providing a more specific, next-level filter for inbound requests, Spring Security uses filter chains to process properly formed requests that make it past the HTTP Firewall.

Simply put, for most applications a developer specifies a chain of filter conditions through which an inbound request passes until it matches one. When a request matches a filter, its corresponding conditions are evaluated to determine if the request will be fulfilled. For example, if a request for a particular API endpoint arrives and matches a filter condition in the filter chain, the user who made the request may be checked to verify they have the proper role/authority to access the requested resource. If so, the request is processed; if not, it is rejected, usually with a *403 Forbidden* status code.

If a request passes through all defined filters in the chain without matching any, the request is discarded.

Request and Response Headers

The IETF and W3C have created a number of specifications and standards for HTTP-based exchanges, several of which relate to the secure exchange of information. There are several headers defined for interactions between user agents—command line utilities, web browsers, etc.—and server or cloud-based applications/services. These headers are used to request or signal specific behavior and have defined allowed values and behavioral responses, and Spring Security makes extensive use of these header details to strengthen your Spring Boot application's security posture.

Realizing it's true that different user agents may support some or all of these standards and specifications, and even then fully or partially, Spring Security embraces a best-possible-coverage approach by checking for all known header options and applying them across the board, looking for them in requests and supplying them in responses, as applicable.

Implementing Forms-Based Authentication and Authorization with Spring Security

Innumerable applications that use the "something you know" method of authentication are used every day. Whether for apps internal to an organization, web applications provided directly to consumers via the internet, or apps native to a mobile device, typing in a user ID and password is a familiar routine for developers and non-developers alike. And in most of those cases, the security this provides is more than sufficient for the task at hand.

Spring Security provides Spring Boot applications with superb out-of-the-box (OOTB) support for password authentication via autoconfiguration and easy-to-grasp abstractions. This section demonstrates the various stepping-off points by refactoring the `Aircraft Positions` application to incorporate forms-based authentication using Spring Security.

Adding Spring Security Dependencies

When creating a new Spring Boot project, it's a simple matter to add one more dependency via the Spring Initializr—that of *Spring Security*—and to enable a top-tier level of security without additional configuration to a fledgling app, as shown in Figure 10-1.

Figure 10-1. Spring Security dependency within Spring Initializr

Updating an existing application is only slightly less simple. I'll add the same two complementary dependencies that Initializr adds, one for Spring Security itself and one for testing it, to `Aircraft Positions`'s *pom.xml* Maven build file:

```
<dependency>
    <groupId>org.springframework.boot</groupId>
    <artifactId>spring-boot-starter-security</artifactId>
</dependency>
<dependency>
```

```
<groupId>org.springframework.security</groupId>
<artifactId>spring-security-test</artifactId>
<scope>test</scope>
</dependency>
```

Notes About Test Coverage

In order to focus specifically on the key concepts of Spring Security in this chapter, I will somewhat reluctantly set aside the tests that have been and would normally be created when adding additional capabilities. This decision is solely an information-sharing decision to streamline chapter content and is not a development process decision.

To continue with builds in this and subsequent chapters, it may be necessary to add -DskipTests if building from the command line or to be sure to select the application's configuration (rather than a test) from a drop-down menu if building from an IDE.

With Spring Security on the classpath and no code or configuration changes to the application, I restart Aircraft Positions for a quick functionality check. This provides a great opportunity to see what Spring Security does on a developer's behalf OOTB.

With both PlaneFinder and Aircraft Positions running, I return to the terminal and again exercise Aircraft Positions's *aircraft* endpoint, as shown here:

```
mheckler-a01 :: ~ » http :8080/aircraft
HTTP/1.1 401
Cache-Control: no-cache, no-store, max-age=0, must-revalidate
Expires: 0
Pragma: no-cache
Set-Cookie: JSESSIONID=347DD039FE008DE50F457B890F2149C0; Path=/; HttpOnly
WWW-Authenticate: Basic realm="Realm"
X-Content-Type-Options: nosniff
X-Frame-Options: DENY
X-XSS-Protection: 1; mode=block

{
    "error": "Unauthorized",
    "message": "",
    "path": "/aircraft",
    "status": 401,
    "timestamp": "2020-10-10T17:26:31.599+00:00"
}
```

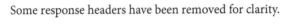 Some response headers have been removed for clarity.

As you can see, I no longer have access to the */aircraft* endpoint, receiving a *401 Unauthorized* response to my request. Since the */aircraft* endpoint is currently the only means of accessing information from the `Aircraft Positions` application, this effectively means the application is secured in its entirety from unwanted access. This is great news, but it's important to understand both how this happened and how to restore desired access for valid users.

As I mentioned earlier, Spring Security adopts a mindset of "secure by default" to the extent possible at every level of configuration—even zero configuration—by the developer employing it in a Spring Boot application. When Spring Boot finds Spring Security on the classpath, security is configured using sensible defaults. Even with no user(s) defined or password(s) specified or any other effort made by the developer, the inclusion of Spring Security in the project indicates a goal of a secure application.

As you can imagine, this is very little to go on. But Spring Boot+Security autoconfiguration creates a number of essential beans to implement basic security capabilities based on forms authentication and user authorization using user IDs and passwords. The next questions to quite reasonably flow from that logical assumption are these: What user(s)? What password(s)?

Returning to the startup log for the `Aircraft Positions` application, one can find the answer to one of those questions in this line:

```
Using generated security password: 1ad8a0fc-1a0c-429e-8ed7-ba0e3c3649ef
```

If no user ID(s) and password(s) are specified in the application or no means are provided to access them by other means, a security-enabled Spring Boot app defaults to a single user account `user` with a unique password that is generated anew each time the application is started. Returning to the terminal window, I try to access the application once again, this time with the provided credentials:

```
mheckler-a01 :: ~ » http :8080/aircraft
    --auth user:1ad8a0fc-1a0c-429e-8ed7-ba0e3c3649ef
HTTP/1.1 200
Cache-Control: no-cache, no-store, max-age=0, must-revalidate
Expires: 0
Pragma: no-cache
Set-Cookie: JSESSIONID=94B52FD39656A17A015BC64CF6BF7475; Path=/; HttpOnly
X-Content-Type-Options: nosniff
X-Frame-Options: DENY
X-XSS-Protection: 1; mode=block

[
```

```json
{
    "altitude": 40000,
    "barometer": 1013.6,
    "bds40_seen_time": "2020-10-10T17:48:02Z",
    "callsign": "SWA2057",
    "category": "A3",
    "flightno": "WN2057",
    "heading": 243,
    "id": 1,
    "is_adsb": true,
    "is_on_ground": false,
    "last_seen_time": "2020-10-10T17:48:06Z",
    "lat": 38.600372,
    "lon": -90.42375,
    "polar_bearing": 207.896382,
    "polar_distance": 24.140226,
    "pos_update_time": "2020-10-10T17:48:06Z",
    "reg": "N557WN",
    "route": "IND-DAL-MCO",
    "selected_altitude": 40000,
    "speed": 395,
    "squawk": "2161",
    "type": "B737",
    "vert_rate": -64
},
{
    "altitude": 3500,
    "barometer": 0.0,
    "bds40_seen_time": null,
    "callsign": "N6884J",
    "category": "A1",
    "flightno": "",
    "heading": 353,
    "id": 2,
    "is_adsb": true,
    "is_on_ground": false,
    "last_seen_time": "2020-10-10T17:47:45Z",
    "lat": 39.062851,
    "lon": -90.084965,
    "polar_bearing": 32.218696,
    "polar_distance": 7.816637,
    "pos_update_time": "2020-10-10T17:47:45Z",
    "reg": "N6884J",
    "route": "",
    "selected_altitude": 0,
    "speed": 111,
    "squawk": "1200",
    "type": "P28A",
    "vert_rate": -64
},
{
    "altitude": 39000,
    "barometer": 0.0,
    "bds40_seen_time": null,
    "callsign": "ATN3425",
    "category": "A5",
```

```
        "flightno": "",
        "heading": 53,
        "id": 3,
        "is_adsb": true,
        "is_on_ground": false,
        "last_seen_time": "2020-10-10T17:48:06Z",
        "lat": 39.424159,
        "lon": -90.419739,
        "polar_bearing": 337.033437,
        "polar_distance": 30.505314,
        "pos_update_time": "2020-10-10T17:48:06Z",
        "reg": "N419AZ",
        "route": "AFW-ABE",
        "selected_altitude": 0,
        "speed": 524,
        "squawk": "2224",
        "type": "B763",
        "vert_rate": 0
    },
    {
        "altitude": 45000,
        "barometer": 1012.8,
        "bds40_seen_time": "2020-10-10T17:48:06Z",
        "callsign": null,
        "category": "A2",
        "flightno": "",
        "heading": 91,
        "id": 4,
        "is_adsb": true,
        "is_on_ground": false,
        "last_seen_time": "2020-10-10T17:48:06Z",
        "lat": 39.433982,
        "lon": -90.50061,
        "polar_bearing": 331.287125,
        "polar_distance": 32.622134,
        "pos_update_time": "2020-10-10T17:48:05Z",
        "reg": "N30GD",
        "route": "",
        "selected_altitude": 44992,
        "speed": 521,
        "squawk": null,
        "type": "GLF4",
        "vert_rate": 64
    }
]
```

 As before, some response headers have been removed for clarity.

Using the correct default user ID and the generated password, I receive a *200 OK* response and once again have access to the */aircraft* endpoint, and thus the Aircraft Positions application.

Important Information About Response Headers

As I mentioned very briefly earlier, several IETF and W3C standard header options have been formalized and/or recommended for use by browsers and other user agents to improve application security. Spring Security adopts and implements these rigorously in an effort to provide the most complete security coverage possible using every available means.

Spring Security's response header defaults that comply with these standards and recommendations include the following:

Cache Control:: The Cache-Control header is set to no-cache with a no-store directive and a max-age of 0 and must-revalidate directive; additionally, a Pragma header is returned with a no-cache directive, and an Expires header is given a 0 value. All of these mechanisms are specified to eliminate possible gaps in browser/user agent feature coverage to ensure best-possible control over caching, i.e., to disable it in all cases so that once a user logs out of a site, a hostile actor can't simply click the Back button of the browser and return to the secure site logged in with the victim's credentials. Content Type Options:: The X-Content-Type-Options header is set to nosniff to disable content sniffing. Browsers can (and often have) attempted to "sniff" the type of content requested and display it accordingly. For example, if a .jpg is requested, a browser might render it as a graphical image. This sounds like it could be a nice feature, and indeed it can be; but if malicious code is embedded within the sniffed content, it can be processed surreptitiously, bypassing otherwise rigorous security measures. Spring Security provides a setting of nosniff by default, closing this attack vector. Frame Options:: The X-Frame-Options header is set to a value of DENY in order to prevent browsers from displaying content within iframes. Dubbed *clickjacking*, the resultant attack can occur when an invisible frame is placed over a displayed control, resulting in the user initiating an undesired action instead of the one intended, thus "hijacking" the user's click. Spring Security disables frame support by default, thus closing the avenue to clickjacking attacks. XSS Protection:: The X-XSS-Protection header is set to a value of 1 to enable browser protection against Cross Site Scripting (XSS) attacks. Once enabled however, there are many ways for a browser to respond to perceived attacks; Spring Security defaults to a setting of mode=block, the most secure setting, to assure that a browser's well-meaning attempt to modify and process the content safely doesn't leave the user vulnerable. Blocking the content closes that potential vulnerability.

Note that if you use a content delivery network, you may need to adjust the XSS settings to ensure correct handling. That setting, like the others, is fully developer-configurable. In the absence of specific directions from you, the developer, Spring

---

Security will always strive to adopt a *secure by default* posture to the greatest extent possible given the information available.

Returning to the `Aircraft Positions` application, there are a few concerns with the current state of application security. First among them is that by having only a single defined user, multiple individuals that need to access the application must all use that single account. This is antithetical to the security principle of accountability and even authentication, as no single individual uniquely proves they are who they say they are. Returning to accountability, how can one determine who committed or contributed to a breach if one occurs? Not to mention that if a breach were to occur, locking the only user account would disable access for all users; there is currently no way to avoid it.

A secondary concern with the existing security configuration is the way the single password is handled. With each application startup, a new password is automatically generated, which must then be shared with all users. And while application scaling hasn't yet been discussed, each instance of `Aircraft Positions` that is started will generate a unique password, requiring that particular password from a user attempting to log into that particular app instance. Clearly some improvements can and should be made.

Adding Authentication

Spring Security employs the concept of a `UserDetailsService` as the centerpiece of its authentication capability. `UserDetailsService` is an interface with a single method `loadUserByUsername(String username)` that (when implemented) returns an object that fulfills the `UserDetails` interface, from which can be obtained key information such as the user's name, password, authorities granted to the user, and account status. This flexibility allows for numerous implementations using various technologies; as long as a `UserDetailsService` returns `UserDetails`, the application doesn't need to be aware of underlying implementation details.

To create a `UserDetailsService` bean, I create a configuration class in which to define a bean creation method.

Bean Creation

While bean creation methods can be placed within any `@Configuration`-annotated class (as mentioned previously), including those with meta-annotations that include `@Configuration` like the main application class, it is cleaner to create a configuration class for related groups of beans. If the application is small and the number of beans is as well, this could be a single class.

With rare exceptions for the smallest and most disposable of applications, I typically do not place bean creation methods in the @SpringBootApplication-annotated main application class. Placing them in separate class(es) simplifies testing by reducing the number of beans that must be created or mocked, and for the occasional circumstance in which a developer may wish to deactivate a group of beans—such as an @Component or @Configuration class that loads data or performs similar function(s)—removing or commenting out the single class-level annotation disables that functionality while leaving the capability easily accessible. While "comment and keep" should not be used with abandon, it makes a great deal of sense in narrowly defined circumstances.

This separate class will come in handy for the next iteration as well, making it easier and faster to iterate due to the natural separation of concerns.

First, I create a class called SecurityConfig and annotate it with @Configuration to enable Spring Boot to find and execute bean creation methods within. The bean necessary for authentication is one that implements the UserDetailsService interface, so I create a method authentication() to create and return that bean. Here is a first, intentionally incomplete pass at the code:

```java
import org.springframework.context.annotation.Bean;
import org.springframework.context.annotation.Configuration;
import org.springframework.security.core.userdetails.User;
import org.springframework.security.core.userdetails.UserDetails;
import org.springframework.security.core.userdetails.UserDetailsService;
import org.springframework.security.provisioning.InMemoryUserDetailsManager;

@Configuration
public class SecurityConfig {
    @Bean
    UserDetailsService authentication() {
        UserDetails peter = User.builder()
                .username("peter")
                .password("ppassword")
                .roles("USER")
                .build();

        UserDetails jodie = User.builder()
                .username("jodie")
                .password("jpassword")
                .roles("USER", "ADMIN")
                .build();

        System.out.println("   >>> Peter's password: " + peter.getPassword());
        System.out.println("   >>> Jodie's password: " + jodie.getPassword());

        return new InMemoryUserDetailsManager(peter, jodie);
    }
}
```

Within the `UserDetailService authentication()` method, I create two application objects that implement the `UserDetails` interface requirements using the `User` class's `builder()` method and specifying username, password, and roles/authorities the user possesses. I then `build()` these users and assign each of them to a local variable.

Next, I display the passwords *for demonstration purposes only*. This helps to demonstrate another concept in this chapter but is *for demonstration purposes only*.

 Logging passwords is an antipattern of the worst kind. Never log passwords in production applications.

Finally, I create an `InMemoryUserDetailsManager` using the two created `User` objects and return it as a Spring bean. An `InMemoryUserDetailsManager` implements interfaces `UserDetailsManager` and `UserDetailsPasswordService`, enabling user management tasks like determining if a particular user exists; creating, updating, and deleting the user; and changing/updating the user's password. I use `InMemoryUserDetailsManager` for its clarity in demonstrating the concept (due to no external dependencies), but any bean that implements the `UserDetailsService` interface can be provided as the authentication bean.

Restarting `Aircraft Positions`, I attempt to authenticate and retrieve a list of current aircraft positions, with the following results (some headers removed for brevity):

```
mheckler-a01 :: ~ » http :8080/aircraft --auth jodie:jpassword
HTTP/1.1 401
Cache-Control: no-cache, no-store, max-age=0, must-revalidate
Content-Length: 0
Expires: 0
Pragma: no-cache
WWW-Authenticate: Basic realm="Realm"
X-Content-Type-Options: nosniff
X-Frame-Options: DENY
X-XSS-Protection: 1; mode=block
```

This prompts a bit of troubleshooting. Returning to the IDE, there is a helpful bit of information in the stack trace:

```
java.lang.IllegalArgumentException: There is no PasswordEncoder
    mapped for the id "null"
        at org.springframework.security.crypto.password
        .DelegatingPasswordEncoder$UnmappedIdPasswordEncoder
            .matches(DelegatingPasswordEncoder.java:250)
                ~[spring-security-core-5.3.4.RELEASE.jar:5.3.4.RELEASE]
```

This provides a hint at the root of the problem. Examining the logged passwords (kind reminder: logging passwords is *for demonstration purposes only*) provides confirmation:

```
>>> Peter's password: ppassword
>>> Jodie's password: jpassword
```

Clearly these passwords are in plain text, with no encoding whatsoever being performed. The next step toward working and secure authentication is to add a password encoder for use within the `SecurityConfig` class, as shown in the following:

```
private final PasswordEncoder pwEncoder =
        PasswordEncoderFactories.createDelegatingPasswordEncoder();
```

One of the challenges of creating and maintaining secure applications is that, of necessity, security is ever evolving. Recognizing this, Spring Security doesn't simply have a designated encoder it plugs in; rather, it uses a factory with several available encoders and delegates to one for encoding and decoding chores.

Of course, this means that one must serve as a default in the event one isn't specified, as in the previous example. Currently *BCrypt* is the (excellent) default, but the flexible, delegated nature of Spring Security's encoder architecture is such that one encoder can be replaced easily by another as standards evolve and/or requirements change. The elegance of this approach allows for a frictionless migration of credentials from one encoder to another when an application user logs into the application, again reducing tasks that don't directly provide value to an organization but are nevertheless critical to perform in a correct and timely manner.

Now that I have an encoder in place, the next step is to use it to encrypt the user passwords. This is done very simply by plugging in a call to the password encoder's `encode()` method, passing the plain text password and receiving in return the encrypted result.

Technically speaking, encrypting a value also encodes that value, but all encoders do not encrypt. For example, hashing encodes a value but does not necessarily encrypt it. That said, every encoding algorithm supported by Spring Security also encrypts; to support legacy applications, however, some supported algorithms are far less secure than others. Always choose a current recommended Spring Security encoder or opt for the default one provided by `PasswordEncoderFactories.createDelegatingPasswordEn coder()`.

The revised, authenticating version of the `SecurityConfig` class follows:

```
import org.springframework.context.annotation.Bean;
import org.springframework.context.annotation.Configuration;
import org.springframework.security.core.userdetails.User;
```

```java
import org.springframework.security.core.userdetails.UserDetails;
import org.springframework.security.core.userdetails.UserDetailsService;
import org.springframework.security.crypto.factory.PasswordEncoderFactories;
import org.springframework.security.crypto.password.PasswordEncoder;
import org.springframework.security.provisioning.InMemoryUserDetailsManager;

@Configuration
public class SecurityConfig {
    private final PasswordEncoder pwEncoder =
            PasswordEncoderFactories.createDelegatingPasswordEncoder();

    @Bean
    UserDetailsService authentication() {
        UserDetails peter = User.builder()
                .username("peter")
                .password(pwEncoder.encode("ppassword"))
                .roles("USER")
                .build();

        UserDetails jodie = User.builder()
                .username("jodie")
                .password(pwEncoder.encode("jpassword"))
                .roles("USER", "ADMIN")
                .build();

        System.out.println("   >>> Peter's password: " + peter.getPassword());
        System.out.println("   >>> Jodie's password: " + jodie.getPassword());

        return new InMemoryUserDetailsManager(peter, jodie);
    }
}
```

I restart Aircraft Positions, then attempt once again to authenticate and retrieve a list of current aircraft positions with the following results (some headers and results removed for brevity):

```
mheckler-a01 :: ~ » http :8080/aircraft --auth jodie:jpassword
HTTP/1.1 200
Cache-Control: no-cache, no-store, max-age=0, must-revalidate
Expires: 0
Pragma: no-cache
X-Content-Type-Options: nosniff
X-Frame-Options: DENY
X-XSS-Protection: 1; mode=block

[
    {
        "altitude": 24250,
        "barometer": 0.0,
        "bds40_seen_time": null,
        "callsign": null,
        "category": "A2",
        "flightno": "",
        "heading": 118,
        "id": 1,
```

```
            "is_adsb": true,
            "is_on_ground": false,
            "last_seen_time": "2020-10-12T16:13:26Z",
            "lat": 38.325119,
            "lon": -90.154159,
            "polar_bearing": 178.56009,
            "polar_distance": 37.661127,
            "pos_update_time": "2020-10-12T16:13:24Z",
            "reg": "N168ZZ",
            "route": "FMY-SUS",
            "selected_altitude": 0,
            "speed": 404,
            "squawk": null,
            "type": "LJ60",
            "vert_rate": 2880
        }
    ]
```

These results confirm that authentication is now successful (an intentional failing scenario using an incorrect password is omitted due to space considerations) and valid users can once again access the exposed API.

Returning to examine the logged, and now encoded, passwords, I note values similar to the following in the IDE's output:

```
>>> Peter's password:
    {bcrypt}$2a$10$rLKBzRBvtTtNcV9o8JHzFeaIskJIPXnYgVtCPs5H0GINZtk1WzsBu
>>> Jodie's password: {
    bcrypt}$2a$10$VR33/dlbSsEPPq6nlpnE/.ZQt0M4.bjvO5UYmw0ZW1aptO4G8dEkW
```

The logged values confirm that both example passwords specified in the code have been encoded successfully by the delegated password encoder using *BCrypt*.

A Note About Encoded Password Format

Based on the format of the encoded password, the correct password encoder will be selected automatically to encode (for comparison) the password supplied by the user attempting to authenticate. Spring Security prepends the encoded value with a key indicating which algorithm was used for convenience, which sometimes gives developers pause. Is that potentially giving away vital information in the event the (encrypted) password is obtained by a hostile actor? Wouldn't that knowledge make it easier to decrypt?

The short answer is no. The strength lies in the encryption itself, not from any perceived obscurity.

How can I be certain of this?

Most methods of encryption already have "tells" that indicate what was used to encrypt a value. Note the two passwords listed previously. Both encoded values begin with the string of characters $2a$10$, and indeed, all *BCrypt*-encrypted values do.

While it's possible to have an encryption algorithm that does not signal which mechanism was used in the resultant encoded value, this would be the exception rather than the rule.

Authorization

The `Aircraft Positions` application now successfully authenticates users and allows only said users to access its exposed API. There is a rather large issue with the current security configuration, though: access to any part of the API means access to all of it, regardless of roles/authority the user possesses—or more accurately, regardless of roles *not* possessed.

As a very simple example of this security flaw, I add another endpoint to `Aircraft Position` 's API by cloning, renaming, and remapping the existing `getCurrentAircraftPositions()` method in the `PositionController` class as a second endpoint. Once complete, `PositionController` appears as follows:

```
import lombok.AllArgsConstructor;
import org.springframework.web.bind.annotation.GetMapping;
import org.springframework.web.bind.annotation.RestController;

@AllArgsConstructor
@RestController
public class PositionController {
    private final PositionRetriever retriever;

    @GetMapping("/aircraft")
    public Iterable<Aircraft> getCurrentAircraftPositions() {
        return retriever.retrieveAircraftPositions();
    }

    @GetMapping("/aircraftadmin")
    public Iterable<Aircraft> getCurrentAircraftPositionsAdminPrivs() {
        return retriever.retrieveAircraftPositions();
    }
}
```

The goal is to allow only users having the "ADMIN" role access to the second method, `getCurrentAircraftPositionsAdminPrivs()`. While in this version of this example the values returned are identical to those returned by the `getCurrentAircraftPositions()`, this will likely not remain the case as the application expands, and the concept applies regardless.

Restarting the `Aircraft Positions` application and returning to the command line, I login first as user Jodie to verify access to the new endpoint, as expected (first endpoint access confirmed but omitted due to space; some headers and results also omitted for brevity):

```
mheckler-a01 :: ~ » http :8080/aircraftadmin --auth jodie:jpassword
HTTP/1.1 200
Cache-Control: no-cache, no-store, max-age=0, must-revalidate
Expires: 0
Pragma: no-cache
X-Content-Type-Options: nosniff
X-Frame-Options: DENY
X-XSS-Protection: 1; mode=block

[
    {
        "altitude": 24250,
        "barometer": 0.0,
        "bds40_seen_time": null,
        "callsign": null,
        "category": "A2",
        "flightno": "",
        "heading": 118,
        "id": 1,
        "is_adsb": true,
        "is_on_ground": false,
        "last_seen_time": "2020-10-12T16:13:26Z",
        "lat": 38.325119,
        "lon": -90.154159,
        "polar_bearing": 178.56009,
        "polar_distance": 37.661127,
        "pos_update_time": "2020-10-12T16:13:24Z",
        "reg": "N168ZZ",
        "route": "FMY-SUS",
        "selected_altitude": 0,
        "speed": 404,
        "squawk": null,
        "type": "LJ60",
        "vert_rate": 2880
    },
    {
        "altitude": 38000,
        "barometer": 1013.6,
        "bds40_seen_time": "2020-10-12T20:24:48Z",
        "callsign": "SWA1828",
        "category": "A3",
        "flightno": "WN1828",
        "heading": 274,
        "id": 2,
        "is_adsb": true,
        "is_on_ground": false,
        "last_seen_time": "2020-10-12T20:24:48Z",
        "lat": 39.348862,
        "lon": -90.751668,
        "polar_bearing": 310.510201,
        "polar_distance": 35.870036,
        "pos_update_time": "2020-10-12T20:24:48Z",
        "reg": "N8567Z",
        "route": "TPA-BWI-OAK",
        "selected_altitude": 38016,
        "speed": 397,
```

```
                "squawk": "7050",
                "type": "B738",
                "vert_rate": -128
        }
    ]
```

Next, I log in as Peter. Peter should not have access to the getCurrentAircraftPositionsAdminPrivs() method, mapped to */aircraftadmin*. But that isn't the case; currently Peter—an authenticated user—can access everything:

```
mheckler-a01 :: ~ » http :8080/aircraftadmin --auth peter:ppassword
HTTP/1.1 200
Cache-Control: no-cache, no-store, max-age=0, must-revalidate
Expires: 0
Pragma: no-cache
X-Content-Type-Options: nosniff
X-Frame-Options: DENY
X-XSS-Protection: 1; mode=block

[
    {
        "altitude": 24250,
        "barometer": 0.0,
        "bds40_seen_time": null,
        "callsign": null,
        "category": "A2",
        "flightno": "",
        "heading": 118,
        "id": 1,
        "is_adsb": true,
        "is_on_ground": false,
        "last_seen_time": "2020-10-12T16:13:26Z",
        "lat": 38.325119,
        "lon": -90.154159,
        "polar_bearing": 178.56009,
        "polar_distance": 37.661127,
        "pos_update_time": "2020-10-12T16:13:24Z",
        "reg": "N168ZZ",
        "route": "FMY-SUS",
        "selected_altitude": 0,
        "speed": 404,
        "squawk": null,
        "type": "LJ60",
        "vert_rate": 2880
    },
    {
        "altitude": 38000,
        "barometer": 1013.6,
        "bds40_seen_time": "2020-10-12T20:24:48Z",
        "callsign": "SWA1828",
        "category": "A3",
        "flightno": "WN1828",
        "heading": 274,
        "id": 2,
        "is_adsb": true,
```

```
        "is_on_ground": false,
        "last_seen_time": "2020-10-12T20:24:48Z",
        "lat": 39.348862,
        "lon": -90.751668,
        "polar_bearing": 310.510201,
        "polar_distance": 35.870036,
        "pos_update_time": "2020-10-12T20:24:48Z",
        "reg": "N8567Z",
        "route": "TPA-BWI-OAK",
        "selected_altitude": 38016,
        "speed": 397,
        "squawk": "7050",
        "type": "B738",
        "vert_rate": -128
    }
]
```

To enable the `Aircraft Positions` application to not simply authenticate users but also to check user authorization to access particular resources, I refactor `SecurityConfig` to perform that task.

The first step is to replace the class-level annotation `@Configuration` with `@EnableWebSecurity`. `@EnableWebSecurity` is a meta-annotation that includes the removed `@Configuration`, still allowing for bean creation methods within the annotated class; but it also includes the `@EnableGlobalAuthentication` annotation that enables a great deal more security autoconfiguration to be done by Spring Boot for the application. This positions `Aircraft Positions` well for the next step of defining the authorization mechanism itself.

I refactor the `SecurityConfig` class to extend `WebSecurityConfigurerAdapter`, an abstract class with numerous member variables and methods useful for extending the basic configuration of an application's web security. In particular, `WebSecurityConfigurerAdapter` has a `configure(HttpSecurity http)` method that provides a basic implementation for user authorization:

```
protected void configure(HttpSecurity http) throws Exception {
    // Logging statement omitted

    http
        .authorizeRequests()
            .anyRequest().authenticated()
            .and()
        .formLogin().and()
        .httpBasic();
}
```

In the preceding implementation, the following directives are issued:

- Authorize any request from an authenticated user.

- Simple login and logout forms (overridable ones created by the developer) will be provided.

- HTTP Basic Authentication is enabled for nonbrowser user agents (command line tools, for example).

This provides a reasonable security posture if no authorization specifics are supplied by the developer. The next step is to provide more specifics and thus override this behavior.

I use IntelliJ for Mac's CTRL+O keyboard shortcut or click the right mouse button and then Generate to open the Generate menu, then select the Override methods... option to display overridable/implementable methods. Selecting the method with signature configure(http:HttpSecurity):void produces the following method:

```
@Override
protected void configure(HttpSecurity http) throws Exception {
    super.configure(http);
}
```

I then replace the call to the superclass's method with the following code:

```
// User authorization
@Override
protected void configure(HttpSecurity http) throws Exception {
    http.authorizeRequests()
            .mvcMatchers("/aircraftadmin/**").hasRole("ADMIN")
            .anyRequest().authenticated()
            .and()
            .formLogin()
            .and()
            .httpBasic();
}
```

This implementation of the configure(HttpSecurity http) method performs the following actions:

- Using a String pattern matcher, the request path is compared for a match with /aircraftadmin and all paths below.

- If the match is successful, the user is authorized to make the request if the user has the "ADMIN" role/authority.

- Any other request is fulfilled for any authenticated user

- Simple login and logout forms (overridable ones created by the developer) will be provided

- HTTP Basic Authentication is enabled for nonbrowser user agents (command line tools, etc.).

This minimal authorization mechanism places two filters in the security filter chain: one to check for a path match and admin privileges and one for all other paths and an authenticated user. A tiered approach allows for complex scenarios to be captured in fairly simple, easy-to-reason-about logic.

The final version (for forms-based security) of the SecurityConfig class looks like this:

```
import org.springframework.context.annotation.Bean;
import org.springframework.security.config.annotation.web.builders.HttpSecurity;
import org.springframework.security.config.annotation.web.configuration
    .EnableWebSecurity;
import org.springframework.security.config.annotation.web.configuration
    .WebSecurityConfigurerAdapter;
import org.springframework.security.core.userdetails.User;
import org.springframework.security.core.userdetails.UserDetails;
import org.springframework.security.core.userdetails.UserDetailsService;
import org.springframework.security.crypto.factory.PasswordEncoderFactories;
import org.springframework.security.crypto.password.PasswordEncoder;
import org.springframework.security.provisioning.InMemoryUserDetailsManager;

@EnableWebSecurity
public class SecurityConfig extends WebSecurityConfigurerAdapter {
    private final PasswordEncoder pwEncoder =
            PasswordEncoderFactories.createDelegatingPasswordEncoder();

    @Bean
    UserDetailsService authentication() {
        UserDetails peter = User.builder()
                .username("peter")
                .password(pwEncoder.encode("ppassword"))
                .roles("USER")
                .build();

        UserDetails jodie = User.builder()
                .username("jodie")
                .password(pwEncoder.encode("jpassword"))
                .roles("USER", "ADMIN")
                .build();

        System.out.println("   >>> Peter's password: " + peter.getPassword());
        System.out.println("   >>> Jodie's password: " + jodie.getPassword());

        return new InMemoryUserDetailsManager(peter, jodie);
    }

    @Override
    protected void configure(HttpSecurity http) throws Exception {
        http.authorizeRequests()
                .mvcMatchers("/aircraftadmin/**").hasRole("ADMIN")
                .anyRequest().authenticated()
                .and()
                .formLogin()
                .and()
```

```
                .httpBasic();
    }
}
```

Additional Notes on Security

It's absolutely critical that *more-specific criteria are placed ahead of less-specific criteria.*

Each request passes through the security filter chain until it matches a filter, at which point the request is processed in accordance with the specified conditions. If, for example, the `.anyRequest().authenticated()` condition were placed before `.mvcMatchers("/aircraftadmin/**").hasRole("ADMIN")`, any request would match, again providing access to all exposed resources—including all resources under */aircraftadmin*—to all authenticated users.

Placing `.mvcMatchers("/aircraftadmin/**").hasRole("ADMIN")` (and any other more specific criteria) before the criteria for `anyRequest()` returns `anyRequest()` to a catch-all state, a very useful position when done intentionally to allow access to areas of the application that all authenticated users should have, such as a common landing page, menus, etc.

Note also that there are some small differences in annotations, class/bean names, return types, and approaches to authentication and authorization between Spring MVC-based (nonreactive) and Spring WebFlux-based (reactive) Spring Boot apps, but there is a very high degree of overlap. These will be addressed to some extent in the following section.

Now to confirm that all works as intended. I restart the `Aircraft Positions` application and access the */aircraftadmin* endpoint as Jodie from the command line (first endpoint access confirmed but omitted due to space; some headers and results also omitted for brevity):

```
mheckler-a01 :: ~ » http :8080/aircraftadmin --auth jodie:jpassword
HTTP/1.1 200
Cache-Control: no-cache, no-store, max-age=0, must-revalidate
Expires: 0
Pragma: no-cache
X-Content-Type-Options: nosniff
X-Frame-Options: DENY
X-XSS-Protection: 1; mode=block

[
    {
        "altitude": 36000,
        "barometer": 1012.8,
        "bds40_seen_time": "2020-10-13T19:16:10Z",
        "callsign": "UPS2806",
        "category": "A5",
        "flightno": "5X2806",
```

```
        "heading": 289,
        "id": 1,
        "is_adsb": true,
        "is_on_ground": false,
        "last_seen_time": "2020-10-13T19:16:14Z",
        "lat": 38.791122,
        "lon": -90.21286,
        "polar_bearing": 189.515723,
        "polar_distance": 9.855602,
        "pos_update_time": "2020-10-13T19:16:12Z",
        "reg": "N331UP",
        "route": "SDF-DEN",
        "selected_altitude": 36000,
        "speed": 374,
        "squawk": "6652",
        "type": "B763",
        "vert_rate": 0
    },
    {
        "altitude": 25100,
        "barometer": 1012.8,
        "bds40_seen_time": "2020-10-13T19:16:13Z",
        "callsign": "ASH5937",
        "category": "A3",
        "flightno": "AA5937",
        "heading": 44,
        "id": 2,
        "is_adsb": true,
        "is_on_ground": false,
        "last_seen_time": "2020-10-13T19:16:13Z",
        "lat": 39.564148,
        "lon": -90.102459,
        "polar_bearing": 5.201331,
        "polar_distance": 36.841422,
        "pos_update_time": "2020-10-13T19:16:13Z",
        "reg": "N905J",
        "route": "DFW-BMI-DFW",
        "selected_altitude": 11008,
        "speed": 476,
        "squawk": "6270",
        "type": "CRJ9",
        "vert_rate": -2624
    }
]
```

Jodie is able to access the *aircraftadmin* endpoint as expected owing to having the "ADMIN" role. Next, I try using Peter's login. Note that the first endpoint access was confirmed but omitted due to space; some headers were also omitted for brevity:

```
mheckler-a01 :: ~ » http :8080/aircraftadmin --auth peter:ppassword
HTTP/1.1 403
Cache-Control: no-cache, no-store, max-age=0, must-revalidate
Expires: 0
Pragma: no-cache
X-Content-Type-Options: nosniff
```

```
X-Frame-Options: DENY
X-XSS-Protection: 1; mode=block

{
    "error": "Forbidden",
    "message": "",
    "path": "/aircraftadmin",
    "status": 403,
    "timestamp": "2020-10-13T19:18:10.961+00:00"
}
```

This is exactly what should have occurred, since Peter only has the "USER" role and not "ADMIN." The system works.

Code Checkout Checkup

Please check out branch *chapter10forms* from the code repository for a complete forms-based example.

Implementing OpenID Connect and OAuth2 for Authentication and Authorization

While forms-based authentication and internal authorization is useful for a large number of applications, numerous use cases exist in which "something you know" methods of authentication are less than ideal or even insufficient for the desired or required level of security. Some examples include but are not limited to the following:

- Free services that require authentication but that don't need to know anything about the user (or don't want to know, for legal or other reasons)
- Situations in which single-factor authentication isn't considered secure enough, desiring and/or requiring Multi-Factor Authentication (MFA) support
- Concerns about creating and maintaining secure software infrastructure for managing passwords, roles/authorities, and other necessary mechanisms
- Concerns over liability in the event of compromise

There is no simple answer to any of these concerns or goals, but several companies have built and maintain robust and secure infrastructure assets for authentication and authorization and offer it for general use at low or no cost. Companies like Okta, a leading security vendor, and others whose businesses require proven user validation and permissions verification: Facebook, GitHub, and Google, to name a few. Spring Security supports all of these options and more via OpenID Connect and OAuth2.

OAuth2 was created to provide a means for third-party authorization of users for specified resources, such as cloud-based services, shared storage, and applications.

OpenID Connect builds on OAuth2 to add consistent, standardized authentication using one or more factors from the following:

- Something you know, for example, a password
- Something you have, like a hardware key
- Something you are, such as a biometric identifier

Spring Boot and Spring Security support autoconfiguration out of the box for OpenID Connect and OAuth2 implementations offered by Facebook, GitHub, Google, and Okta, with additional providers easily configurable due to the published standards for OpenID Connect and OAuth2 and Spring Security's extensible architecture. I use Okta's libraries and authentication+authorization mechanisms for the examples that follow, but differences between providers are mostly variations on a theme. Feel free to use the security provider that best suits your needs.

Various Application/Service Roles for OpenID Connect and OAuth2

While this section speaks directly to roles fulfilled by various services using OpenID Connect and OAuth2 for authentication and authorization, respectively, it can really apply in whole or part to any type of third-party authentication and authorization mechanism(s).

Applications/services fulfill three primary roles:

- Client
- Authorization server
- Resource server

Typically one or more services are considered to be clients, applications/services with which an end user interacts and that works with one or more security providers to authenticate and obtain authorization (roles/authorities) granted to the user for various resources.

There are one or more authorization servers that handle user authentication and return to the client(s) the authorities a user possesses. Authorization servers handle the issuance of timed authorizations and, optionally, renewals.

Resource servers provide access to protected resources based on authorities presented by clients.

Spring Security enables developers to create all three types of applications/services, but for the purposes of this book, I focus on creating a client and a resource server. The Spring Authorization Server (*https://oreil.ly/spraut*) is currently considered an experimental project but is maturing quickly, and it will be extremely useful for a number of use cases; however, for many organizations and for many of the goals listed previously, authorization services provided by a third party continue to make the most sense. As with all decisions, your requirements should determine your path.

In this example, I refactor `Aircraft Positions` to serve as an OpenID Connect and OAuth2 client application, working with Okta's capabilities to validate the user and obtain the user's authorities to access resources exposed by a resource server. I then refactor PlaneFinder to provide its resources—as an OAuth2 resource server—based on credentials supplied with requests from the `Aircraft Positions` (client) application.

Aircraft Positions Client Application

I typically begin with the application farthest back in the stack, but in this case, I believe the opposite approach has more merit due to the flows associated with a user gaining (or being denied) access to a resource.

A user accesses a client application that uses some mechanism to authenticate them. Once authenticated, user requests for resources are relayed to so-called resource servers that hold and manage said resources. This is a logical flow that most of us follow repeatedly and find very familiar. By enabling security in the same order—client, then resource server—it neatly aligns with our own, expected flow.

Adding OpenID Connect and OAuth2 dependencies to Aircraft Positions

As with forms-based security, it's simple to add additional dependencies via the Spring Initializr when creating a new Spring Boot client project to get started with OpenID Connect and OAuth2 in a greenfield client application, as shown in Figure 10-2.

Figure 10-2. Dependencies for OpenID Connect and OAuth2 Client application using Okta within Spring Initializr

Updating an existing application requires only a bit more effort. Since I'm replacing the current forms-based security, I first remove the existing dependency for Spring Security that I added in the previous section. Then I add the same two dependencies that Initializr adds for OpenID Connect and OAuth2, one for the OAuth2 Client (which includes the OpenID Connect authentication piece and other necessary components) and one for Okta, since we'll be using their infrastructure to authenticate and manage authorities, to `Aircraft Positions`'s *pom.xml* Maven build file:

```
<!--   Comment out or remove this   -->
<!--<dependency>-->
<!--    <groupId>org.springframework.boot</groupId>-->
<!--    <artifactId>spring-boot-starter-security</artifactId>-->
<!--</dependency>-->

<!--    Add these                    -->
<dependency>
    <groupId>org.springframework.boot</groupId>
    <artifactId>spring-boot-starter-oauth2-client</artifactId>
</dependency>
<dependency>
    <groupId>com.okta.spring</groupId>
    <artifactId>okta-spring-boot-starter</artifactId>
    <version>1.4.0</version>
</dependency>
```

 The current included version of Okta's Spring Boot Starter library is 1.4.0. This is the version that has been tested and verified to work well with the current version of Spring Boot. When adding dependencies to a build file manually, a good practice for developers to make habit is to visit the Spring Initializr (*https://start.spring.io*), select the current (at that time) version of Boot, add the Okta (or other specifically versioned) dependency, and *Explore* the project to confirm the current recommended version number.

Once I refresh the build, it's time to refactor the code to enable `Aircraft Positions` to authenticate with Okta and obtain user authorities.

Refactoring Aircraft Positions for authentication and authorization

There are really three things required to configure the current `Aircraft Positions` as an OAuth2 client app:

- Remove the forms-based security configuration.
- Add OAuth2 configuration to the created `WebClient` used to access PlaneFinder endpoints.
- Specify OpenID Connect+OAuth2 registered client credentials and a URI for the security provider (in this case, Okta).

I tackle the first two together, beginning by removing the body of the `SecurityCon fig` class in its entirety. If access control to resources provided locally by `Aircraft`

Positions is still desired or required, SecurityConfig can of course remain as it is or with some slight modification; however, for this example, PlaneFinder fulfills the role of resource server and as such should control or deny access to requested resources of value. Aircraft Positions acts simply as a user client that works with security infrastructure to enable a user to authenticate, then passes requests for resources to resource server(s).

I replace the @EnableWebSecurity annotation with @Configuration, as the autoconfiguration for local authentication is no longer needed. Also gone is extends WebSecurityConfigurerAdapter from the class header, since this particular iteration of the Aircraft Positions application doesn't restrict requests to its endpoints, instead passing the user's authorities with requests to PlaneFinder so it can compare those authorities against those allowed for each resource and act accordingly.

Next, I create a WebClient bean within the SecurityConfig class for use throughout the Aircraft Positions application. This is not a hard requirement at this point, as I could simply incorporate the OAuth2 configuration into the creation of the Web Client assigned to the member variable within PositionRetriever, and there are valid arguments for doing so. That said, PositionRetriever needs access to a Web Client, but configuring the WebClient to handle OpenID Connect and OAuth2 configuration runs pretty far afield of the core mission of PositionRetriever: to retrieve aircraft positions.

Creating and configuring a WebClient for authentication and authorization fits very well within the scope of a class named SecurityConfig:

```
import org.springframework.context.annotation.Bean;
import org.springframework.context.annotation.Configuration;
import org.springframework.security.oauth2.client.registration
    .ClientRegistrationRepository;
import org.springframework.security.oauth2.client.web
    .OAuth2AuthorizedClientRepository;
import org.springframework.security.oauth2.client.web.reactive.function.client
    .ServletOAuth2AuthorizedClientExchangeFilterFunction;
import org.springframework.web.reactive.function.client.WebClient;

@Configuration
public class SecurityConfig {
    @Bean
    WebClient client(ClientRegistrationRepository regRepo,
                    OAuth2AuthorizedClientRepository cliRepo) {
        ServletOAuth2AuthorizedClientExchangeFilterFunction filter =
                new ServletOAuth2AuthorizedClientExchangeFilterFunction
                    (regRepo, cliRepo);

        filter.setDefaultOAuth2AuthorizedClient(true);

        return WebClient.builder()
                .baseUrl("http://localhost:7634/")
```

```
                .apply(filter.oauth2Configuration())
                .build();
    }
}
```

Two beans are autowired into the `client()` bean creation method:

- The `ClientRegistrationRepository`, a list of OAuth2 clients specified for use by the application, usually in a properties file like *application.yml*
- `OAuth2AuthorizedClientRepository`, a list of OAuth2 clients that represent an authenticated user and manage that user's `OAuth2AccessToken`

Within the method to create and configure the `WebClient` bean, I perform the following actions:

1. I initialize a filter function with the two injected repositories.
2. I confirm that the default authorized client should be used. This is typically the case—after all, the authenticated user is typically the resource owner who wishes to gain access to the resource—but optionally, a different authorized client could be desired for use cases involving delegated access. . I specify the URL and apply the filter configured for OAuth2 to the `WebClient` builder and build the Web Client, returning it as a Spring bean and adding it to the `ApplicationContext`. The OAuth2-enabled `WebClient` is now available for use throughout the Air craft Positions application.

Since the `WebClient` bean is now created by the application via a bean creation method, I now remove the statement creating and directly assigning a `WebClient` object to a member variable within the `PositionRetriever` class and replace it with a simple member variable declaration. With the Lombok `@AllArgsConstructor` annotation on the class, Lombok automatically adds a `WebClient` parameter to the "all arguments constructor" it generates for the class. Since a `WebClient` bean is available in the `ApplicationContext`, Spring Boot autowires it into `PositionRetriever` where it is assigned to the `WebClient` member variable automatically. The newly refactored `PositionRetriever` class now looks like this:

```
import lombok.AllArgsConstructor;
import org.springframework.stereotype.Component;
import org.springframework.web.reactive.function.client.WebClient;

@AllArgsConstructor
@Component
public class PositionRetriever {
    private final AircraftRepository repository;
    private final WebClient client;

    Iterable<Aircraft> retrieveAircraftPositions() {
```

```
        repository.deleteAll();

        client.get()
                .uri("/aircraft")
                .retrieve()
                .bodyToFlux(Aircraft.class)
                .filter(ac -> !ac.getReg().isEmpty())
                .toStream()
                .forEach(repository::save);

        return repository.findAll();
    }
}
```

Earlier in this section I mentioned the use of a `ClientRegistrationRepository`, a list of OAuth2 clients specified for use by the application. There are many ways to populate this repository, but entries are usually specified as application properties. In this example, I add the following information to `Aircraft Position`'s *application.yml* file (dummy values shown here):

```
spring:
  security:
    oauth2:
      client:
        registration:
          okta:
            client-id: <your_assigned_client_id_here>
            client-secret: <your_assigned_client_secret_here>
        provider:
          okta:
            issuer-uri: https://<your_assigned_subdomain_here>
                         .oktapreview.com/oauth2/default
```

Obtaining Client and Issuer Details from an OpenID Connect + OAuth2 Provider

Since this section is focused on how to properly develop Spring Boot applications securely by interacting with security infrastructure provided by trusted third parties, providing detailed steps for creating accounts with those numerous security providers, registering applications, and defining user authorities for various resources falls somewhat outside of the defined scope of this chapter. Fortunately, the procedures required to perform those external actions are covered within the Spring Security OAuth2 sample repository. Follow this link to Configure Okta as an Authentication Provider (*https://oreil.ly/sbokta*); similar steps for other supported providers are included in the same document.

With that information in place, the `Aircraft Positions` application's `ClientRegis trationRepository` will have a single entry for Okta that it will use automatically when a user attempts to access the application.

If multiple entries are defined, a web page will be presented upon first request, prompting the user to choose a provider.

I make one other small change to `Aircraft Positions` (and a small downstream change to `PositionRetriever`), only to better demonstrate successful and unsuccessful user authorization. I replicate the sole endpoint currently defined in the `Position Controller` class, rename it, and assign it a mapping implying "admin only" access:

```java
import lombok.AllArgsConstructor;
import org.springframework.web.bind.annotation.GetMapping;
import org.springframework.web.bind.annotation.RestController;

@AllArgsConstructor
@RestController
public class PositionController {
    private final PositionRetriever retriever;

    @GetMapping("/aircraft")
    public Iterable<Aircraft> getCurrentAircraftPositions() {
        return retriever.retrieveAircraftPositions("aircraft");
    }

    @GetMapping("/aircraftadmin")
    public Iterable<Aircraft> getCurrentAircraftPositionsAdminPrivs() {
        return retriever.retrieveAircraftPositions("aircraftadmin");
    }
}
```

To accommodate access to both PlaneFinder endpoints using a single method in `PositionRetriever`, I change its `retrieveAircraftPositions()` method to accept a dynamic path parameter `String endpoint` and use it when building the client request. The updated `PositionRetriever` class looks like this:

```java
import lombok.AllArgsConstructor;
import org.springframework.stereotype.Component;
import org.springframework.web.reactive.function.client.WebClient;

@AllArgsConstructor
@Component
public class PositionRetriever {
    private final AircraftRepository repository;
    private final WebClient client;

    Iterable<Aircraft> retrieveAircraftPositions(String endpoint) {
        repository.deleteAll();

        client.get()
                .uri((null != endpoint) ? endpoint : "")
                .retrieve()
                .bodyToFlux(Aircraft.class)
```

```
            .filter(ac -> !ac.getReg().isEmpty())
            .toStream()
            .forEach(repository::save);

        return repository.findAll();
    }
}
```

`Aircraft Positions` is now a fully configured OpenID Connect and OAuth2 client application. Next, I refactor PlaneFinder to serve as an OAuth2 resource server, providing resources upon request to authorized users.

PlaneFinder Resource Server

With any refactoring involving a change of dependencies, the place to begin is with the build file.

Adding OpenID Connect and OAuth2 Dependencies to Aircraft Positions

As mentioned before, it's easy to simply add another dependency or two via the Spring Initializr when creating a new Spring Boot OAuth2 resource server in a greenfield client application, as shown in Figure 10-3.

Figure 10-3. Dependencies for OAuth2 Resource Server using Okta within Spring Initializr

Investigating Those Dependencies

Since I've chosen to use Okta for OpenID Connect and OAuth2 mechanisms (security infrastructure and libraries) in these examples, I could accomplish the same results by adding *only* the Okta Spring Boot starter dependency to the project. The Okta dependency brings along with it all other necessary libraries for both OAuth2 client apps and resource servers:

- Spring Security Config
- Spring Security Core
- Spring Security OAuth2 Client

- Spring Security Core
- Spring Security JOSE
- Spring Security Resource Server
- Spring Security Web

Adding the dependency from the Initializr for the OAuth2 Resource Server doesn't add any extra baggage to a new application because it includes the same dependencies minus the one for OAuth2 Client; the Okta dependencies are a superset. I do it primarily as a visual cue and a good practice to avoid chasing dependencies in the event I later decide to change authentication and authorization providers. That said, I recommend you always inspect your application's dependency tree and remove unnecessary ones.

Updating the existing PlaneFinder application is straightforward enough. I add the same two dependencies that Initializr adds for the OAuth2 Resource Server and for Okta, since we'll be using their infrastructure to verify authorities, to PlaneFinder's *pom.xml* Maven build file:

```
<dependency>
    <groupId>org.springframework.boot</groupId>
    <artifactId>spring-boot-starter-oauth2-resource-server</artifactId>
</dependency>
<dependency>
    <groupId>com.okta.spring</groupId>
    <artifactId>okta-spring-boot-starter</artifactId>
    <version>1.4.0</version>
</dependency>
```

Once I refresh the build, it's time to refactor the code to enable PlaneFinder to verify user authorities provided with inbound requests to verify user permissions and grant (or deny) access to PlaneFinder resources.

Refactoring PlaneFinder for resource authorization

Much of the work to enable OpenID Connect and OAuth2 authentication and authorization using Okta for our distributed system has already been accomplished by this point. Refactoring PlaneFinder to correctly perform the duties of an OAuth2 resource server requires minimal effort:

- Incorporating JWT (JSON Web Token) support
- Comparing the authorities delivered within the JWTs (pronounced "jots") to those required for access to designated resources

Both of these tasks can be accomplished by creating a single `SecurityWebFilter Chain` bean that Spring Security will use for retrieving, verifying, and comparing the contents of the inbound request's JWT with required authorities.

Once again I create a `SecurityConfig` class and annotate it with `@Configuration` to provide a distinct place for bean creation methods. Next, I create a `securityWebFilterChain()` method as follows:

```java
import org.springframework.context.annotation.Bean;
import org.springframework.context.annotation.Configuration;
import org.springframework.security.config.web.server.ServerHttpSecurity;
import org.springframework.security.web.server.SecurityWebFilterChain;

@Configuration
public class SecurityConfig {
    @Bean
    public SecurityWebFilterChain securityWebFilterChain(ServerHttpSecurity http) {
        http
                .authorizeExchange()
                .pathMatchers("/aircraft/**").hasAuthority("SCOPE_closedid")
                .pathMatchers("/aircraftadmin/**").hasAuthority("SCOPE_openid")
                .and().oauth2ResourceServer().jwt();

        return http.build();
    }
}
```

To create the filter chain, I autowire the existing `ServerHttpSecurity` bean provided by Spring Boot's security autoconfiguration. This bean is used with WebFlux-enabled applications, i.e., when `spring-boot-starter-webflux` is on the classpath.

Applications without WebFlux on the classpath would use the `HttpSecurity` bean and its corresponding methods instead, as was done in the forms-based authentication example earlier in this chapter.

Next, I configure the `ServerHttpSecurity` bean's security criteria, specifying how requests should be handled. To do so, I provide two resource paths to match against requests and their required user authorities; I also enable OAuth2 resource server support using JWTs to bear the user information.

JWTs are sometimes referred to as *bearer tokens* because they bear the user's authorization for access to resources.

Finally, I build the `SecurityWebFilterChain` from the `ServerHttpSecurity` bean and return it, making it available as a bean throughout the PlaneFinder application.

When a request arrives, the filter chain compares the requested resource's path to paths specified in the chain until a match is found. Once a match is made, the application verifies the token validity with the OAuth2 provider—Okta, in this case—and then compares the contained authorities with those required for access to the mapped resources. If there is a valid match, access is granted; if not, the application returns a *403 Forbidden* status code.

You might have noticed that the second `pathMatcher` specifies a resource path that doesn't (yet) exist in PlaneFinder. I add this path to the `PlaneController` class solely to be able to provide examples of both successful and failed authority checks.

OAuth2 providers may include several default authorities, including *openid*, *email*, *profile*, and more. In the example filter chain, I check a nonexistent (for my provider and OAuth2 authority configuration) authority of *closedid*; consequently, any request for a resource with a path beginning with */aircraft* will fail. As currently written, any inbound request for resources beginning with a path of */aircraftadmin* and bearing a valid token will succeed.

 Spring Security prepends "SCOPE_" to OAuth2 provider-supplied authorities, mapping Spring Security's internal concept of scopes 1:1 with OAuth2 authorities. For developers using Spring Security with OAuth2, this is important to be aware of but is a distinction without a practical difference.

To complete the code refactoring, I now add the */aircraftadmin* endpoint mapping referenced in the previous path matcher to PlaneFinder's `PlaneController` class, simply copying the functionality of the existing */aircraft* endpoint in order to demonstrate two endpoints with different access criteria:

```java
import org.springframework.messaging.handler.annotation.MessageMapping;
import org.springframework.stereotype.Controller;
import org.springframework.web.bind.annotation.GetMapping;
import org.springframework.web.bind.annotation.ResponseBody;
import reactor.core.publisher.Flux;

import java.io.IOException;
import java.time.Duration;

@Controller
public class PlaneController {
    private final PlaneFinderService pfService;

    public PlaneController(PlaneFinderService pfService) {
        this.pfService = pfService;
    }
```

```
@ResponseBody
@GetMapping("/aircraft")
public Flux<Aircraft> getCurrentAircraft() throws IOException {
    return pfService.getAircraft();
}

@ResponseBody
@GetMapping("/aircraftadmin")
public Flux<Aircraft> getCurrentAircraftByAdmin() throws IOException {
    return pfService.getAircraft();
}

@MessageMapping("acstream")
public Flux<Aircraft> getCurrentACStream() throws IOException {
    return pfService.getAircraft().concatWith(
            Flux.interval(Duration.ofSeconds(1))
                    .flatMap(l -> pfService.getAircraft()));
}
```

Finally, I must indicate to the application where to go to access the OAuth2 provider in order to validate the incoming JWTs. There may be variations in how this is done, as the specification for OAuth2 provider endpoints has some latitude, but Okta helpfully implements an issuer URI to act as a central URI for configuration from which other necessary URIs can be obtained. This reduces the burden on application developers to adding a single property.

I've converted the *application.properties* file from a key-value pairs format to *application.yml*, allowing for a structured tree of properties, reducing repetition a bit. Note that this is optional but useful when duplication in property keys begins to manifest:

```
spring:
  security:
    oauth2:
      resourceserver:
        jwt:
          issuer-uri: https://<your_assigned_subdomain_here>.oktapreview.com/
              oauth2/default
  rsocket:
    server:
      port: 7635

server:
  port: 7634
```

With all elements now in place, I restart both the PlaneFinder OAuth2 resource server and the Aircraft Positions OpenID Connect + OAuth2 client application to verify the results. Loading the address for Aircraft Positions's */aircraftadmin* API endpoint (*http://localhost:8080/aircraftadmin*) in a browser, I'm redirected to Okta for authentication, as shown in Figure 10-4.

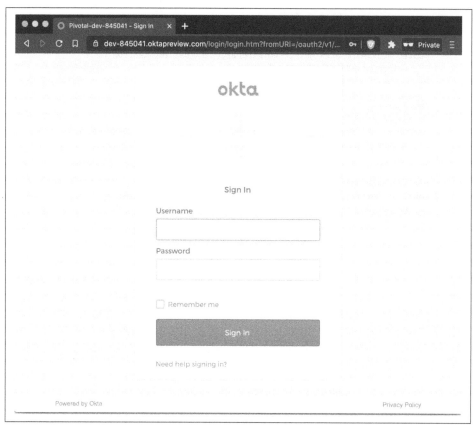

Figure 10-4. Login prompt provided by OpenID Connect provider (Okta)

Once I provide my valid user credentials, Okta redirects the authenticated user (me) to the client application, `Aircraft Positions`. The endpoint I requested in turn requests aircraft positions from PlaneFinder, passing along the JWT supplied to it by Okta. Once PlaneFinder matches the path requested to a resource path and verifies the JWT and its contained authorities, it responds with current aircraft positions to the `Aircraft Positions` client app, which in turn provides them to me, as shown in Figure 10-5.

```
[
  {
    "id": 1,
    "callsign": "N684CA",
    "squawk": "5635",
    "reg": "N684CA",
    "flightno": "",
    "route": "",
    "type": "P46T",
    "category": "A1",
    "altitude": 28000,
    "heading": 305,
    "speed": 204,
    "lat": 38.85692,
    "lon": -90.475281,
    "barometer": 1013.6,
    "vert_rate": 0,
    "selected_altitude": 28000,
    "polar_distance": 15.178367,
    "polar_bearing": 246.770022,
    "is_adsb": true,
    "is_on_ground": false,
    "last_seen_time": "2020-10-18T17:18:41Z",
    "pos_update_time": "2020-10-18T17:18:39Z",
    "bds40_seen_time": "2020-10-18T17:18:38Z"
  },
  {
    "id": 2,
    "callsign": null,
    "squawk": null,
    "reg": "N11TS",
    "flightno": "",
    "route": "FAT-SDF",
    "type": "F2TH",
    "category": "A2",
    "altitude": 41000,
    "heading": 97,
    "speed": 547,
    "lat": 38.552282,
    "lon": -90.286316,
    "barometer": 0,
```

Figure 10-5. Successful return current aircraft positions

What happens if I request a resource for which I have no authorization? To see an example of a failed authorization, I attempt to access AircraftPosition's /aircraft endpoint at *http://localhost:8080/aircraft*, with the results shown in Figure 10-6. Note that since I've already authenticated, I needn't reauthenticate to continue accessing the Aircraft Positions application.

Figure 10-6. Results of failed authorization

Note that the response doesn't provide much information regarding the failure to retrieve results. It is generally considered a good security practice to avoid leaking details that could provide potential hostile actors with information that is helpful toward an eventual compromise. Visiting the logs for Aircraft Positions, however, I see the following additional information:

```
Forbidden: 403 Forbidden from GET http://localhost:7634/aircraft with root cause
```

This is exactly the response expected, since PlaneFinder's filter that matched requests for resources at or under */aircraft* expected the undefined authority *closedid*, which of course wasn't supplied.

These examples were distilled to the maximum extent possible, but they represent the key aspects of OpenID Connect authentication and OAuth2 authorization using a respected third-party security provider. Everything else that can be done to customize and extend this type of authentication and authorization for Spring Boot applications builds upon these fundamental principles and steps.

Going with the Flow

The examples in this section utilize the Authorization Code Flow resulting in an Authorization Code Grant. The Authorization Code Flow is the process around which secure web applications are typically constructed and also serves as the center-piece of the Authorization Code Flow with PKCE (Proof Key for Code Exchange) recommended for native applications.

There are other flows, notably the Resource Owner Password Flow, the Implicit Flow, and the Client Credentials Flow, but these other flows and their limitations and particular use cases are beyond the scope of this chapter.

Code Checkout Checkup

For complete chapter code, please check out branch *chapter10end* from the code repository.

Summary

Understanding the concepts of authentication and authorization are critical to building secure applications, providing the foundations for user verification and access control. Spring Security combines options for authentication and authorization with other mechanisms like the HTTP Firewall, filter chains, extensive use of IETF and W3C standards and options for exchanges, and more to help lock down applications. Adopting a secure out-of-the-box mindset, Spring Security leverages Boot's powerful autoconfiguration to evaluate developer inputs and available dependencies to deliver maximal security for Spring Boot applications with minimal effort.

This chapter discussed several core aspects of security and how they apply to applications. I demonstrated multiple ways to incorporate Spring Security into Spring Boot apps to strengthen an application's security posture, closing dangerous gaps in coverage and reducing attack surface area.

The next chapter examines ways to deploy your Spring Boot application to various target destinations and discusses their relative merits. I also demonstrate how to create these deployment artifacts, provide options for their optimal execution, and show how to verify their components and provenance.

## CHAPTER 11

Deploying Your Spring Boot Application

In software development, deployment is the on-ramp to production for an application.

Regardless of any capabilities an application may promise its end users, until said users can actually use the application, it is effectively an academic what-if exercise. Figuratively and often very literally, deployment is the payoff.

Referencing the Spring Initializr, many developers are aware that Spring Boot applications can be created as WAR files or JAR files. Most of those same developers also know that there are many good reasons (several of which were mentioned earlier in this book) to eschew the WAR option and create executable JAR files, and few good reasons to do the opposite. What many developers may not realize is that even when building a Spring Boot executable JAR, there are numerous options for deployment to fulfill various requirements and use cases.

In this chapter, I examine ways to deploy your Spring Boot application with options useful for different target destinations and discuss their relative merits. I then demonstrate how to create these deployment artifacts, explain options for optimal execution, and show how to verify their components and provenance. You almost certainly have more and better tools for deploying your Spring Boot applications than you realized.

Code Checkout Checkup

Please check out branch *chapter11begin* from the code repository to begin.

Revisiting the Spring Boot Executable JAR

As discussed way back in Chapter 1, Spring Boot's executable JAR provides maximum utility and versatility in a single, self-contained, testable, and deployable unit. It's fast to create and iterate, dynamically self-configurable to changes in its environment, and simple in the extreme to distribute and maintain.

Every cloud provider offers an application hosting option that enjoys widespread use for prototyping through production deployments, and most of those application platforms expect a largely self-contained deployable application, offering only the barest of environmental essentials. A Spring Boot JAR fits quite naturally into these clean environments, requiring only the presence of a JDK for frictionless execution; some platforms even specify Spring Boot by name due to its seamless fit for app hosting. By bringing mechanisms with it for external interactions involving HTTP exchanges, messaging, and more, a Spring Boot application can eliminate installation, configuration, and maintenance of an application server or other externalities. This dramatically reduces developer workload and application platform overhead.

Since a Spring Boot application possesses full control over dependent libraries, it eliminates fear of external dependency changes. Scheduled updates to an application server, servlet engine, database or messaging libraries, or any of a number of other critical components have crashed countless non-Boot applications over the years. In those applications that rely on external components maintained by the underlying app platform, developers must be hypervigilant for unplanned outages due to the world shifting under their feet, simply due to a dot-release change of a single dependent library. Exciting times.

With a Spring Boot application, upgrades to any dependencies—whether core Spring libraries or second- (or third- , or fourth- , etc.) tier dependencies—are much less painful and stressful as well. The app developer upgrades and tests the application and deploys an update (typically using a blue-green deployment (*https://en.wikipedia.org/wiki/Blue-green_deployment*)) only when satisfied that everything is working as expected. Since dependencies are no longer external to the application but instead bundled with it, the developer has full control over dependency versions and upgrade timing.

Spring Boot JARs have another useful trick up their sleeve, courtesy of the Spring Boot Maven and Gradle plug-ins: the ability to create what is sometimes called a "fully executable" JAR. The quotes are intentional and are present in official documentation as well because a JDK is still required for the application to function. So what is meant by a "fully executable" Spring Boot application, and how does one create it?

Let's begin with the how.

Building a "Fully Executable" Spring Boot JAR

I'll use PlaneFinder for this example. For purposes of comparison, I build the project from the command line without changes using mvn `clean package`. This results in the following JAR being created in the project's *target* directory (result trimmed to fit page):

```
» ls -lb target/*.jar

-rw-r--r--  1 markheckler  staff  27085204 target/planefinder-0.0.1-SNAPSHOT.jar
```

This Spring Boot JAR is referred to as an *executable JAR* because it consists of the entire application without need for external downstream dependencies; all it requires to execute is a JVM provided by an installed JDK. Running the app in its current state looks something like this (results trimmed and edited to fit page):

```
» java -jar target/planefinder-0.0.1-SNAPSHOT.jar


  .   ____          _            __ _ _
 /\\ / ___'_ __ _ _(_)_ __  __ _ \ \ \ \
( ( )\___ | '_ | '_| | '_ \/ _` | \ \ \ \
 \\/  ___)| |_)| | | | | || (_| |  ) ) ) )
  '  |____| .__|_| |_|_| |_\__, | / / / /
 =========|_|==============|___/=/_/_/_/
 :: Spring Boot ::                (v2.4.0)

: Starting PlanefinderApplication v0.0.1-SNAPSHOT
: No active profile set, falling back to default profiles: default
: Bootstrapping Spring Data R2DBC repositories in DEFAULT mode.
: Finished Spring Data repository scanning in 132 ms. Found 1 R2DBC
  repository interfaces.
: Netty started on port(s): 7634
: Netty RSocket started on port(s): 7635
: Started PlanefinderApplication in 2.75 seconds (JVM running for 3.106)
```

This works as expected, of course, and it serves as a baseline for what comes next. I now revisit PlaneFinder's *pom.xml* to add the indicated XML snippet to the existing section for the spring-boot-maven-plug-in, as shown in Figure 11-1.

```
<build>
    <plugins>
        <plugin>
            <groupId>org.springframework.boot</groupId>
            <artifactId>spring-boot-maven-plugin</artifactId>
            <version>2.4.0</version>
            <configuration>
                <executable>true</executable>
            </configuration>
        </plugin>
    </plugins>
</build>
```

Figure 11-1. Plugins section of PlaneFinder pom.xml file

Returning to the terminal, I again build the project from the command line using mvn
clean package. This time, there is a notable difference in the resultant JAR created
within the project's *target* directory, as indicated in the following output (result trimmed to fit page):

```
» ls -lb target/*.jar

-rwxr--r-- 1 markheckler  staff  27094314 target/planefinder-0.0.1-SNAPSHOT.jar
```

It's ever so slightly larger than Boot's standard executable JAR, to the tune of 9,110
byte, or just under 9 KB. What does this gain you?

Java JAR files are read from end to beginning—yes, you read that correctly—until an
end-of-file marker is found. When creating a so-called "fully executable JAR," the
Spring Boot Maven plug-in ingeniously prepends a script to the beginning of the
usual Spring Boot executable JAR that enables it to be run like any other executable
binary (assuming the presence of a JDK) on a Unix- or Linux-based system, including registering it with init.d or systemd. Examining PlaneFinder's JAR in an editor
results in the following (only a portion of the script header is shown for brevity; it is
quite extensive):

```
#!/bin/bash
#
#  .   ___                    _           ___ _ _
#  /\\ / __'_ _ _ _(_)_ _  _ _  __ \ \ \ \
# ( ( )\__ | '_ | '_| | '_ \/ _` | \ \ \ \
#  \\/  ___)| |_)| | | | | || (_| |  ) ) ) )
#  '  |____| .__|_| |_|_| |_\__, | / / / /
#  =========|_|==============|___/=/_/_/_/
#  :: Spring Boot Startup Script ::
#
```

```
### BEGIN INIT INFO
# Provides:          planefinder
# Required-Start:    $remote_fs $syslog $network
# Required-Stop:     $remote_fs $syslog $network
# Default-Start:     2 3 4 5
# Default-Stop:      0 1 6
# Short-Description: planefinder
# Description:       Data feed for SBUR
# chkconfig:         2345 99 01
### END INIT INFO

...

# Action functions
start() {
  if [[ -f "$pid_file" ]]; then
    pid=$(cat "$pid_file")
    isRunning "$pid" && { echoYellow "Already running [$pid]"; return 0; }
  fi
  do_start "$@"
}

do_start() {
  working_dir=$(dirname "$jarfile")
  pushd "$working_dir" > /dev/null
  if [[ ! -e "$PID_FOLDER" ]]; then
    mkdir -p "$PID_FOLDER" &> /dev/null
    if [[ -n "$run_user" ]]; then
      chown "$run_user" "$PID_FOLDER"
    fi
  fi
  if [[ ! -e "$log_file" ]]; then
    touch "$log_file" &> /dev/null
    if [[ -n "$run_user" ]]; then
      chown "$run_user" "$log_file"
    fi
  fi
  if [[ -n "$run_user" ]]; then
    checkPermissions || return $?
    if [ $USE_START_STOP_DAEMON = true ] && type start-stop-daemon > \
        /dev/null 2>&1; then
      start-stop-daemon --start --quiet \
        --chuid "$run_user" \
        --name "$identity" \
        --make-pidfile --pidfile "$pid_file" \
        --background --no-close \
        --startas "$javaexe" \
        --chdir "$working_dir" \
        -"${arguments[@]}" \
        >> "$log_file" 2>&1
      await_file "$pid_file"
    else
      su -s /bin/sh -c "$javaexe $(printf "\"%s\" " "${arguments[@]}") >> \
        \"$log_file\" 2>&1 & echo \$!" "$run_user" > "$pid_file"
    fi
```

```
      pid=$(cat "$pid_file")
    else
      checkPermissions || return $?
      "$javaexe" "${arguments[@]}" >> "$log_file" 2>&1 &
      pid=$!
      disown $pid
      echo "$pid" > "$pid_file"
    fi
    [[ -z $pid ]] && { echoRed "Failed to start"; return 1; }
    echoGreen "Started [$pid]"
}

stop() {
  working_dir=$(dirname "$jarfile")
  pushd "$working_dir" > /dev/null
  [[ -f $pid_file ]] ||
    { echoYellow "Not running (pidfile not found)"; return 0; }
  pid=$(cat "$pid_file")
  isRunning "$pid" || { echoYellow "Not running (process ${pid}).
    Removing stale pid file."; rm -f "$pid_file"; return 0; }
  do_stop "$pid" "$pid_file"
}

do_stop() {
  kill "$1" &> /dev/null || { echoRed "Unable to kill process $1"; return 1; }
  for ((i = 1; i <= STOP_WAIT_TIME; i++)); do
    isRunning "$1" || { echoGreen "Stopped [$1]"; rm -f "$2"; return 0; }
    [[ $i -eq STOP_WAIT_TIME/2 ]] && kill "$1" &> /dev/null
    sleep 1
  done
  echoRed "Unable to kill process $1";
  return 1;
}

force_stop() {
  [[ -f $pid_file ]] ||
    { echoYellow "Not running (pidfile not found)"; return 0; }
  pid=$(cat "$pid_file")
  isRunning "$pid" ||
    { echoYellow "Not running (process ${pid}). Removing stale pid file.";
    rm -f "$pid_file"; return 0; }
  do_force_stop "$pid" "$pid_file"
}

do_force_stop() {
  kill -9 "$1" &> /dev/null ||
      { echoRed "Unable to kill process $1"; return 1; }
  for ((i = 1; i <= STOP_WAIT_TIME; i++)); do
    isRunning "$1" || { echoGreen "Stopped [$1]"; rm -f "$2"; return 0; }
    [[ $i -eq STOP_WAIT_TIME/2 ]] && kill -9 "$1" &> /dev/null
    sleep 1
  done
  echoRed "Unable to kill process $1";
  return 1;
}
```

```
restart() {
  stop && start
}

force_reload() {
  working_dir=$(dirname "$jarfile")
  pushd "$working_dir" > /dev/null
  [[ -f $pid_file ]] || { echoRed "Not running (pidfile not found)";
      return 7; }
  pid=$(cat "$pid_file")
  rm -f "$pid_file"
  isRunning "$pid" || { echoRed "Not running (process ${pid} not found)";
      return 7; }
  do_stop "$pid" "$pid_file"
  do_start
}

status() {
  working_dir=$(dirname "$jarfile")
  pushd "$working_dir" > /dev/null
  [[ -f "$pid_file" ]] || { echoRed "Not running"; return 3; }
  pid=$(cat "$pid_file")
  isRunning "$pid" || { echoRed "Not running (process ${pid} not found)";
      return 1; }
  echoGreen "Running [$pid]"
  return 0
}

run() {
  pushd "$(dirname "$jarfile")" > /dev/null
  "$javaexe" "${arguments[@]}"
  result=$?
  popd > /dev/null
  return "$result"
}

# Call the appropriate action function
case "$action" in
start)
  start "$@"; exit $?;;
stop)
  stop "$@"; exit $?;;
force-stop)
  force_stop "$@"; exit $?;;
restart)
  restart "$@"; exit $?;;
force-reload)
  force_reload "$@"; exit $?;;
status)
  status "$@"; exit $?;;
run)
  run "$@"; exit $?;;
*)
  echo "Usage: $0 {start|stop|force-stop|restart|force-reload|status|run}";
    exit 1;
esac
```

```
exit 0
<binary portion omitted>
```

The Spring Boot Maven (or Gradle, if chosen as the build system) plug-in also sets file owner permissions to read, write, and execute (rwx) for the output JAR. Doing so enables it to be executed as indicated previously and allows the header script to locate the JDK, prepare the application for execution, and run it as demonstrated here (results trimmed and edited to fit page):

```
» target/planefinder-0.0.1-SNAPSHOT.jar


  .   ___          _            __ _ _
 /\\ / ___'_ __ _ _(_)_ __  __ _ \ \ \ \
( ( )\___ | '_ | '_| | '_ \/ _` | \ \ \ \
 \\/  ___)| |_)| | | | | || (_| |  ) ) ) )
  '  |____| .__|_| |_|_| |_\__, | / / / /
 =========|_|==============|___/=/_/_/_/
 :: Spring Boot ::              (v2.4.0)

: Starting PlanefinderApplication v0.0.1-SNAPSHOT
: No active profile set, falling back to default profiles: default
: Bootstrapping Spring Data R2DBC repositories in DEFAULT mode.
: Finished Spring Data repository scanning in 185 ms.
  Found 1 R2DBC repository interfaces.
: Netty started on port(s): 7634
: Netty RSocket started on port(s): 7635
: Started PlanefinderApplication in 2.938 seconds (JVM running for 3.335)
```

Now that I've demonstrated how, it's time to discuss what this option brings to the table.

What Does It Mean?

The ability to create a Spring Boot "fully executable" JAR is not a solution to all problems, but it does provide a unique capability for deeper integration with underlying Unix- and Linux-based systems when necessary. Adding a Spring Boot application to supply startup functionality becomes trivial thanks to the embedded startup script and execute permissions.

If you don't need or can't make use of that capability in your current application environments, you should continue to simply create typical Spring Boot executable JAR output that makes use of java -jar. This is simply another tool in your toolbox, included at no cost and requiring nearly no effort from you to implement, for when you find you need it.

Exploding JARs

Spring Boot's innovative approach of nesting dependent JAR files completely intact and unchanged within the Boot executable JAR lends itself brilliantly to subsequent actions like extraction. Reversing the process that was involved in adding them to the Spring Boot executable JAR produces the component artifacts in their original, unaltered state. It sounds simple because it *is* simple.

There are many reasons you might want to rehydrate a Spring Boot executable JAR into its various, separate parts:

- Extracted Boot applications offer slightly faster execution. This is rarely reason enough to rehydrate, but it is a nice bonus.

- Extracted dependencies are easily replaceable discrete units. App updates can be done more quickly and/or with lower bandwidth because only the changed files must be redeployed.

- Many cloud platforms, such as Heroku and any build or brand/derivative of Cloud Foundry, do this as part of the app deployment process. Mirroring local and remote environments to the maximum extent possible can aid in consistency and, when necessary, diagnosis of any issues.

Both standard Spring Boot executable JARs and "fully executable" JARs can be rehydrated in the following manner, using `jar -xvf <spring_boot_jar>` (most file entries removed for brevity):

```
» mkdir expanded
» cd expanded
» jar -xvf ../target/planefinder-0.0.1-SNAPSHOT.jar
  created: META-INF/
 inflated: META-INF/MANIFEST.MF
  created: org/
  created: org/springframework/
  created: org/springframework/boot/
  created: org/springframework/boot/loader/
  created: org/springframework/boot/loader/archive/
  created: org/springframework/boot/loader/data/
  created: org/springframework/boot/loader/jar/
  created: org/springframework/boot/loader/jarmode/
  created: org/springframework/boot/loader/util/
  created: BOOT-INF/
  created: BOOT-INF/classes/
  created: BOOT-INF/classes/com/
  created: BOOT-INF/classes/com/thehecklers/
  created: BOOT-INF/classes/com/thehecklers/planefinder/
  created: META-INF/maven/
  created: META-INF/maven/com.thehecklers/
  created: META-INF/maven/com.thehecklers/planefinder/
 inflated: BOOT-INF/classes/schema.sql
 inflated: BOOT-INF/classes/application.properties
 inflated: META-INF/maven/com.thehecklers/planefinder/pom.xml
 inflated: META-INF/maven/com.thehecklers/planefinder/pom.properties
  created: BOOT-INF/lib/
 inflated: BOOT-INF/classpath.idx
```

```
    inflated: BOOT-INF/layers.idx
  »
```

Once files are extracted, I find it useful to examine the structure a bit more visually using the *nix `tree` command:

```
» tree
.
├── BOOT-INF
│   ├── classes
│   │   ├── application.properties
│   │   ├── com
│   │   │   └── thehecklers
│   │   │       └── planefinder
│   │   │           ├── Aircraft.class
│   │   │           ├── DbConxInit.class
│   │   │           ├── PlaneController.class
│   │   │           ├── PlaneFinderService.class
│   │   │           ├── PlaneRepository.class
│   │   │           ├── PlanefinderApplication.class
│   │   │           └── User.class
│   │   └── schema.sql
│   ├── classpath.idx
│   ├── layers.idx
│   └── lib
│       ├── h2-1.4.200.jar
│       ├── jackson-annotations-2.11.3.jar
│       ├── jackson-core-2.11.3.jar
│       ├── jackson-databind-2.11.3.jar
│       ├── jackson-dataformat-cbor-2.11.3.jar
│       ├── jackson-datatype-jdk8-2.11.3.jar
│       ├── jackson-datatype-jsr310-2.11.3.jar
│       ├── jackson-module-parameter-names-2.11.3.jar
│       ├── jakarta.annotation-api-1.3.5.jar
│       ├── jul-to-slf4j-1.7.30.jar
│       ├── log4j-api-2.13.3.jar
│       ├── log4j-to-slf4j-2.13.3.jar
│       ├── logback-classic-1.2.3.jar
│       ├── logback-core-1.2.3.jar
│       ├── lombok-1.18.16.jar
│       ├── netty-buffer-4.1.54.Final.jar
│       ├── netty-codec-4.1.54.Final.jar
│       ├── netty-codec-dns-4.1.54.Final.jar
│       ├── netty-codec-http-4.1.54.Final.jar
│       ├── netty-codec-http2-4.1.54.Final.jar
│       ├── netty-codec-socks-4.1.54.Final.jar
│       ├── netty-common-4.1.54.Final.jar
│       ├── netty-handler-4.1.54.Final.jar
│       ├── netty-handler-proxy-4.1.54.Final.jar
│       ├── netty-resolver-4.1.54.Final.jar
│       ├── netty-resolver-dns-4.1.54.Final.jar
│       ├── netty-transport-4.1.54.Final.jar
│       ├── netty-transport-native-epoll-4.1.54.Final-linux-x86_64.jar
│       ├── netty-transport-native-unix-common-4.1.54.Final.jar
│       ├── r2dbc-h2-0.8.4.RELEASE.jar
│       ├── r2dbc-pool-0.8.5.RELEASE.jar
```

```
│       ├── r2dbc-spi-0.8.3.RELEASE.jar
│       ├── reactive-streams-1.0.3.jar
│       ├── reactor-core-3.4.0.jar
│       ├── reactor-netty-core-1.0.1.jar
│       ├── reactor-netty-http-1.0.1.jar
│       ├── reactor-pool-0.2.0.jar
│       ├── rsocket-core-1.1.0.jar
│       ├── rsocket-transport-netty-1.1.0.jar
│       ├── slf4j-api-1.7.30.jar
│       ├── snakeyaml-1.27.jar
│       ├── spring-aop-5.3.1.jar
│       ├── spring-beans-5.3.1.jar
│       ├── spring-boot-2.4.0.jar
│       ├── spring-boot-autoconfigure-2.4.0.jar
│       ├── spring-boot-jarmode-layertools-2.4.0.jar
│       ├── spring-context-5.3.1.jar
│       ├── spring-core-5.3.1.jar
│       ├── spring-data-commons-2.4.1.jar
│       ├── spring-data-r2dbc-1.2.1.jar
│       ├── spring-data-relational-2.1.1.jar
│       ├── spring-expression-5.3.1.jar
│       ├── spring-jcl-5.3.1.jar
│       ├── spring-messaging-5.3.1.jar
│       ├── spring-r2dbc-5.3.1.jar
│       ├── spring-tx-5.3.1.jar
│       ├── spring-web-5.3.1.jar
│       └── spring-webflux-5.3.1.jar
├── META-INF
│   ├── MANIFEST.MF
│   └── maven
│       └── com.thehecklers
│           └── planefinder
│               ├── pom.properties
│               └── pom.xml
└── org
    └── springframework
        └── boot
            └── loader
                ├── ClassPathIndexFile.class
                ├── ExecutableArchiveLauncher.class
                ├── JarLauncher.class
                ├── LaunchedURLClassLoader$DefinePackageCallType.class
                ├── LaunchedURLClassLoader
                │   $UseFastConnectionExceptionsEnumeration.class
                ├── LaunchedURLClassLoader.class
                ├── Launcher.class
                ├── MainMethodRunner.class
                ├── PropertiesLauncher$1.class
                ├── PropertiesLauncher$ArchiveEntryFilter.class
                ├── PropertiesLauncher$ClassPathArchives.class
                ├── PropertiesLauncher$PrefixMatchingArchiveFilter.class
                ├── PropertiesLauncher.class
                ├── WarLauncher.class
                ├── archive
                │   ├── Archive$Entry.class
                │   ├── Archive$EntryFilter.class
```

```
                    │   ├── Archive.class
                    │   ├── ExplodedArchive$AbstractIterator.class
                    │   ├── ExplodedArchive$ArchiveIterator.class
                    │   ├── ExplodedArchive$EntryIterator.class
                    │   ├── ExplodedArchive$FileEntry.class
                    │   ├── ExplodedArchive$SimpleJarFileArchive.class
                    │   ├── ExplodedArchive.class
                    │   ├── JarFileArchive$AbstractIterator.class
                    │   ├── JarFileArchive$EntryIterator.class
                    │   ├── JarFileArchive$JarFileEntry.class
                    │   ├── JarFileArchive$NestedArchiveIterator.class
                    │   └── JarFileArchive.class
                    ├── data
                    │   ├── RandomAccessData.class
                    │   ├── RandomAccessDataFile$1.class
                    │   ├── RandomAccessDataFile$DataInputStream.class
                    │   ├── RandomAccessDataFile$FileAccess.class
                    │   └── RandomAccessDataFile.class
                    ├── jar
                    │   ├── AbstractJarFile$JarFileType.class
                    │   ├── AbstractJarFile.class
                    │   ├── AsciiBytes.class
                    │   ├── Bytes.class
                    │   ├── CentralDirectoryEndRecord$1.class
                    │   ├── CentralDirectoryEndRecord$Zip64End.class
                    │   ├── CentralDirectoryEndRecord$Zip64Locator.class
                    │   ├── CentralDirectoryEndRecord.class
                    │   ├── CentralDirectoryFileHeader.class
                    │   ├── CentralDirectoryParser.class
                    │   ├── CentralDirectoryVisitor.class
                    │   ├── FileHeader.class
                    │   ├── Handler.class
                    │   ├── JarEntry.class
                    │   ├── JarEntryCertification.class
                    │   ├── JarEntryFilter.class
                    │   ├── JarFile$1.class
                    │   ├── JarFile$JarEntryEnumeration.class
                    │   ├── JarFile.class
                    │   ├── JarFileEntries$1.class
                    │   ├── JarFileEntries$EntryIterator.class
                    │   ├── JarFileEntries.class
                    │   ├── JarFileWrapper.class
                    │   ├── JarURLConnection$1.class
                    │   ├── JarURLConnection$JarEntryName.class
                    │   ├── JarURLConnection.class
                    │   ├── StringSequence.class
                    │   └── ZipInflaterInputStream.class
                    ├── jarmode
                    │   ├── JarMode.class
                    │   ├── JarModeLauncher.class
                    │   └── TestJarMode.class
                    └── util
                        └── SystemPropertyUtils.class

        19 directories, 137 files
        »
```

Viewing the JAR contents using `tree` offers a nice hierarchical display of the application's composition. It also calls out the numerous dependencies that combine to provide the capabilities chosen for this application. Listing the files under *BOOT-INF/lib* confirms that the component libraries remain unchanged through the building of the Spring Boot JAR and subsequent extraction of its contents, even down to original component JAR timestamps, as shown here (most entries removed for brevity):

```
» ls -l BOOT-INF/lib
total 52880
-rw-r--r--  1 markheckler  staff  2303679 Oct 14  2019 h2-1.4.200.jar
-rw-r--r--  1 markheckler  staff    68215 Oct  1 22:20 jackson-annotations-
2.11.3.jar
-rw-r--r--  1 markheckler  staff   351495 Oct  1 22:25 jackson-core-
2.11.3.jar
-rw-r--r--  1 markheckler  staff  1421699 Oct  1 22:38 jackson-databind-
2.11.3.jar
-rw-r--r--  1 markheckler  staff    58679 Oct  2 00:17 jackson-dataformat-cbor-
2.11.3.jar
-rw-r--r--  1 markheckler  staff    34335 Oct  2 00:25 jackson-datatype-jdk8-
2.11.3.jar
-rw-r--r--  1 markheckler  staff   111008 Oct  2 00:25 jackson-datatype-jsr310-
2.11.3.jar
-rw-r--r--  1 markheckler  staff     9267 Oct  2 00:25 jackson-module-parameter-
names-2.11.3.jar
...
-rw-r--r--  1 markheckler  staff   374303 Nov 10 09:01 spring-aop-5.3.1.jar
-rw-r--r--  1 markheckler  staff   695851 Nov 10 09:01 spring-beans-5.3.1.jar
-rw-r--r--  1 markheckler  staff  1299025 Nov 12 13:56 spring-boot-2.4.0.jar
-rw-r--r--  1 markheckler  staff  1537971 Nov 12 13:55 spring-boot-
autoconfigure-2.4.0.jar
-rw-r--r--  1 markheckler  staff    32912 Feb  1  1980 spring-boot-jarmode-
layertools-2.4.0.jar
-rw-r--r--  1 markheckler  staff  1241939 Nov 10 09:01 spring-context-5.3.1.jar
-rw-r--r--  1 markheckler  staff  1464734 Feb  1  1980 spring-core-5.3.1.jar
-rw-r--r--  1 markheckler  staff  1238966 Nov 11 12:03 spring-data-commons-
2.4.1.jar
-rw-r--r--  1 markheckler  staff   433079 Nov 11 12:08 spring-data-r2dbc-
1.2.1.jar
-rw-r--r--  1 markheckler  staff   339745 Nov 11 12:05 spring-data-relational-
2.1.1.jar
-rw-r--r--  1 markheckler  staff   282565 Nov 10 09:01 spring-expression-
5.3.1.jar
-rw-r--r--  1 markheckler  staff    23943 Nov 10 09:01 spring-jcl-5.3.1.jar
-rw-r--r--  1 markheckler  staff   552895 Nov 10 09:01 spring-messaging-
5.3.1.jar
-rw-r--r--  1 markheckler  staff   133156 Nov 10 09:01 spring-r2dbc-5.3.1.jar
-rw-r--r--  1 markheckler  staff   327956 Nov 10 09:01 spring-tx-5.3.1.jar
-rw-r--r--  1 markheckler  staff  1546053 Nov 10 09:01 spring-web-5.3.1.jar
-rw-r--r--  1 markheckler  staff   901591 Nov 10 09:01 spring-webflux-5.3.1.jar
»
```

Once all files are extracted from the Spring Boot JAR, there are a few ways to run the application. The recommended approach is to use `JarLauncher`, which maintains a consistent classloading order across executions, as shown below (results trimmed and edited to fit page):

```
» java org.springframework.boot.loader.JarLauncher
```

```
  .   ___          _            __ _ _
 /\\ / ___'_ __ _ _(_)_ __  __ _ \ \ \ \
( ( )\___ | '_ | '_| | '_ \/ _` | \ \ \ \
 \\/  ___)| |_)| | | | | || (_| |  ) ) ) )
  '  |____| .__|_| |_|_| |_\__, | / / / /
 =========|_|==============|___/=/_/_/_/
 :: Spring Boot ::                (v2.4.0)
```

```
: Starting PlanefinderApplication v0.0.1-SNAPSHOT
: No active profile set, falling back to default profiles: default
: Bootstrapping Spring Data R2DBC repositories in DEFAULT mode.
: Finished Spring Data repository scanning in 95 ms. Found 1 R2DBC
  repository interfaces.
: Netty started on port(s): 7634
: Netty RSocket started on port(s): 7635
: Started PlanefinderApplication in 1.935 seconds (JVM running for 2.213)
```

In this case, PlaneFinder started just over a full second faster expanded than in the Spring Boot "fully executable" JAR. This positive alone may or may not outweigh the advantages of a single, fully self-contained deployable unit; it likely will not. But combined with the ability to only push deltas when a small number of files change and (if applicable) better alignment between local and remote environments, the ability to run exploded Spring Boot applications can be a very useful option.

Deploying Spring Boot Applications to Containers

As mentioned earlier, some cloud platforms—both on-premises/private and public cloud—take deployable applications and create a container image on a developer's behalf using widely optimized defaults and settings provided by the app's developer. These images are then used to create (and destroy) containers with the running application based on the application's replication settings and utilization. Platforms like Heroku and numerous versions of Cloud Foundry enable a developer to push a Spring Boot executable JAR, and provide any desired configuration settings (or simply accept the defaults), and the rest is handled by the platform. Other platforms like VMware's Tanzu Application Service for Kubernetes incorporate this as well, and the feature list is increasing in both scope and fluid execution.

There are many platforms and deployment targets that don't support this level of frictionless developer enablement. Whether you or your organization has committed to one of those other offerings, or if you have other requirements that guide you in a different direction, Spring Boot has you covered.

While you can handcraft your own container images for your Spring Boot applications, it isn't optimal; doing so adds no value to the application itself and has usually been considered a necessary evil (at best) to go from dev to prod. No more.

Leveraging many of the same tools used by the previously mentioned platforms to intelligently containerize applications, Spring Boot incorporates within its Maven and Gradle plug-ins the capability to build painlessly and frictionlessly fully compliant Open Container Initiative (OCI) images used by Docker, Kubernetes, and every major container engine/mechanism. Built upon industry-leading Cloud Native Buildpacks (*https://buildpacks.io*) and the Paketo (*https://paketo.io*) buildpacks initiative, the Spring Boot build plug-ins provide the option to create an OCI image using a locally installed and locally running Docker daemon and push it to a local or designated remote image repository.

Using the Spring Boot plug-in to create an image from your application is opinionated in all the best ways as well, using a conceptual "autoconfiguration" to optimize image creation by layering image contents, separating code/libraries based on each code unit's anticipated frequency of change. Staying true to the Spring Boot philosophy behind autoconfiguration and opinions, Boot also provides a way to override and guide the layering process should you need to customize your configuration. This is rarely necessary or even desirable, but it's easily accomplished should your needs fall within one of those rare, exceptional cases.

The default settings produce the following layers for all versions of Spring Boot from 2.4.0 Milestone 2 onward:

dependencies
    Includes regularly released dependencies, i.e., GA versions

spring-boot-loader
    Includes all files found under *org/springframework/boot/loader*

snapshot-dependencies
    Forward-looking releases not yet considered GA

application
    Application classes and related resources (templates, properties files, scripts, etc.)

Code volatility, or its propensity and frequency of change, typically increases as you move through this list of layers from top to bottom. By creating separate layers in which to place similarly volatile code, subsequent image creation is much more efficient and thus much faster to complete. This *drastically* reduces the time and resources required to rebuild the deployable artifact over the life of the application.

Creating a Container Image from an IDE

Creating a layered container image from a Spring Boot application can be done from within an IDE very easily. I use IntelliJ for this example, but nearly all major IDEs have similar capabilities.

 A local version of Docker—Docker Desktop for Mac in my case—must be running to create images.

To create the image, I open the Maven panel by expanding the tab labeled *Maven* in IntelliJ's right margin, then expand *Plugins*, choose and expand the *spring-boot* plug-in, and double-click the *spring-boot:build-image* option to execute the goal, as shown in Figure 11-2.

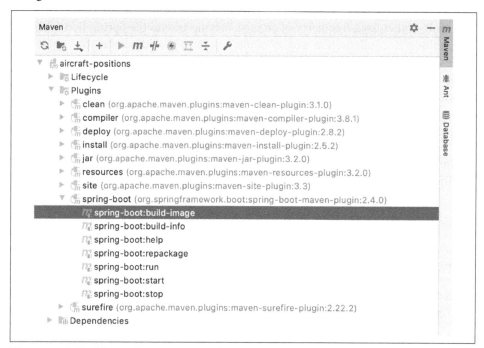

Figure 11-2. Building a Spring Boot application container image from IntelliJ's Maven panel

Creating the image produces a rather lengthy log of actions. Of particular interest are entries listed here:

```
[INFO]    [creator]    Paketo Executable JAR Buildpack 3.1.3
[INFO]    [creator]        https://github.com/paketo-buildpacks/executable-jar
```

```
[INFO]      [creator]           Writing env.launch/CLASSPATH.delim
[INFO]      [creator]           Writing env.launch/CLASSPATH.prepend
[INFO]      [creator]         Process types:
[INFO]      [creator]           executable-jar: java org.springframework.boot.
     loader.JarLauncher
[INFO]      [creator]           task:           java org.springframework.boot.
     loader.JarLauncher
[INFO]      [creator]           web:            java org.springframework.boot.
     loader.JarLauncher
[INFO]      [creator]
[INFO]      [creator]     Paketo Spring Boot Buildpack 3.5.0
[INFO]      [creator]       https://github.com/paketo-buildpacks/spring-boot
[INFO]      [creator]       Creating slices from layers index
[INFO]      [creator]         dependencies
[INFO]      [creator]         spring-boot-loader
[INFO]      [creator]         snapshot-dependencies
[INFO]      [creator]         application
[INFO]      [creator]       Launch Helper: Contributing to layer
[INFO]      [creator]         Creating /layers/paketo-buildpacks_spring-boot/
     helper/exec.d/spring-cloud-bindings
[INFO]      [creator]         Writing profile.d/helper
[INFO]      [creator]       Web Application Type: Contributing to layer
[INFO]      [creator]         Reactive web application detected
[INFO]      [creator]         Writing env.launch/BPL_JVM_THREAD_COUNT.default
[INFO]      [creator]       Spring Cloud Bindings 1.7.0: Contributing to layer
[INFO]      [creator]         Downloading from
     https://repo.spring.io/release/org/springframework/cloud/
     spring-cloud-bindings/1.7.0/spring-cloud-bindings-1.7.0.jar
[INFO]      [creator]         Verifying checksum
[INFO]      [creator]         Copying to
     /layers/paketo-buildpacks_spring-boot/spring-cloud-bindings
[INFO]      [creator]       4 application slices
```

As noted earlier, image layers (referred to as *slices* in the preceding listing) and their contents can be modified if necessary for unique circumstances.

Once the image has been created, results like those that follow will complete the log.

```
[INFO] Successfully built image 'docker.io/library/aircraft-positions:
       0.0.1-SNAPSHOT'
[INFO]
[INFO] ------------------------------------------------------------------------
[INFO] BUILD SUCCESS
[INFO] ------------------------------------------------------------------------
[INFO] Total time:  25.851 s
[INFO] Finished at: 2020-11-28T20:09:48-06:00
[INFO] ------------------------------------------------------------------------
```

Creating a Container Image from the Command Line

It's of course also possible—and simple—to create the same container image from the command line. Prior to doing so, I do want to make a small change to the naming settings for the resultant image.

As a matter of convenience, I prefer to create images that align with my Docker Hub (*https://hub.docker.com*) account and naming conventions, and your choice of image repository likely has similar, specific conventions. Spring Boot's build plug-ins accept *<configuration>* section details that smooth the step of pushing the image to repository/catalog. I add a single, properly tagged line to the *<plug-ins>* section of Aircraft Position's *pom.xml* file to match my requirements/preferences:

```
<build>
  <plug-ins>
    <plug-in>
      <groupId>org.springframework.boot</groupId>
      <artifactId>spring-boot-maven-plug-in</artifactId>
      <configuration>
        <image>
          <name>hecklerm/${project.artifactId}</name>
        </image>
      </configuration>
    </plug-in>
  </plug-ins>
</build>
```

Next, I issue the following command from the project directory in the terminal window to re-create the application container image and soon thereafter receive the results shown:

```
» mvn spring-boot:build-image


... (Intermediate logged results omitted for brevity)


[INFO] Successfully built image 'docker.io/hecklerm/aircraft-positions:latest'
[INFO]
[INFO] ------------------------------------------------------------------------
[INFO] BUILD SUCCESS
[INFO] ------------------------------------------------------------------------
[INFO] Total time:  13.257 s
[INFO] Finished at: 2020-11-28T20:23:40-06:00
[INFO] ------------------------------------------------------------------------
```

Notice that the image output is no longer *docker.io/library/aircraft-positions:0.0.1-SNAPSHOT* as it was when I built it using defaults from within the IDE. The new image coordinates match those I specified in the *pom.xml*: *docker.io/hecklerm/aircraft-positions:latest*.

Verifying the Image Exists

To verify that the images created in the prior two sections have been loaded into the local repository, I run the following command from the terminal window, filtering by name to get the following results (and trimmed to fit page):

```
» docker images | grep -in aircraft-positions
aircraft-positions            0.0.1-SNAPSHOT   a7ed39a3d52e   277MB
hecklerm/aircraft-positions   latest           924893a0f1a9   277MB
```

Pushing the image shown last in the preceding output—since it now aligns with expected and desired account and naming conventions—to Docker Hub is accomplished as follows, with the following results:

```
» docker push hecklerm/aircraft-positions
The push refers to repository [docker.io/hecklerm/aircraft-positions]
1dc94a70dbaa: Pushed
4672559507f8: Pushed
e3e9839150af: Pushed
5f70bf18a086: Layer already exists
a3abfb734aa5: Pushed
3c14fe2f1177: Pushed
4cc7b4eb8637: Pushed
fcc507beb4cc: Pushed
c2e9ddddd4ef: Pushed
108b6855c4a6: Pushed
ab39aa8fd003: Layer already exists
0b18b1f120f4: Layer already exists
cf6b3a71f979: Pushed
ec0381c8f321: Layer already exists
7b0fc1578394: Pushed
eb0f7cd0acf8: Pushed
1e5c1d306847: Mounted from paketobuildpacks/run
23c4345364c2: Mounted from paketobuildpacks/run
a1efa53a237c: Mounted from paketobuildpacks/run
fe6d8881187d: Mounted from paketobuildpacks/run
23135df75b44: Mounted from paketobuildpacks/run
b43408d5f11b: Mounted from paketobuildpacks/run
latest: digest:
  sha256:a7e5d536a7426d6244401787b153ebf43277fbadc9f43a789f6c4f0aff6d5011
    size: 5122
»
```

Visiting the Docker Hub allows me to confirm successful public deployment of the image, as shown in Figure 11-3.

Figure 11-3. Spring Boot application container image in Docker Hub

Deploying to Docker Hub or any other container image repository available from outside of your local machine is the last step prior to wider (and hopefully production) deployment of your Spring Boot containerized application.

Running the Containerized Application

To run the application, I use the `docker run` command. Your organization likely has a deployment pipeline that moves applications from container images (retrieved from image repositories) to running, containerized applications, but the steps performed are likely the same, albeit with more automation and less typing.

Since I already have a local copy of the image, no remote retrieval will be necessary; otherwise, remote access to the image repository is required for the daemon to retrieve the remote image and/or layers to reconstruct it locally prior to starting a container based upon the image specified.

To run the containerized Aircraft Positions application, I execute the following command and see the following results (trimmed and edited to fit page):

```
» docker run --name myaircraftpositions -p8080:8080
  hecklerm/aircraft-positions:latest
Setting Active Processor Count to 6
WARNING: Container memory limit unset. Configuring JVM for 1G container.
Calculated JVM Memory Configuration: -XX:MaxDirectMemorySize=10M -Xmx636688K
  -XX:MaxMetaspaceSize=104687K -XX:ReservedCodeCacheSize=240M -Xss1M
  (Total Memory: 1G, Thread Count: 50, Loaded Class Count: 16069, Headroom: 0%)
Adding 138 container CA certificates to JVM truststore
Spring Cloud Bindings Enabled
Picked up JAVA_TOOL_OPTIONS:
-Djava.security.properties=/layers/paketo-buildpacks_bellsoft-liberica/
    java-security-properties/java-security.properties
  -agentpath:/layers/paketo-buildpacks_bellsoft-liberica/jvmkill/
    jvmkill-1.16.0-RELEASE.so=printHeapHistogram=1
  -XX:ActiveProcessorCount=6
  -XX:MaxDirectMemorySize=10M
  -Xmx636688K
  -XX:MaxMetaspaceSize=104687K
  -XX:ReservedCodeCacheSize=240M
  -Xss1M
  -Dorg.springframework.cloud.bindings.boot.enable=true


  .   ____          _            __ _ _
 /\\ / ___'_ __ _ _(_)_ __  __ _ \ \ \ \
( ( )\___ | '_ | '_| | '_ \/ _` | \ \ \ \
 \\/  ___)| |_)| | | | | || (_| |  ) ) ) )
  '  |____| .__|_| |_|_| |_\__, | / / / /
 =========|_|==============|___/=/_/_/_/
 :: Spring Boot ::               (v2.4.0)

 : Starting AircraftPositionsApplication v0.0.1-SNAPSHOT
 : Netty started on port(s): 8080
 : Started AircraftPositionsApplication in 10.7 seconds (JVM running for 11.202)
```

Now to take a quick look inside a Spring Boot plug-in-created image.

Utilities for Examining Spring Boot Application Container Images

Numerous utilities exist to work with container images, and much of the functionality provided by them falls well outside the scope of this book. I do want to briefly mention two that I've found useful in certain circumstances: pack and dive.

Pack

To examine the materials that go into the creation of a Spring Boot application container image using Cloud Native (Paketo) Buildpacks—and the buildpacks themselves—one can use the pack utility. pack is the designated CLI for building apps using Cloud Native Buildpacks and can be obtained by various means. I used home brew to retrieve and install it with a simple brew install pack command on my Mac.

Running pack against the image created previously results in the following:

```
» pack inspect-image hecklerm/aircraft-positions
Inspecting image: hecklerm/aircraft-positions

REMOTE:

Stack: io.buildpacks.stacks.bionic

Base Image:
  Reference: f5caea10feb38ae882a9447b521fd1ea1ee93384438395c7ace2d8cfaf808e3d
  Top Layer: sha256:1e5c1d306847275caa0d1d367382dfdcfd4d62b634b237f1d7a2e
             746372922cd

Run Images:
  index.docker.io/paketobuildpacks/run:base-cnb
  gcr.io/paketo-buildpacks/run:base-cnb

Buildpacks:
  ID                                        VERSION
  paketo-buildpacks/ca-certificates         1.0.1
  paketo-buildpacks/bellsoft-liberica       5.2.1
  paketo-buildpacks/executable-jar          3.1.3
  paketo-buildpacks/dist-zip                2.2.2
  paketo-buildpacks/spring-boot             3.5.0

Processes:
  TYPE             SHELL  COMMAND  ARGS
  web (default)    bash   java     org.springframework.boot.loader.JarLauncher
  executable-jar   bash   java     org.springframework.boot.loader.JarLauncher
  task             bash   java     org.springframework.boot.loader.JarLauncher


LOCAL:
```

```
Stack: io.buildpacks.stacks.bionic

Base Image:
  Reference: f5caea10feb38ae882a9447b521fd1ea1ee93384438395c7ace2d8cfaf808e3d
  Top Layer: sha256:1e5c1d306847275caa0d1d367382dfdcfd4d62b634b237f1d7a2e
             746372922cd

Run Images:
  index.docker.io/paketobuildpacks/run:base-cnb
  gcr.io/paketo-buildpacks/run:base-cnb

Buildpacks:
  ID                                      VERSION
  paketo-buildpacks/ca-certificates       1.0.1
  paketo-buildpacks/bellsoft-liberica     5.2.1
  paketo-buildpacks/executable-jar        3.1.3
  paketo-buildpacks/dist-zip              2.2.2
  paketo-buildpacks/spring-boot           3.5.0

Processes:
  TYPE            SHELL   COMMAND  ARGS
  web (default)   bash    java     org.springframework.boot.loader.JarLauncher
  executable-jar  bash    java     org.springframework.boot.loader.JarLauncher
  task            bash    java     org.springframework.boot.loader.JarLauncher
```

Using the pack utility's inspect-image command provides some key bits of information about the image, particularly the following:

- Which Docker base image/Linux version (bionic) was used as the foundation for this image
- Which buildpacks were used to populate the image (five Paketo buildpacks listed)
- What processes will be run and by what means (Java commands executed by the shell)

Note that both local and remote connected repositories are polled for the specified image, and details are provided for both. This is particularly helpful in diagnosing issues caused by an out-of-date container image in one location or the other.

Dive

The dive utility was created by Alex Goodman as a way to "dive" into a container image, viewing the very granular OCI image layers and the tree structure of the entire image filesystem.

dive goes far beneath the application-level layers of the Spring Boot layering construct and into the operating system. I find it less useful than pack due to its focus on the OS versus the application, but it's ideal for verifying the presence or absence of particular files, file permissions, and other essential low-level concerns. It's a rarely used tool but essential when that level of detail and control is needed.

Code Checkout Checkup

For complete chapter code, please check out branch *chapter11end* from the code repository.

Summary

Until an application's users can actually use that application, it is little more than a what-if exercise. Figuratively and often very literally, deployment is the payoff.

Many developers are aware that Spring Boot applications can be created as WAR files or JAR files. Most of those developers also know that there are many good reasons to skip the WAR option and create executable JAR files and few good reasons to do the opposite. What many developers may not realize is that even when building a Spring Boot executable JAR, there are numerous options for deployment to fulfill various requirements and use cases.

In this chapter, I examined several ways to deploy your Spring Boot application with options useful for different target destinations and discussed their relative merits. I then demonstrated how to create those deployment artifacts, explained options for optimal execution, and showed how to verify their components and provenance. Targets included the standard Spring Boot executable JARs, "fully executable" Spring Boot JARs, exploded/expanded JARs, and container images built using Cloud Native (Paketo) Buildpacks that run on Docker, Kubernetes, and every major container engine/mechanism. Spring Boot gives you numerous frictionless deployment options, extending your development superpowers into deployment superpowers as well.

In the next and final chapter, I round out this book and journey by delving a bit further into two slightly deeper topics. If you'd like to know more about testing and debugging reactive applications, you won't want to miss it.

## CHAPTER 12

Going Deeper with Reactive

As previously discussed, reactive programming gives developers a way to make better use of resources in distributed systems, even extending powerful scaling mechanisms across application boundaries and into the communication channels. For developers with experience exclusively with mainstream Java development practices—often called *imperative* Java due to its explicit and sequential logic versus the more declarative approach generally used in reactive programming, although this label, like most, is imperfect—these reactive capabilities may bear some undesired costs. In addition to the expected learning curve, which Spring helps flatten considerably due to parallel and complementary WebMVC and WebFlux implementations, there are also relative limitations in tooling, its maturity, and established practices for essential activities like testing, troubleshooting, and debugging.

While it is true that reactive Java development is in its infancy relative to its imperative cousin, the fact that they are family has allowed a much faster development and maturation of useful tooling and processes. As mentioned, Spring builds similarly on established imperative expertise within its development and community to condense decades of evolution into production-ready components available *now*.

This chapter introduces and explains the current state of the art in testing and diagnosing/debugging issues you might encounter as you begin to deploy reactive Spring Boot applications and demonstrates how to put WebFlux/Reactor to work for you, even before—and to help—you go to production.

Code Checkout Checkup

Please check out branch *chapter12begin* from the code repository to begin.

When Reactive?

Reactive programming, and in particular those applications focusing on reactive streams, enables system-wide scaling that is difficult to match using other means available at this point in time. However, not all applications need to perform at the far reaches of end-to-end scalability, or they may already be performing (or are expected to perform) admirably with relatively predictable loads over impressive time frames. Imperative apps have long fulfilled production demands for organizations globally, and they will not simply cease to do so because a new option arrives.

While reactive programming is unquestionably exciting in terms of the possibilities it offers, the Spring team clearly states that reactive code will not replace all imperative code for the foreseeable future, if ever. As stated in the Spring Framework reference documentation for Spring WebFlux (*https://oreil.ly/SFRefDoc*):

> If you have a large team, keep in mind the steep learning curve in the shift to non-blocking, functional, and declarative programming. A practical way to start without a full switch is to use the reactive WebClient. Beyond that, start small and measure the benefits. We expect that, for a wide range of applications, the shift is unnecessary. If you are unsure what benefits to look for, start by learning about how non-blocking I/O works (for example, concurrency on single-threaded Node.js) and its effects.
>
> —Spring Framework Reference Documentation

In short, adopting reactive programming and Spring WebFlux is a choice—a great choice that provides perhaps the best way to accomplish certain requirements—but still a choice to make after careful consideration of the relevant requirements and demands for the system in question. Reactive or not, Spring Boot provides unsurpassed options to develop business-critical software to handle all of your production workloads.

Testing Reactive Applications

In order to better focus on the key concepts of testing reactive Spring Boot applications, I take several steps to tighten the scope of code under consideration. Like zooming in on a subject you wish to photograph, other project code is still present but is not on the critical path for the information in this section.

Additional Notes on Testing

I covered testing and, to some degree, my testing philosophy in Chapter 9. To delve more deeply into the aspects of testing covered in this chapter, I must share more of my thinking in order for steps taken here to be clear. Since this book is focused primarily on Spring Boot and only secondarily on related topics, I have attempted

---

(and will continue to attempt) to find the "just enough" amount of additional information needed to provide context without unnecessary elaboration. As the reader might imagine, such a balancing point is impossible to find because it differs by reader, but I hope to get as close as humanly possible.

Testing informs code structure. When done as true Test Driven Development (TDD), this structural guidance occurs from the very beginning of application development. Fleshing out tests once code is in place—as I have done in several chapters of this book in order to place full emphasis on the Spring Boot concepts to be shared rather than applicable test harnesses—can result in greater code refactoring efforts to better isolate and decouple behavior to test specific components and outcomes. This may feel disruptive, but it typically results in better code with cleaner boundaries, making it both more testable and more robust.

This chapter's code is no exception. In order to isolate and test properly for desired behavior, some refactoring of existing, working code is in order. It doesn't take long, and the end results are provably better.

For this section I'll zero in specifically on testing externally those APIs that expose reactive streams publishers—`Flux`, `Mono`, and `Publisher` types that could be either `Flux` or `Mono`—instead of the typical blocking `Iterable` or `Object` types. I begin with the class within `Aircraft Positions` that provides the external APIs: `PositionCon troller`.

 If you haven't already checked out the Chapter 12 code as indicated at the beginning of this chapter, please do so now.

But First, Refactoring

While the code within `PositionController` does work, it is a bit of a testing muddle. The first order of business is to provide a cleaner separation of concerns, and I begin by removing the code to create an `RSocketRequester` object to an `@Configuration` class that will create it as a Spring bean, accessible anywhere within the application:

```
import org.springframework.context.annotation.Bean;
import org.springframework.context.annotation.Configuration;
import org.springframework.messaging.rsocket.RSocketRequester;

@Configuration
public class RSocketRequesterConfig {
    @Bean
    RSocketRequester requester(RSocketRequester.Builder builder) {
        return builder.tcp("localhost", 7635);
```

```
        }
    }
```

This streamlines the constructor for `PositionController`, placing the work for creating the `RSocketRequester` where it belongs and well outside of a controller class. To use the `RSocketRequester` bean in `PositionController`, I simply autowire it in using Spring Boot's constructor injection:

```
public PositionController(AircraftRepository repository,
                          RSocketRequester requester) {
    this.repository = repository;
    this.requester = requester;
}
```

 Testing the RSocket connection would require integration testing. While this section focuses on unit testing and not integration testing, it is still essential to decouple the construction of the RSocke tRequester from `PositionController` in order to isolate and properly unit test `PositionController`.

There is another source of logic that falls well outside of controller functionality that remains, this time involving the acquisition, then the storing and retrieving, of aircraft positions using the `AircraftRepository` bean. Typically when complex logic unrelated to a particular class finds its way into that class, it's best to extract it, as I did for the `RSocketRequester` bean. To relocate this somewhat complex and unrelated code outside of `PositionController`, I create a `PositionService` class and define it as a `@Service` bean available throughout the application. The `@Service` annotation is simply a more visually specific description of the oft-used `@Component` annotation:

```
import org.springframework.stereotype.Service;
import org.springframework.web.reactive.function.client.WebClient;
import reactor.core.publisher.Flux;
import reactor.core.publisher.Mono;

@Service
public class PositionService {
    private final AircraftRepository repo;
    private WebClient client = WebClient.create(
        "http://localhost:7634/aircraft");

    public PositionService(AircraftRepository repo) {
        this.repo = repo;
    }

    public Flux<Aircraft> getAllAircraft() {
        return repo.deleteAll()
                .thenMany(client.get()
                        .retrieve()
                        .bodyToFlux(Aircraft.class)
                        .filter(plane -> !plane.getReg().isEmpty()))
```

```
        .flatMap(repo::save)
        .thenMany(repo.findAll());
    }

    public Mono<Aircraft> getAircraftById(Long id) {
        return repo.findById(id);
    }

    public Flux<Aircraft> getAircraftByReg(String reg) {
        return repo.findAircraftByReg(reg);
    }
}
```

 Currently there is no findAircraftByReg() method defined within AircraftRepository. I address that prior to creating tests.

Although more work could be done (especially with regard to the WebClient member variable), it is sufficient for now to remove the complex logic shown in PositionService::getAllAircraft from its former home within PositionController::getCurrentAircraftPositions and inject the PositionSer vice bean into the controller for its use, resulting in a much cleaner and focused controller class:

```
import org.springframework.http.MediaType;
import org.springframework.messaging.rsocket.RSocketRequester;
import org.springframework.stereotype.Controller;
import org.springframework.ui.Model;
import org.springframework.web.bind.annotation.GetMapping;
import org.springframework.web.bind.annotation.ResponseBody;
import reactor.core.publisher.Flux;

@Controller
public class PositionController {
    private final PositionService service;
    private final RSocketRequester requester;

    public PositionController(PositionService service,
            RSocketRequester requester) {
        this.service = service;
        this.requester = requester;
    }

    @GetMapping("/aircraft")
    public String getCurrentAircraftPositions(Model model) {
        model.addAttribute("currentPositions", service.getAllAircraft());

        return "positions";
    }

    @ResponseBody
```

```
@GetMapping(value = "/acstream", produces =
    MediaType.TEXT_EVENT_STREAM_VALUE)
public Flux<Aircraft> getCurrentACPositionsStream() {
    return requester.route("acstream")
            .data("Requesting aircraft positions")
            .retrieveFlux(Aircraft.class);
    }
}
```

Reviewing the existing `PositionController` endpoints shows that they feed a Thymeleaf template (`public String getCurrentAircraftPositions(Model model)`) or require an external RSocket connection (`public Flux<Aircraft> getCurrentACPositionsStream()`). In order to isolate and test the Aircraft Positions application's ability to provide an external API, I need to expand the currently defined endpoints. I add two more endpoints mapped to *acpos* and *acpos/search* to create a basic, but flexible, API leveraging the methods I created within `PositionService`.

I first create a method to retrieve and return as JSON all positions of aircraft currently within range of our PlaneFinder service-enabled device. The `getCurrentACPositions()` method calls `PositionService::getAllAircraft` just as its counterpart `getCurrentAircraftPositions(Model model)`, but it returns JSON object values instead of adding them to the domain object model and redirecting to the template engine for display of an HTML page.

Next, I create a method for searching current aircraft positions by the unique position record identifier and by the aircraft registration number. The record (technically document, since this version of `Aircraft Positions` uses MongoDB) identifier is the database unique ID among the stored positions last retrieved from PlaneFinder. It is useful for retrieving a specific position record; but more useful from an aircraft perspective is the ability to search for an aircraft's unique registration number.

Interestingly, PlaneFinder may report a small number of positions reported by a single aircraft when queried. This is due to near-constant position reports being sent from aircraft in flight. What this means for us is that when searching by an aircraft's unique registration number within currently reported positions, we may actually retrieve 1+ position reports for that flight.

There are various ways to write a search mechanism with flexibility to accept different search criteria of different types returning different numbers of potential results, but I chose to incorporate all options within a single method:

```
@ResponseBody
@GetMapping("/acpos/search")
public Publisher<Aircraft>
        searchForACPosition(@RequestParam Map<String, String> searchParams) {

    if (!searchParams.isEmpty()) {
        Map.Entry<String, String> setToSearch =
                searchParams.entrySet().iterator().next();
```

```
        if (setToSearch.getKey().equalsIgnoreCase("id")) {
            return service.getAircraftById(Long.valueOf(setToSearch.getValue())));
        } else {
            return service.getAircraftByReg(setToSearch.getValue());
        }
    } else {
        return Mono.empty();
    }
}
```

Notes on searchForACPosition's Design and Implementation Decisions

First, @ResponseBody is necessary because I chose to combine REST endpoints with template-driving endpoints in the same Controller class. As mentioned previously, the @RestController meta-annotation includes both @Controller and @Response Body to indicate Object values are returned directly, versus via an HTML page's Domain Object Model (DOM). Since PositionController is annotated with only @Controller, it is necessary to add @ResponseBody to any methods I desire to return Object values directly.

Next, the @RequestParam annotation allows for the user to provide zero or more request parameters by appending a question mark (?) to an endpoint's mapping and specifying parameters in the format key=value, separated by a comma. In this example, I made the conscious choice to check only the first parameter (if any exist) for a key named "id"; if the request includes an id parameter, it is used to request the aircraft position document by its database ID. If the parameter is not id, I default to a search of aircraft registration numbers within the currently reported positions.

There are several tacit assumptions here that I might not make in a production system, including a default search for registrations, the intentional discard of any subsequent search parameters, and more. I leave these as a future exercise for myself and the reader.

One thing of note from the method signature: I return a Publisher, not specifically a Flux or Mono. This is necessary based on my decision to integrate search options into a single method and the fact that while searching for a position document within the database by the database ID will return no more than one match, searching by an aircraft's registration may yield multiple closely grouped position reports. Specifying a return value of Publisher for the method allows me to return either Mono or Flux, since both are specializations of Publisher.

Finally, if no search parameters are supplied by the user, I return an empty Mono using Mono.empty(). Your requirements may dictate the same outcome, or you may choose (or be required) to return a different result, such as all aircraft positions. Whatever the design decision, the Principle of Least Astonishment should inform the outcome.

The final (for now) version of the `PositionController` class should look something like this:

```java
import org.reactivestreams.Publisher;
import org.springframework.http.MediaType;
import org.springframework.messaging.rsocket.RSocketRequester;
import org.springframework.stereotype.Controller;
import org.springframework.ui.Model;
import org.springframework.web.bind.annotation.GetMapping;
import org.springframework.web.bind.annotation.RequestParam;
import org.springframework.web.bind.annotation.ResponseBody;
import reactor.core.publisher.Flux;
import reactor.core.publisher.Mono;

import java.util.Map;

@Controller
public class PositionController {
    private final PositionService service;
    private final RSocketRequester requester;

    public PositionController(PositionService service,
            RSocketRequester requester) {
        this.service = service;
        this.requester = requester;
    }

    @GetMapping("/aircraft")
    public String getCurrentAircraftPositions(Model model) {
        model.addAttribute("currentPositions", service.getAllAircraft());

        return "positions";
    }

    @ResponseBody
    @GetMapping("/acpos")
    public Flux<Aircraft> getCurrentACPositions() {
        return service.getAllAircraft();
    }

    @ResponseBody
    @GetMapping("/acpos/search")
    public Publisher<Aircraft> searchForACPosition(@RequestParam Map<String,
            String> searchParams) {

        if (!searchParams.isEmpty()) {
            Map.Entry<String, String> setToSearch =
                searchParams.entrySet().iterator().next();

            if (setToSearch.getKey().equalsIgnoreCase("id")) {
                return service.getAircraftById(Long.valueOf
                    (setToSearch.getValue()));
            } else {
                return service.getAircraftByReg(setToSearch.getValue());
            }
```

```
        } else {
            return Mono.empty();
        }
    }

    @ResponseBody
    @GetMapping(value = "/acstream", produces =
            MediaType.TEXT_EVENT_STREAM_VALUE)
    public Flux<Aircraft> getCurrentACPositionsStream() {
        return requester.route("acstream")
                .data("Requesting aircraft positions")
                .retrieveFlux(Aircraft.class);
    }
}
```

Next, I return to the `PositionService` class. As mentioned earlier, its `public Flux<Aircraft> getAircraftByReg(String reg)` method references a currently undefined method in `AircraftRepository`. To fix that, I add a `Flux<Aircraft> findAircraftByReg(String reg)` method to the `AircraftRepository` interface definition:

```
import org.springframework.data.repository.reactive.ReactiveCrudRepository;
import reactor.core.publisher.Flux;

public interface AircraftRepository extends
        ReactiveCrudRepository<Aircraft, Long> {
    Flux<Aircraft> findAircraftByReg(String reg);
}
```

This interesting bit of code, this single method signature, demonstrates the powerful Spring Data concept of query derivation using a set of widely applicable conventions: operators like `find`, `search`, or `get`, the specified type of objects stored/retrieved/managed (in this case `Aircraft`), and member variable names like `reg`. By declaring a method signature with parameters+types and return type using the method naming conventions mentioned, Spring Data can build the method implementation for you.

If you want or need to provide more specifics or hints, it's also possible to annotate the method signature with `@Query` and supply desired or required details. That isn't necessary for this case, as stating we wish to search aircraft positions by registration number and return 0+ values in a reactive streams `Flux` is ample information for Spring Data to create the implementation.

Returning to `PositionService`, the IDE now happily reports `repo.findAircraftByReg(reg)` as a valid method call.

Another design decision I made for this example was to have both getAircraftByXxx methods query the current position documents. This may be considered to assume some position documents exist in the database or that the user isn't concerned with a fresh retrieval if the database doesn't already contain any positions within. Your requirements may drive a different choice, such as verifying some positions are present prior to searching and if not executing a fresh retrieval with a call to getAllAircraft.

And Now, the Testing

In the earlier chapter on testing, standard Object types were used to test expected outcomes. I did use WebClient and WebTestClient, but only as the tool of choice for interacting with all HTTP-based endpoints, regardless of whether they returned reactive streams publisher types or not. Now, it's time to properly test those reactive streams semantics.

Using the existing PositionControllerTest class as a starting point, I retool it to accommodate the new reactive endpoints exposed by its counterpart class Position Controller. Here are the class-level details:

```
@WebFluxTest(controllers = {PositionController.class})
class PositionControllerTest {
    @Autowired
    private WebTestClient client;

    @MockBean
    private PositionService service;
    @MockBean
    private RSocketRequester requester;

    private Aircraft ac1, ac2, ac3;

    ...

}
```

First, I make the class-level annotation @WebFluxTest(controllers = {PositionCon troller.class}). I still use the reactive WebTestClient and wish to restrict the scope of this test class to WebFlux capabilities, so loading a full Spring Boot application context is unnecessary and wasteful of time and resources.

Second, I autowire a WebTestClient bean. In the earlier chapter on testing, I directly injected the WebTestClient bean into a single test method, but since it now will be needed in multiple methods, it makes more sense to create a member variable from which to reference it.

Third, I create mock beans using Mockito's @MockBean annotation. I mock the RSocketRequester bean simply because PositionController—which we request (and need) to be loaded in the class-level annotation—requires a bean, real or mocked, of an RSocketRequester. I mock the PositionService bean in order to mock and use its behavior within this class's tests. Mocking PositionService allows me to assure its proper behavior, exercise a consumer of its outputs (PositionCon troller), and compare the actual results with known expected results.

Finally, I create three Aircraft instances for use in the contained tests.

Prior to executing a JUnit @Test method, a method annotated with @BeforeEach is run to configure the scenario and expected results. This is the setUp() method I use to prepare the testing environment before each test method:

```
@BeforeEach
void setUp(ApplicationContext context) {
    // Spring Airlines flight 001 en route, flying STL to SFO,
    // at 30000' currently over Kansas City
    ac1 = new Aircraft(1L, "SAL001", "sqwk", "N12345", "SAL001",
            "STL-SFO", "LJ", "ct",
            30000, 280, 440, 0, 0,
            39.2979849, -94.71921, 0D, 0D, 0D,
            true, false,
            Instant.now(), Instant.now(), Instant.now());

    // Spring Airlines flight 002 en route, flying SFO to STL,
    // at 40000' currently over Denver
    ac2 = new Aircraft(2L, "SAL002", "sqwk", "N54321", "SAL002",
            "SFO-STL", "LJ", "ct",
            40000, 65, 440, 0, 0,
            39.8560963, -104.6759263, 0D, 0D, 0D,
            true, false,
            Instant.now(), Instant.now(), Instant.now());

    // Spring Airlines flight 002 en route, flying SFO to STL,
    // at 40000' currently just past DEN
    ac3 = new Aircraft(3L, "SAL002", "sqwk", "N54321", "SAL002",
            "SFO-STL", "LJ", "ct",
            40000, 65, 440, 0, 0,
            39.8412964, -105.0048267, 0D, 0D, 0D,
            true, false,
            Instant.now(), Instant.now(), Instant.now());


    Mockito.when(service.getAllAircraft()).thenReturn(Flux.just(ac1, ac2, ac3));
    Mockito.when(service.getAircraftById(1L)).thenReturn(Mono.just(ac1));
    Mockito.when(service.getAircraftById(2L)).thenReturn(Mono.just(ac2));
    Mockito.when(service.getAircraftById(3L)).thenReturn(Mono.just(ac3));
    Mockito.when(service.getAircraftByReg("N12345"))
        .thenReturn(Flux.just(ac1));
    Mockito.when(service.getAircraftByReg("N54321"))
        .thenReturn(Flux.just(ac2, ac3));
}
```

I assign an aircraft position for the aircraft with registration N12345 to the `ac1` member variable. For `ac2` and `ac3`, I assign positions very close to each other for the same aircraft, N54321, simulating a frequent case of closely updated position reports arriving from PlaneFinder.

The last several lines of the `setUp()` method define the behavior that the `Position Service` mock bean will provide when its methods are called in various ways. Similar to the method mocks in the earlier chapter on testing, the only difference of import is the types of return values; since the actual `PositionService` methods return Reactor `Publisher` types of `Flux` and `Mono`, so must the mock methods.

Test for retrieving all aircraft positions

Finally, I create a method to test the `PositionController` method `getCurrentACPositions()`:

```
@Test
void getCurrentACPositions() {
    StepVerifier.create(client.get()
            .uri("/acpos")
            .exchange()
            .expectStatus().isOk()
            .expectHeader().contentType(MediaType.APPLICATION_JSON)
            .returnResult(Aircraft.class)
            .getResponseBody())
        .expectNext(ac1)
        .expectNext(ac2)
        .expectNext(ac3)
        .verifyComplete();
}
```

Testing reactive streams applications can bring myriad challenges to what is often considered a pretty mundane (if prone to omission) effort of setting expected results, obtaining actual results, and comparing the two to determine test success or failure. Though multiple results *can* be obtained in an effectively instantaneous manner, just as with a blocking type of `Iterable`, reactive streams `Publishers` don't wait for a complete result set prior to returning it as a single unit. From a machine perspective, it's the difference between receiving one group of five all at once (for example) or receiving five results very quickly, but individually.

The core of Reactor's testing tools is the `StepVerifier` and its utility methods. `Step Verifier` subscribes to a `Publisher` and, as the name implies, enables the developer to consider results obtained as discrete values and verify each one. In the test for `getCurrentACPositions`, I perform the following actions:

- Create a StepVerifier.
- Supply it a Flux produced by the following steps:
  - — Use the WebTestClient bean.
  - — Access the PositionController::getCurrentACPositions method mapped to the */acpos* endpoint.
  - — Initiate the exchange().
  - — Verify a response status of 200 OK.
  - — Verify the response header has a content type of "application/json".
  - — Return the result items as instances of the Aircraft class.
  - — GET the response.
- Evaluate the actual first value against the expected first value ac1.
- Evaluate the actual second value against the expected second value ac2.
- Evaluate the actual third value against the expected third value ac3.
- Verify all actions and receipt of Publisher completion signal.

This is quite an exhaustive evaluation of expected behavior, including conditions and values returned. Running the test results in output similar to the following (trimmed to fit page):

```
  .   ___          _            __ _ _
 /\\ / ___'_ __ _ _(_)_ __  __ _ \ \ \ \
( ( )\___ | '_ | '_| | '_ \/ _` | \ \ \ \
 \\/  ___)| |_)| | | | | || (_| |  ) ) ) )
  '  |____| .__|_| |_|_| |_\__, | / / / /
 =========|_|==============|___/=/_/_/_/
 :: Spring Boot ::              (v2.4.0)

 : Starting PositionControllerTest on mheckler-a01.vmware.com with PID 21211
 : No active profile set, falling back to default profiles: default
 : Started PositionControllerTest in 2.19 seconds (JVM running for 2.879)

 Process finished with exit code 0
```

Run from the IDE, the result will look similar to that shown in Figure 12-1.

Test Results	303 ms
▼ ✓ PositionControllerTest	303 ms
✓ getCurrentACPositions()	303 ms

Figure 12-1. Successful test

Testing Aircraft Positions search capabilities

Testing the search functionality within `PositionController::searchForACPosition` requires a minimum of two separate tests due to the ability to handle searches for aircraft positions by database document ID and aircraft registration numbers.

To test searching by database document identifier, I create the following unit test:

```
@Test
void searchForACPositionById() {
    StepVerifier.create(client.get()
            .uri("/acpos/search?id=1")
            .exchange()
            .expectStatus().isOk()
            .expectHeader().contentType(MediaType.APPLICATION_JSON)
            .returnResult(Aircraft.class)
            .getResponseBody())
        .expectNext(ac1)
        .verifyComplete();
}
```

This is similar to the unit test for all aircraft positions. There are two notable exceptions:

- The specified URI references the search endpoint and includes the search parameter `id=1` to retrieve `ac1`.

- The expected result is only `ac1`, as indicated in the `expectNext(ac1)` chained operation.

To test searching for aircraft positions by an aircraft registration number, I create the following unit test, using a registration that I've mocked to include two corresponding position documents:

```
@Test
void searchForACPositionByReg() {
    StepVerifier.create(client.get()
            .uri("/acpos/search?reg=N54321")
            .exchange()
            .expectStatus().isOk()
            .expectHeader().contentType(MediaType.APPLICATION_JSON)
            .returnResult(Aircraft.class)
            .getResponseBody())
        .expectNext(ac2)
        .expectNext(ac3)
        .verifyComplete();
}
```

The differences between this test and the previous one are minimal:

- The URI includes the search parameter `reg=N54321` and should result in the return of both `ac2` and `ac3`, both of which contain reported positions for the aircraft with registration number N54321.

- Expected results are verified to be `ac2` and `ac3` with the `expectNext(ac2)` and `expectNext(ac3)` chained operations.

The final state of the `PositionControllerTest` class is shown in the following listing:

```java
import org.junit.jupiter.api.AfterEach;
import org.junit.jupiter.api.BeforeEach;
import org.junit.jupiter.api.Test;
import org.mockito.Mockito;
import org.springframework.beans.factory.annotation.Autowired;
import org.springframework.boot.test.autoconfigure.web.reactive.WebFluxTest;
import org.springframework.boot.test.mock.mockito.MockBean;
import org.springframework.http.MediaType;
import org.springframework.messaging.rsocket.RSocketRequester;
import org.springframework.test.web.reactive.server.WebTestClient;
import reactor.core.publisher.Flux;
import reactor.core.publisher.Mono;
import reactor.test.StepVerifier;

import java.time.Instant;

@WebFluxTest(controllers = {PositionController.class})
class PositionControllerTest {
    @Autowired
    private WebTestClient client;

    @MockBean
    private PositionService service;
    @MockBean
    private RSocketRequester requester;

    private Aircraft ac1, ac2, ac3;

    @BeforeEach
    void setUp() {
        // Spring Airlines flight 001 en route, flying STL to SFO, at 30000'
        // currently over Kansas City
        ac1 = new Aircraft(1L, "SAL001", "sqwk", "N12345", "SAL001",
                "STL-SFO", "LJ", "ct",
                30000, 280, 440, 0, 0,
                39.2979849, -94.71921, 0D, 0D, 0D,
                true, false,
                Instant.now(), Instant.now(), Instant.now());

        // Spring Airlines flight 002 en route, flying SFO to STL, at 40000'
        // currently over Denver
        ac2 = new Aircraft(2L, "SAL002", "sqwk", "N54321", "SAL002",
                "SFO-STL", "LJ", "ct",
                40000, 65, 440, 0, 0,
                39.8560963, -104.6759263, 0D, 0D, 0D,
                true, false,
                Instant.now(), Instant.now(), Instant.now());

        // Spring Airlines flight 002 en route, flying SFO to STL, at 40000'
        // currently just past DEN
```

```java
        ac3 = new Aircraft(3L, "SAL002", "sqwk", "N54321", "SAL002",
                "SFO-STL", "LJ", "ct",
                40000, 65, 440, 0, 0,
                39.8412964, -105.0048267, 0D, 0D, 0D,
                true, false,
                Instant.now(), Instant.now(), Instant.now());


        Mockito.when(service.getAllAircraft())
                .thenReturn(Flux.just(ac1, ac2, ac3));
        Mockito.when(service.getAircraftById(1L))
                .thenReturn(Mono.just(ac1));
        Mockito.when(service.getAircraftById(2L))
                .thenReturn(Mono.just(ac2));
        Mockito.when(service.getAircraftById(3L))
                .thenReturn(Mono.just(ac3));
        Mockito.when(service.getAircraftByReg("N12345"))
                .thenReturn(Flux.just(ac1));
        Mockito.when(service.getAircraftByReg("N54321"))
                .thenReturn(Flux.just(ac2, ac3));
    }

    @AfterEach
    void tearDown() {
    }

    @Test
    void getCurrentACPositions() {
        StepVerifier.create(client.get()
                .uri("/acpos")
                .exchange()
                .expectStatus().isOk()
                .expectHeader().contentType(MediaType.APPLICATION_JSON)
                .returnResult(Aircraft.class)
                .getResponseBody())
            .expectNext(ac1)
            .expectNext(ac2)
            .expectNext(ac3)
            .verifyComplete();
    }

    @Test
    void searchForACPositionById() {
        StepVerifier.create(client.get()
                .uri("/acpos/search?id=1")
                .exchange()
                .expectStatus().isOk()
                .expectHeader().contentType(MediaType.APPLICATION_JSON)
                .returnResult(Aircraft.class)
                .getResponseBody())
            .expectNext(ac1)
            .verifyComplete();
    }

    @Test
    void searchForACPositionByReg() {
```

```
StepVerifier.create(client.get()
        .uri("/acpos/search?reg=N54321")
        .exchange()
        .expectStatus().isOk()
        .expectHeader().contentType(MediaType.APPLICATION_JSON)
        .returnResult(Aircraft.class)
        .getResponseBody())
    .expectNext(ac2)
    .expectNext(ac3)
    .verifyComplete();
    }
}
```

Executing all tests within the `PositionControllerTest` class provides the gratifying results shown in Figure 12-2.

Test Results	325 ms
▼ ✓ PositionControllerTest	325 ms
✓ searchForACPositionByReg()	302 ms
✓ getCurrentACPositions()	11 ms
✓ searchForACPositionById()	12 ms

Figure 12-2. Successful execution of all unit tests

> `StepVerifier` enables more testing possibilities, a few of which have been hinted at in this section. Of particular interest is the `StepVerifier::withVirtualTime` method that enables tests of publishers that emit values sporadically to be compressed, producing results instantaneously that might ordinarily be spaced over extensive periods of time. `StepVerifier::withVirtualTime` accepts a `Supplier<Publisher>` instead of a `Publisher` directly, but otherwise the mechanics of its use are quite similar.

These are essential elements of testing reactive Spring Boot applications. But what happens when you encounter issues in production? What tools does Reactor offer for identification and resolution of issues when your app goes live?

Diagnosing and Debugging Reactive Applications

When things go sideways in typical Java applications, there is usually a stacktrace. A useful (if sometimes voluminous) stacktrace can be produced by imperative code for several reasons, but at a high level, two factors enable this helpful information to be collected and shown:

- Sequential execution of code that typically dictates how to do something (imperative)

- Execution of that sequential code occurs within a single thread

There are exceptions to every rule, but generally speaking, this is the common combination that allows for the capture of steps executed sequentially up to the time an error was encountered: everything happens one step at a time in a single swimlane. It may not leverage full system resources as effectively, and it generally doesn't, but it makes isolating and resolving issues a much simpler affair.

Enter reactive streams. Project Reactor and other reactive streams implementations use schedulers to manage and use those other threads. Resources that would typically have remained idle or underutilized can be put to work to enable reactive applications to scale far beyond their blocking counterparts. I would refer you to the Reactor Core documentation (*https://projectreactor.io/docs/core/release/reference*) for more details regarding Schedulers and the options available for controlling how they can be used and tuned, but suffice it to say for now that Reactor does a fine job handling scheduling automatically in the vast majority of circumstances.

This does highlight one challenge with producing a meaningful execution trace for a reactive Spring Boot (or any reactive) application, however. One can't expect to simply follow a single thread's activity and produce a meaningful sequential list of code executed.

Compounding the difficulty of tracing execution due to this thread-hopping optimizing feature is that reactive programming separates code *assembly* from code *execution*. As mentioned in Chapter 8, in most cases for most Publisher types, nothing happens until you *subscribe*.

Simply put, it's unlikely that you will ever see a production failure that points to an issue with the code where you declaratively assembled the Publisher (whether Flux or Mono) pipeline of operations. Failures nearly universally occur at the point the pipeline becomes active: producing, processing, and passing values to a Subscriber.

This distancing between code assembly and execution and Reactor's ability to utilize multiple threads to complete a chain of operations necessitates better tooling to effectively troubleshoot errors that surface at runtime. Fortunately, Reactor provides several excellent options.

Hooks.onOperatorDebug()

This is not to imply that troubleshooting reactive applications using existing stack-trace results is impossible, only that it could be significantly improved upon. As with most things, the proof is in the code—or in this case, the logged, post failure output.

To simulate a failure in a reactive Publisher chain of operators, I revisit the Position ControllerTest class and change one line of code in the setUp() method run before each test's execution:

```
Mockito.when(service.getAllAircraft()).thenReturn(Flux.just(ac1, ac2, ac3));
```

I replace the properly operating Flux produced by the mock getAllAircraft() method with one that includes an error in the resultant stream of values:

```
Mockito.when(service.getAllAircraft()).thenReturn(
    Flux.just(ac1, ac2, ac3)
        .concatWith(Flux.error(new Throwable("Bad position report")))
);
```

Next, I execute the test for getCurrentACPositions() to see the results of our intentional Flux sabotage (wrapped to fit page):

```
500 Server Error for HTTP GET "/acpos"

java.lang.Throwable: Bad position report
        at com.thehecklers.aircraftpositions.PositionControllerTest
.setUp(PositionControllerTest.java:59) ~[test-classes/:na]
        Suppressed: reactor.core.publisher.FluxOnAssembly$OnAssemblyException:
Error has been observed at the following site(s):
        |_ checkpoint → Handler com.thehecklers.aircraftpositions
.PositionController
        #getCurrentACPositions() [DispatcherHandler]
        |_ checkpoint → HTTP GET "/acpos" [ExceptionHandlingWebHandler]
Stack trace:
                at com.thehecklers.aircraftpositions.PositionControllerTest
.setUp(PositionControllerTest.java:59) ~[test-classes/:na]
                at java.base/jdk.internal.reflect.NativeMethodAccessorImpl
.invoke0(Native Method) ~[na:na]
                at java.base/jdk.internal.reflect.NativeMethodAccessorImpl
.invoke(NativeMethodAccessorImpl.java:62) ~[na:na]
                at java.base/jdk.internal.reflect.DelegatingMethodAccessorImpl
.invoke(DelegatingMethodAccessorImpl.java:43) ~[na:na]
                at java.base/java.lang.reflect.Method
.invoke(Method.java:564) ~[na:na]
                at org.junit.platform.commons.util.ReflectionUtils
.invokeMethod(ReflectionUtils.java:686)
                ~[junit-platform-commons-1.6.2.jar:1.6.2]
                at org.junit.jupiter.engine.execution.MethodInvocation
.proceed(MethodInvocation.java:60)
                        ~[junit-jupiter-engine-5.6.2.jar:5.6.2]
                at org.junit.jupiter.engine.execution.InvocationInterceptorChain
$ValidatingInvocation.proceed(InvocationInterceptorChain.java:131)
                ~[junit-jupiter-engine-5.6.2.jar:5.6.2]
                at org.junit.jupiter.engine.extension.TimeoutExtension
.intercept(TimeoutExtension.java:149)
                ~[junit-jupiter-engine-5.6.2.jar:5.6.2]
                at org.junit.jupiter.engine.extension.TimeoutExtension
.interceptLifecycleMethod(TimeoutExtension.java:126)
                ~[junit-jupiter-engine-5.6.2.jar:5.6.2]
                at org.junit.jupiter.engine.extension.TimeoutExtension
.interceptBeforeEachMethod(TimeoutExtension.java:76)
                ~[junit-jupiter-engine-5.6.2.jar:5.6.2]
                at org.junit.jupiter.engine.execution
.ExecutableInvoker$ReflectiveInterceptorCall.lambda$ofVoidMethod
                $0(ExecutableInvoker.java:115)
```

```
    ~[junit-jupiter-engine-5.6.2.jar:5.6.2]
        at org.junit.jupiter.engine.execution.ExecutableInvoker
.lambda$invoke$0(ExecutableInvoker.java:105)
    ~[junit-jupiter-engine-5.6.2.jar:5.6.2]
        at org.junit.jupiter.engine.execution.InvocationInterceptorChain
$InterceptedInvocation.proceed(InvocationInterceptorChain.java:106)
    ~[junit-jupiter-engine-5.6.2.jar:5.6.2]
        at org.junit.jupiter.engine.execution.InvocationInterceptorChain
.proceed(InvocationInterceptorChain.java:64)
    ~[junit-jupiter-engine-5.6.2.jar:5.6.2]
        at org.junit.jupiter.engine.execution.InvocationInterceptorChain
.chainAndInvoke(InvocationInterceptorChain.java:45)
    ~[junit-jupiter-engine-5.6.2.jar:5.6.2]
        at org.junit.jupiter.engine.execution.InvocationInterceptorChain
.invoke(InvocationInterceptorChain.java:37)
    ~[junit-jupiter-engine-5.6.2.jar:5.6.2]
        at org.junit.jupiter.engine.execution.ExecutableInvoker
.invoke(ExecutableInvoker.java:104)
    ~[junit-jupiter-engine-5.6.2.jar:5.6.2]
        at org.junit.jupiter.engine.execution.ExecutableInvoker
.invoke(ExecutableInvoker.java:98)
    ~[junit-jupiter-engine-5.6.2.jar:5.6.2]
        at org.junit.jupiter.engine.descriptor.ClassBasedTestDescriptor
.invokeMethodInExtensionContext(ClassBasedTestDescriptor.java:481)
    ~[junit-jupiter-engine-5.6.2.jar:5.6.2]
        at org.junit.jupiter.engine.descriptor.ClassBasedTestDescriptor
.lambda$synthesizeBeforeEachMethodAdapter
    $18(ClassBasedTestDescriptor.java:466)
    ~[junit-jupiter-engine-5.6.2.jar:5.6.2]
        at org.junit.jupiter.engine.descriptor.TestMethodTestDescriptor
.lambda$invokeBeforeEachMethods$2(TestMethodTestDescriptor.java:169)
    ~[junit-jupiter-engine-5.6.2.jar:5.6.2]
        at org.junit.jupiter.engine.descriptor.TestMethodTestDescriptor
.lambda$invokeBeforeMethodsOrCallbacksUntilExceptionOccurs
    $5(TestMethodTestDescriptor.java:197)
     ~[junit-jupiter-engine-5.6.2.jar:5.6.2]
        at org.junit.platform.engine.support.hierarchical.ThrowableCollector
.execute(ThrowableCollector.java:73)
     ~[junit-platform-engine-1.6.2.jar:1.6.2]
        at org.junit.jupiter.engine.descriptor.TestMethodTestDescriptor
.invokeBeforeMethodsOrCallbacksUntilExceptionOccurs
    (TestMethodTestDescriptor.java:197)
     ~[junit-jupiter-engine-5.6.2.jar:5.6.2]
        at org.junit.jupiter.engine.descriptor.TestMethodTestDescriptor
.invokeBeforeEachMethods(TestMethodTestDescriptor.java:166)
     ~[junit-jupiter-engine-5.6.2.jar:5.6.2]
        at org.junit.jupiter.engine.descriptor.TestMethodTestDescriptor
.execute(TestMethodTestDescriptor.java:133)
     ~[junit-jupiter-engine-5.6.2.jar:5.6.2]
        at org.junit.jupiter.engine.descriptor.TestMethodTestDescriptor
.execute(TestMethodTestDescriptor.java:71)
     ~[junit-jupiter-engine-5.6.2.jar:5.6.2]
        at org.junit.platform.engine.support.hierarchical.NodeTestTask
.lambda$executeRecursively$5(NodeTestTask.java:135)
     ~[junit-platform-engine-1.6.2.jar:1.6.2]
        at org.junit.platform.engine.support.hierarchical.ThrowableCollector
```

```
            .execute(ThrowableCollector.java:73)
                ~[junit-platform-engine-1.6.2.jar:1.6.2]
                    at org.junit.platform.engine.support.hierarchical.NodeTestTask
            .lambda$executeRecursively$7(NodeTestTask.java:125)
                ~[junit-platform-engine-1.6.2.jar:1.6.2]
                    at org.junit.platform.engine.support.hierarchical.Node
            .around(Node.java:135) ~[junit-platform-engine-1.6.2.jar:1.6.2]
                    at org.junit.platform.engine.support.hierarchical.NodeTestTask
            .lambda$executeRecursively$8(NodeTestTask.java:123)
                ~[junit-platform-engine-1.6.2.jar:1.6.2]
                    at org.junit.platform.engine.support.hierarchical.ThrowableCollector
            .execute(ThrowableCollector.java:73)
                ~[junit-platform-engine-1.6.2.jar:1.6.2]
                    at org.junit.platform.engine.support.hierarchical.NodeTestTask
            .executeRecursively(NodeTestTask.java:122)
                ~[junit-platform-engine-1.6.2.jar:1.6.2]
                    at org.junit.platform.engine.support.hierarchical.NodeTestTask
            .execute(NodeTestTask.java:80)
                ~[junit-platform-engine-1.6.2.jar:1.6.2]
                    at java.base/java.util.ArrayList.forEach(ArrayList.java:1510) ~[na:na]
                    at org.junit.platform.engine.support.hierarchical
            .SameThreadHierarchicalTestExecutorService
                .invokeAll(SameThreadHierarchicalTestExecutorService.java:38)
                    ~[junit-platform-engine-1.6.2.jar:1.6.2]
                    at org.junit.platform.engine.support.hierarchical.NodeTestTask
            .lambda$executeRecursively$5(NodeTestTask.java:139)
                ~[junit-platform-engine-1.6.2.jar:1.6.2]
                    at org.junit.platform.engine.support.hierarchical.ThrowableCollector
            .execute(ThrowableCollector.java:73)
                ~[junit-platform-engine-1.6.2.jar:1.6.2]
                    at org.junit.platform.engine.support.hierarchical.NodeTestTask
            .lambda$executeRecursively$7(NodeTestTask.java:125)
                ~[junit-platform-engine-1.6.2.jar:1.6.2]
                    at org.junit.platform.engine.support.hierarchical.Node
            .around(Node.java:135) ~[junit-platform-engine-1.6.2.jar:1.6.2]
                    at org.junit.platform.engine.support.hierarchical.NodeTestTask
            .lambda$executeRecursively$8(NodeTestTask.java:123)
                ~[junit-platform-engine-1.6.2.jar:1.6.2]
                    at org.junit.platform.engine.support.hierarchical.ThrowableCollector
            .execute(ThrowableCollector.java:73)
                ~[junit-platform-engine-1.6.2.jar:1.6.2]
                    at org.junit.platform.engine.support.hierarchical.NodeTestTask
            .executeRecursively(NodeTestTask.java:122)
                ~[junit-platform-engine-1.6.2.jar:1.6.2]
                    at org.junit.platform.engine.support.hierarchical.NodeTestTask
            .execute(NodeTestTask.java:80)
                ~[junit-platform-engine-1.6.2.jar:1.6.2]
                    at java.base/java.util.ArrayList.forEach(ArrayList.java:1510) ~[na:na]
                    at org.junit.platform.engine.support.hierarchical
            .SameThreadHierarchicalTestExecutorService
                .invokeAll(SameThreadHierarchicalTestExecutorService.java:38)
                    ~[junit-platform-engine-1.6.2.jar:1.6.2]
                    at org.junit.platform.engine.support.hierarchical.NodeTestTask
            .lambda$executeRecursively$5(NodeTestTask.java:139)
                ~[junit-platform-engine-1.6.2.jar:1.6.2]
                    at org.junit.platform.engine.support.hierarchical.ThrowableCollector
```

```
.execute(ThrowableCollector.java:73)
    ~[junit-platform-engine-1.6.2.jar:1.6.2]
        at org.junit.platform.engine.support.hierarchical.NodeTestTask
.lambda$executeRecursively$7(NodeTestTask.java:125)
    ~[junit-platform-engine-1.6.2.jar:1.6.2]
        at org.junit.platform.engine.support.hierarchical.Node
.around(Node.java:135) ~[junit-platform-engine-1.6.2.jar:1.6.2]
        at org.junit.platform.engine.support.hierarchical.NodeTestTask
.lambda$executeRecursively$8(NodeTestTask.java:123)
    ~[junit-platform-engine-1.6.2.jar:1.6.2]
        at org.junit.platform.engine.support.hierarchical.ThrowableCollector
.execute(ThrowableCollector.java:73)
    ~[junit-platform-engine-1.6.2.jar:1.6.2]
        at org.junit.platform.engine.support.hierarchical.NodeTestTask
.executeRecursively(NodeTestTask.java:122)
    ~[junit-platform-engine-1.6.2.jar:1.6.2]
        at org.junit.platform.engine.support.hierarchical.NodeTestTask
.execute(NodeTestTask.java:80)
    ~[junit-platform-engine-1.6.2.jar:1.6.2]
        at org.junit.platform.engine.support.hierarchical
.SameThreadHierarchicalTestExecutorService
    .submit(SameThreadHierarchicalTestExecutorService.java:32)
        ~[junit-platform-engine-1.6.2.jar:1.6.2]
        at org.junit.platform.engine.support.hierarchical
.HierarchicalTestExecutor.execute(HierarchicalTestExecutor.java:57)
    ~[junit-platform-engine-1.6.2.jar:1.6.2]
        at org.junit.platform.engine.support.hierarchical
.HierarchicalTestEngine.execute(HierarchicalTestEngine.java:51)
    ~[junit-platform-engine-1.6.2.jar:1.6.2]
        at org.junit.platform.launcher.core.DefaultLauncher
.execute(DefaultLauncher.java:248)
    ~[junit-platform-launcher-1.6.2.jar:1.6.2]
        at org.junit.platform.launcher.core.DefaultLauncher
.lambda$execute$5(DefaultLauncher.java:211)
    ~[junit-platform-launcher-1.6.2.jar:1.6.2]
        at org.junit.platform.launcher.core.DefaultLauncher
.withInterceptedStreams(DefaultLauncher.java:226)
    ~[junit-platform-launcher-1.6.2.jar:1.6.2]
        at org.junit.platform.launcher.core.DefaultLauncher
.execute(DefaultLauncher.java:199)
    ~[junit-platform-launcher-1.6.2.jar:1.6.2]
        at org.junit.platform.launcher.core.DefaultLauncher
.execute(DefaultLauncher.java:132)
    ~[junit-platform-launcher-1.6.2.jar:1.6.2]
        at com.intellij.junit5.JUnit5IdeaTestRunner
.startRunnerWithArgs(JUnit5IdeaTestRunner.java:69)
    ~[junit5-rt.jar:na]
        at com.intellij.rt.junit.IdeaTestRunner$Repeater
.startRunnerWithArgs(IdeaTestRunner.java:33)
    ~[junit-rt.jar:na]
        at com.intellij.rt.junit.JUnitStarter
.prepareStreamsAndStart(JUnitStarter.java:230)
    ~[junit-rt.jar:na]
        at com.intellij.rt.junit.JUnitStarter
.main(JUnitStarter.java:58) ~[junit-rt.jar:na]
```

```
java.lang.AssertionError: Status expected:<200 OK>
    but was:<500 INTERNAL_SERVER_ERROR>

> GET /acpos
> WebTestClient-Request-Id: [1]

No content

< 500 INTERNAL_SERVER_ERROR Internal Server Error
< Content-Type: [application/json]
< Content-Length: [142]
```

{"timestamp":"2020-11-09T15:41:12.516+00:00","path":"/acpos","status":500,
      "error":"Internal Server Error","message":"","requestId":"699a523c"}

```
    at org.springframework.test.web.reactive.server.ExchangeResult
.assertWithDiagnostics(ExchangeResult.java:209)
    at org.springframework.test.web.reactive.server.StatusAssertions
.assertStatusAndReturn(StatusAssertions.java:227)
    at org.springframework.test.web.reactive.server.StatusAssertions
.isOk(StatusAssertions.java:67)
    at com.thehecklers.aircraftpositions.PositionControllerTest
.getCurrentACPositions(PositionControllerTest.java:90)
    at java.base/jdk.internal.reflect.NativeMethodAccessorImpl
.invoke0(Native Method)
    at java.base/jdk.internal.reflect.NativeMethodAccessorImpl
.invoke(NativeMethodAccessorImpl.java:62)
    at java.base/jdk.internal.reflect.DelegatingMethodAccessorImpl
.invoke(DelegatingMethodAccessorImpl.java:43)
    at java.base/java.lang.reflect.Method.invoke(Method.java:564)
    at org.junit.platform.commons.util.ReflectionUtils
.invokeMethod(ReflectionUtils.java:686)
    at org.junit.jupiter.engine.execution.MethodInvocation
.proceed(MethodInvocation.java:60)
    at org.junit.jupiter.engine.execution.InvocationInterceptorChain
$ValidatingInvocation.proceed(InvocationInterceptorChain.java:131)
    at org.junit.jupiter.engine.extension.TimeoutExtension
.intercept(TimeoutExtension.java:149)
    at org.junit.jupiter.engine.extension.TimeoutExtension
.interceptTestableMethod(TimeoutExtension.java:140)
    at org.junit.jupiter.engine.extension.TimeoutExtension
.interceptTestMethod(TimeoutExtension.java:84)
    at org.junit.jupiter.engine.execution.ExecutableInvoker
$ReflectiveInterceptorCall
    .lambda$ofVoidMethod$0(ExecutableInvoker.java:115)
    at org.junit.jupiter.engine.execution.ExecutableInvoker
.lambda$invoke$0(ExecutableInvoker.java:105)
    at org.junit.jupiter.engine.execution.InvocationInterceptorChain
$InterceptedInvocation.proceed(InvocationInterceptorChain.java:106)
    at org.junit.jupiter.engine.execution.InvocationInterceptorChain
.proceed(InvocationInterceptorChain.java:64)
    at org.junit.jupiter.engine.execution.InvocationInterceptorChain
.chainAndInvoke(InvocationInterceptorChain.java:45)
    at org.junit.jupiter.engine.execution.InvocationInterceptorChain
.invoke(InvocationInterceptorChain.java:37)
```

```
        at org.junit.jupiter.engine.execution.ExecutableInvoker
.invoke(ExecutableInvoker.java:104)
        at org.junit.jupiter.engine.execution.ExecutableInvoker
.invoke(ExecutableInvoker.java:98)
        at org.junit.jupiter.engine.descriptor.TestMethodTestDescriptor
.lambda$invokeTestMethod$6(TestMethodTestDescriptor.java:212)
        at org.junit.platform.engine.support.hierarchical.ThrowableCollector
.execute(ThrowableCollector.java:73)
        at org.junit.jupiter.engine.descriptor.TestMethodTestDescriptor
.invokeTestMethod(TestMethodTestDescriptor.java:208)
        at org.junit.jupiter.engine.descriptor.TestMethodTestDescriptor
.execute(TestMethodTestDescriptor.java:137)
        at org.junit.jupiter.engine.descriptor.TestMethodTestDescriptor
.execute(TestMethodTestDescriptor.java:71)
        at org.junit.platform.engine.support.hierarchical.NodeTestTask
.lambda$executeRecursively$5(NodeTestTask.java:135)
        at org.junit.platform.engine.support.hierarchical.ThrowableCollector
.execute(ThrowableCollector.java:73)
        at org.junit.platform.engine.support.hierarchical.NodeTestTask
.lambda$executeRecursively$7(NodeTestTask.java:125)
        at org.junit.platform.engine.support.hierarchical.Node.around(Node.java:135)
        at org.junit.platform.engine.support.hierarchical.NodeTestTask
.lambda$executeRecursively$8(NodeTestTask.java:123)
        at org.junit.platform.engine.support.hierarchical.ThrowableCollector
.execute(ThrowableCollector.java:73)
        at org.junit.platform.engine.support.hierarchical.NodeTestTask
.executeRecursively(NodeTestTask.java:122)
        at org.junit.platform.engine.support.hierarchical.NodeTestTask
.execute(NodeTestTask.java:80)
        at java.base/java.util.ArrayList.forEach(ArrayList.java:1510)
        at org.junit.platform.engine.support.hierarchical
.SameThreadHierarchicalTestExecutorService
        .invokeAll(SameThreadHierarchicalTestExecutorService.java:38)
        at org.junit.platform.engine.support.hierarchical.NodeTestTask
.lambda$executeRecursively$5(NodeTestTask.java:139)
        at org.junit.platform.engine.support.hierarchical.ThrowableCollector
.execute(ThrowableCollector.java:73)
        at org.junit.platform.engine.support.hierarchical.NodeTestTask
.lambda$executeRecursively$7(NodeTestTask.java:125)
        at org.junit.platform.engine.support.hierarchical.Node.around(Node.java:135)
        at org.junit.platform.engine.support.hierarchical.NodeTestTask
.lambda$executeRecursively$8(NodeTestTask.java:123)
        at org.junit.platform.engine.support.hierarchical.ThrowableCollector
.execute(ThrowableCollector.java:73)
        at org.junit.platform.engine.support.hierarchical.NodeTestTask
.executeRecursively(NodeTestTask.java:122)
        at org.junit.platform.engine.support.hierarchical.NodeTestTask
.execute(NodeTestTask.java:80)
        at java.base/java.util.ArrayList.forEach(ArrayList.java:1510)
        at org.junit.platform.engine.support.hierarchical
.SameThreadHierarchicalTestExecutorService
        .invokeAll(SameThreadHierarchicalTestExecutorService.java:38)
        at org.junit.platform.engine.support.hierarchical.NodeTestTask
.lambda$executeRecursively$5(NodeTestTask.java:139)
        at org.junit.platform.engine.support.hierarchical.ThrowableCollector
.execute(ThrowableCollector.java:73)
```

```
        at org.junit.platform.engine.support.hierarchical.NodeTestTask
.lambda$executeRecursively$7(NodeTestTask.java:125)
        at org.junit.platform.engine.support.hierarchical.Node.around(Node.java:135)
        at org.junit.platform.engine.support.hierarchical.NodeTestTask
.lambda$executeRecursively$8(NodeTestTask.java:123)
        at org.junit.platform.engine.support.hierarchical.ThrowableCollector
.execute(ThrowableCollector.java:73)
        at org.junit.platform.engine.support.hierarchical.NodeTestTask
.executeRecursively(NodeTestTask.java:122)
        at org.junit.platform.engine.support.hierarchical.NodeTestTask
.execute(NodeTestTask.java:80)
        at org.junit.platform.engine.support.hierarchical
.SameThreadHierarchicalTestExecutorService
        .submit(SameThreadHierarchicalTestExecutorService.java:32)
        at org.junit.platform.engine.support.hierarchical.HierarchicalTestExecutor
.execute(HierarchicalTestExecutor.java:57)
        at org.junit.platform.engine.support.hierarchical.HierarchicalTestEngine
.execute(HierarchicalTestEngine.java:51)
        at org.junit.platform.launcher.core.DefaultLauncher
.execute(DefaultLauncher.java:248)
        at org.junit.platform.launcher.core.DefaultLauncher
.lambda$execute$5(DefaultLauncher.java:211)
        at org.junit.platform.launcher.core.DefaultLauncher
.withInterceptedStreams(DefaultLauncher.java:226)
        at org.junit.platform.launcher.core.DefaultLauncher
.execute(DefaultLauncher.java:199)
        at org.junit.platform.launcher.core.DefaultLauncher
.execute(DefaultLauncher.java:132)
        at com.intellij.junit5.JUnit5IdeaTestRunner
.startRunnerWithArgs(JUnit5IdeaTestRunner.java:69)
        at com.intellij.rt.junit.IdeaTestRunner$Repeater
.startRunnerWithArgs(IdeaTestRunner.java:33)
        at com.intellij.rt.junit.JUnitStarter
.prepareStreamsAndStart(JUnitStarter.java:230)
        at com.intellij.rt.junit.JUnitStarter
.main(JUnitStarter.java:58)
Caused by: java.lang.AssertionError: Status expected:<200 OK>
        but was:<500 INTERNAL_SERVER_ERROR>
        at org.springframework.test.util.AssertionErrors
.fail(AssertionErrors.java:59)
        at org.springframework.test.util.AssertionErrors
.assertEquals(AssertionErrors.java:122)
        at org.springframework.test.web.reactive.server.StatusAssertions
.lambda$assertStatusAndReturn$4(StatusAssertions.java:227)
        at org.springframework.test.web.reactive.server.ExchangeResult
.assertWithDiagnostics(ExchangeResult.java:206)
        ... 66 more
```

As you can see, the volume of information for a single bad value is quite difficult to digest. Useful information is present, but it's overwhelmed by excessive, less-helpful data.

I reluctantly but deliberately included the full output resulting from the preceding Flux error to show how difficult it can be to navigate the usual output when a Publisher encounters an error and to contrast it with how dramatically available tools reduce the noise and boost the signal of key information. Getting to the core of the problem reduces frustration in development, but it is absolutely critical when troubleshooting business-critical applications in production.

Project Reactor includes configurable life cycle callbacks called *hooks*, available via its Hooks class. One operator that is particularly useful for increasing the signal to noise ratio when things go awry is onOperatorDebug().

Calling Hooks.onOperatorDebug() prior to instantiation of the failing Publisher enables assembly-time instrumentation of all subsequent instances of type Publisher (and subtypes). In order to ensure capture of the necessary information at the necessary time(s), the call is usually placed in the application's main method as follows:

```
import org.springframework.boot.SpringApplication;
import org.springframework.boot.autoconfigure.SpringBootApplication;
import reactor.core.publisher.Hooks;

@SpringBootApplication
public class AircraftPositionsApplication {

        public static void main(String[] args) {
                Hooks.onOperatorDebug();
                SpringApplication.run(AircraftPositionsApplication.class, args);
        }

}
```

Since I am demonstrating this capability from a test class, I instead insert Hooks.onOperatorDebug(); on the line immediately preceding assembly of the intentionally failing Publisher:

```
Hooks.onOperatorDebug();
Mockito.when(service.getAllAircraft()).thenReturn(
        Flux.just(ac1, ac2, ac3)
                .concatWith(Flux.error(new Throwable("Bad position report"))))
);
```

This single addition doesn't eliminate the somewhat voluminous stacktrace—there are still rare occasions in which any additional bit of data provided can be helpful—but for the vast majority of cases, the tree summary added to the log by onOperatorDebug() as a backtrace results in faster issue identification and resolution. The backtrace summary for the same error I introduced in the getCurrentACPosi tions() test is shown in Figure 12-3 in order to preserve full details and formatting.

```
java.lang.Throwable: Bad position report
    at com.thehecklers.aircraftpositions.PositionControllerTest.setUp(PositionControllerTest.java:67) ~[test-classes/:na]
    Suppressed: reactor.core.publisher.FluxOnAssembly$OnAssemblyException:
Assembly trace from producer [reactor.core.publisher.FluxError] :
    reactor.core.publisher.Flux.error(Flux.java:871)
    com.thehecklers.aircraftpositions.PositionControllerTest.setUp(PositionControllerTest.java:68)
Error has been observed at the following site(s):
    |_          Flux.error → at com.thehecklers.aircraftpositions.PositionControllerTest.setUp(PositionControllerTest.java:68)
    |_     Flux.concatWith → at com.thehecklers.aircraftpositions.PositionControllerTest.setUp(PositionControllerTest.java:68)
    |_                     → at com.thehecklers.aircraftpositions.PositionService$MockitoMock$883678645.getAllAircraft(null:-1)
    |_           Flux.from → at org.springframework.http.codec.json.AbstractJackson2Encoder.encode(AbstractJackson2Encoder.java:178)
    |_     Flux.collectList → at org.springframework.http.codec.json.AbstractJackson2Encoder.encode(AbstractJackson2Encoder.java:179)
    |_     Flux.collectList → at org.springframework.http.codec.json.AbstractJackson2Encoder.encode(AbstractJackson2Encoder.java:179)
    |_            Mono.map → at org.springframework.http.codec.json.AbstractJackson2Encoder.encode(AbstractJackson2Encoder.java:180)
    |_            Mono.map → at org.springframework.http.codec.json.AbstractJackson2Encoder.encode(AbstractJackson2Encoder.java:180)
    |_           Mono.flux → at org.springframework.http.codec.json.AbstractJackson2Encoder.encode(AbstractJackson2Encoder.java:181)
    |_           Mono.flux → at org.springframework.http.codec.json.AbstractJackson2Encoder.encode(AbstractJackson2Encoder.java:181)
    |_           Flux.from → at org.springframework.http.server.reactive.ChannelSendOperator.<init>(ChannelSendOperator.java:57)
    |_       Mono.doOnError → at org.springframework.http.server.reactive.AbstractServerHttpResponse.writeWith(AbstractServerHttpResponse.java:221)
    |_                     → at org.springframework.http.codec.EncoderHttpMessageWriter.write(EncoderHttpMessageWriter.java:203)
    |_                     → at org.springframework.web.reactive.result.method.annotation.AbstractMessageWriterResultHandler.writeBody
(AbstractMessageWriterResultHandler.java:184)
    |_                     → at org.springframework.web.reactive.result.method.annotation.ResponseBodyResultHandler.handleResult(ResponseBodyResultHandler.java:86)
    |_          checkpoint → Handler com.thehecklers.aircraftpositions.PositionController#getCurrentACPositions() [DispatcherHandler]
    |_         Mono.flatMap → at org.springframework.web.reactive.DispatcherHandler.lambda$handleResult$5(DispatcherHandler.java:171)
    |_ Mono.onErrorResume → at org.springframework.web.reactive.DispatcherHandler.handleResult(DispatcherHandler.java:171)
    |_         Mono.flatMap → at org.springframework.web.reactive.DispatcherHandler.handle(DispatcherHandler.java:147)
    |_                     → at org.springframework.web.server.handler.DefaultWebFilterChain.lambda$filter$0(DefaultWebFilterChain.java:120)
    |_          Mono.defer → at org.springframework.web.server.handler.DefaultWebFilterChain.filter(DefaultWebFilterChain.java:119)
    |_          Mono.defer → at org.springframework.web.server.handler.DefaultWebFilterChain.filter(DefaultWebFilterChain.java:119)
    |_                     → at org.springframework.web.server.handler.FilteringWebHandler.handle(FilteringWebHandler.java:59)
    |_                     → at org.springframework.web.server.handler.WebHandlerDecorator.handle(WebHandlerDecorator.java:56)
    |_          Mono.error → at org.springframework.web.server.handler.ExceptionHandlingWebHandler$CheckpointInsertingHandler.handle(ExceptionHandlingWebHandler
.java:98)
    |_          Mono.error → at org.springframework.web.server.handler.ExceptionHandlingWebHandler$CheckpointInsertingHandler.handle(ExceptionHandlingWebHandler
.java:98)
    |_          checkpoint → HTTP GET "/acpos" [ExceptionHandlingWebHandler]
    |_                     → at org.springframework.web.server.handler.ExceptionHandlingWebHandler.lambda$handle$0(ExceptionHandlingWebHandler.java:73)
    |_ Mono.onErrorResume → at org.springframework.web.server.handler.ExceptionHandlingWebHandler.handle(ExceptionHandlingWebHandler.java:77)
    |_ Mono.onErrorResume → at org.springframework.web.server.handler.ExceptionHandlingWebHandler.handle(ExceptionHandlingWebHandler.java:77)
```

Figure 12-3. Debugging backtrace

At the top of the tree is the incriminating evidence: a Flux error has been introduced using concatWith on line 68 of PositionControllerTest.java. Thanks to Hooks.onOperatorDebug(), the time it took to identify this issue and its specific location has been reduced from several minutes (or more) to a few seconds.

Instrumenting all assembly instructions for all subsequent Publisher occurrences doesn't come without a cost, however; using hooks to instrument your code is relatively runtime-expensive, as debug mode is global and impacts every chained operator of every reactive streams Publisher executed once enabled. Let's consider another alternative.

Checkpoints

Rather than populate every possible backtrace of every possible Publisher, one can set checkpoints near key operators to assist with troubleshooting. Inserting a check point() operator into the chain works like enabling a hook but only for that segment of that chain of operators.

There are three variants of checkpoints:

- Standard checkpoints that include a backtrace

- Light checkpoints that accept a descriptive `String` parameter and do not include backtrace

- Standard checkpoints with backtrace that also accept a descriptive `String` parameter

Let's see them in action.

First, I remove the `Hooks.onOperatorDebug()` statement before the mocked method for `PositionService::getAllAircraft` in the `setUp()` method within `Position ControllerTest`:

```
//Hooks.onOperatorDebug();        Comment out or remove
Mockito.when(service.getAllAircraft()).thenReturn(
    Flux.just(ac1, ac2, ac3)
        .checkpoint()
        .concatWith(Flux.error(new Throwable("Bad position report")))
        .checkpoint()
);
```

Rerunning the test for `getCurrentACPositions()` produces the results shown in Figure 12-4.

```
java.lang.Throwable: Bad position report
    at com.thehecklers.aircraftpositions.PositionControllerTest.setUp(PositionControllerTest.java:68) ~[test-classes/:na]
    Suppressed: reactor.core.publisher.FluxOnAssembly$OnAssemblyException:
Assembly trace from producer [reactor.core.publisher.FluxConcatArray] :
    reactor.core.publisher.Flux.checkpoint(Flux.java:3196)
    com.thehecklers.aircraftpositions.PositionControllerTest.setUp(PositionControllerTest.java:70)
Error has been observed at the following site(s):
    |_       Flux.checkpoint → at com.thehecklers.aircraftpositions.PositionControllerTest.setUp(PositionControllerTest.java:70)
    |_                       → at com.thehecklers.aircraftpositions.PositionService$MockitoMock$1696125553.getAllAircraft(null:-1)
    |_          Flux.from → at org.springframework.http.codec.json.AbstractJackson2Encoder.encode(AbstractJackson2Encoder.java:172)
    |_  Flux.collectList → at org.springframework.http.codec.json.AbstractJackson2Encoder.encode(AbstractJackson2Encoder.java:179)
    |_          Mono.map → at org.springframework.http.codec.json.AbstractJackson2Encoder.encode(AbstractJackson2Encoder.java:188)
    |_         Mono.flux → at org.springframework.http.codec.json.AbstractJackson2Encoder.encode(AbstractJackson2Encoder.java:181)
    |_          Flux.from → at org.springframework.http.server.reactive.ChannelSendOperator.<init>(ChannelSendOperator.java:52)
    |_                    → at org.springframework.http.codec.EncoderHttpMessageWriter.write(EncoderHttpMessageWriter.java:203)
    |_                    → at org.springframework.web.reactive.result.method.annotation.AbstractMessageWriterResultHandler.writeBody
(AbstractMessageWriterResultHandler.java:184)
    |_                    → at org.springframework.web.reactive.result.method.annotation.ResponseBodyResultHandler.handleResult(ResponseBodyResultHandler.java:84)
    |_      checkpoint → Handler com.thehecklers.aircraftpositions.PositionController#getCurrentACPositions() [DispatcherHandler]
    |_                    → at org.springframework.web.server.handler.DefaultWebFilterChain.lambda$filter$0(DefaultWebFilterChain.java:120)
    |_       Mono.defer → at org.springframework.web.server.handler.DefaultWebFilterChain.filter(DefaultWebFilterChain.java:119)
    |_                    → at org.springframework.web.server.handler.FilteringWebHandler.handle(FilteringWebHandler.java:59)
    |_                    → at org.springframework.web.server.handler.WebHandlerDecorator.handle(WebHandlerDecorator.java:56)
    |_       Mono.error → at org.springframework.web.server.handler.ExceptionHandlingWebHandler$CheckpointInsertingHandler.handle(ExceptionHandlingWebHandler
.java:98)
    |_      checkpoint → HTTP GET "/acpos" [ExceptionHandlingWebHandler]
    |_                    → at org.springframework.web.server.handler.ExceptionHandlingWebHandler.lambda$handle$0(ExceptionHandlingWebHandler.java:77)
    |_ Mono.onErrorResume → at org.springframework.web.server.handler.ExceptionHandlingWebHandler.handle(ExceptionHandlingWebHandler.java:77)
```

Figure 12-4. Standard checkpoint output

The checkpoint at the top of the list directs us to the problematic operator: the one immediately preceding the triggered checkpoint. Note that backtrace information is still being collected, as the checkpoint reflects the actual source code file and specific line number for the checkpoint I inserted on line 64 of the `PositionControllerTest` class.

Switching to lightweight checkpoints replaces the collection of backtrace information with a useful `String` description specified by the developer. While backtrace collection for standard checkpoints is limited in scope, it still requires resources beyond the simple storage of a `String`. If done with sufficient detail, light checkpoints provide the same utility in locating problematic operators. Updating the code to leverage light checkpoints is a simple matter:

```
//Hooks.onOperatorDebug();      Comment out or remove
Mockito.when(service.getAllAircraft()).thenReturn(
    Flux.just(ac1, ac2, ac3)
        .checkpoint("All Aircraft: after all good positions reported")
        .concatWith(Flux.error(new Throwable("Bad position report")))
        .checkpoint("All Aircraft: after appending bad position report")
);
```

Re-running the `getCurrentACPositions()` test produces the results shown in Figure 12-5.

```
java.lang.Throwable: Bad position report
    at com.thehecklers.aircraftpositions.PositionControllerTest.setUp(PositionControllerTest.java:48) ~[test-classes/:na]
    Suppressed: reactor.core.publisher.FluxOnAssembly$OnAssemblyException:
Error has been observed at the following site(s):
    |_          checkpoint ⇢ All Aircraft: after appending bad position report
    |_               ⇢ at com.thehecklers.aircraftpositions.PositionService$MockitoMock$1153167644.getAllAircraft(null:-1)
    |_        Flux.from ⇢ at org.springframework.http.codec.json.AbstractJackson2Encoder.encode(AbstractJackson2Encoder.java:178)
    |_    Flux.collectList ⇢ at org.springframework.http.codec.json.AbstractJackson2Encoder.encode(AbstractJackson2Encoder.java:179)
    |_          Mono.map ⇢ at org.springframework.http.codec.json.AbstractJackson2Encoder.encode(AbstractJackson2Encoder.java:180)
    |_         Mono.flux ⇢ at org.springframework.http.codec.json.AbstractJackson2Encoder.encode(AbstractJackson2Encoder.java:181)
    |_         Flux.from ⇢ at org.springframework.http.server.reactive.ChannelSendOperator.<init>(ChannelSendOperator.java:57)
    |_               ⇢ at org.springframework.http.codec.EncoderHttpMessageWriter.write(EncoderHttpMessageWriter.java:203)
    |_               ⇢ at org.springframework.web.reactive.result.method.annotation.AbstractMessageWriterResultHandler.writeBody
(AbstractMessageWriterResultHandler.java:104)
    |_               ⇢ at org.springframework.web.reactive.result.method.annotation.ResponseBodyResultHandler.handleResult(ResponseBodyResultHandler.java:86)
    |_          checkpoint ⇢ Handler com.thehecklers.aircraftpositions.PositionController#getCurrentACPositions() [DispatcherHandler]
    |_               ⇢ at org.springframework.web.server.handler.DefaultWebFilterChain.lambda$filter$0(DefaultWebFilterChain.java:126)
    |_         Mono.defer ⇢ at org.springframework.web.server.handler.DefaultWebFilterChain.filter(DefaultWebFilterChain.java:117)
    |_               ⇢ at org.springframework.web.server.handler.FilteringWebHandler.handle(FilteringWebHandler.java:59)
    |_               ⇢ at org.springframework.web.server.handler.WebHandlerDecorator.handle(WebHandlerDecorator.java:56)
    |_         Mono.error ⇢ at org.springframework.web.server.handler.ExceptionHandlingWebHandler$CheckpointInsertingHandler.handle(ExceptionHandlingWebHandler
.java:98)
    |_          checkpoint ⇢ HTTP GET "/acpos" [ExceptionHandlingWebHandler]
    |_               ⇢ at org.springframework.web.server.handler.ExceptionHandlingWebHandler.lambda$handle$0(ExceptionHandlingWebHandler.java:77)
    |_ Mono.onErrorResume ⇢ at org.springframework.web.server.handler.ExceptionHandlingWebHandler.handle(ExceptionHandlingWebHandler.java:77)
```

Figure 12-5. Light checkpoint output

Although file and line number coordinates are no longer present in the top-listed checkpoint, its clear description makes it easy to find the problem operator in the `Flux` assembly.

Occasionally there will be a requirement to employ an extremely complex chain of operators to build a `Publisher`. In those circumstances, it may be useful to include both a description and full backtrace information for troubleshooting. To demonstrate a very limited example, I refactor the mock method used for `PositionService::getAllAircraft` once more as follows:

```
//Hooks.onOperatorDebug();      Comment out or remove
Mockito.when(service.getAllAircraft()).thenReturn(
    Flux.just(ac1, ac2, ac3)
        .checkpoint("All Aircraft: after all good positions reported", true)
        .concatWith(Flux.error(new Throwable("Bad position report")))
        .checkpoint("All Aircraft: after appending bad position report", true)
);
```

Running the `getCurrentACPositions()` test once again results in the output shown in Figure 12-6.

```
java.lang.Throwable: Bad position report
    at com.thehecklers.aircraftpositions.PositionControllerTest.setUp(PositionControllerTest.java:68) ~[test-classes/:na]
    Suppressed: reactor.core.publisher.FluxOnAssembly$OnAssemblyException:
Assembly trace from producer [reactor.core.publisher.FluxConcatArray], described as [All Aircraft: after appending bad position report] :
    reactor.core.publisher.Flux.checkpoint(Flux.java:3261)
    com.thehecklers.aircraftpositions.PositionControllerTest.setUp(PositionControllerTest.java:70)
Error has been observed at the following site(s):
    |_          Flux.checkpoint → at com.thehecklers.aircraftpositions.PositionControllerTest.setUp(PositionControllerTest.java:70)
    |_                          → at com.thehecklers.aircraftpositions.PositionService$MockitoMock$1850388294.getAllAircraft(null:-1)
    |_              Flux.from → at org.springframework.http.codec.json.AbstractJackson2Encoder.encode(AbstractJackson2Encoder.java:178)
    |_        Flux.collectList → at org.springframework.http.codec.json.AbstractJackson2Encoder.encode(AbstractJackson2Encoder.java:179)
    |_             Mono.map → at org.springframework.http.codec.json.AbstractJackson2Encoder.encode(AbstractJackson2Encoder.java:180)
    |_            Mono.flux → at org.springframework.http.codec.json.AbstractJackson2Encoder.encode(AbstractJackson2Encoder.java:181)
    |_            Flux.from → at org.springframework.http.server.reactive.ChannelSendOperator.<init>(ChannelSendOperator.java:57)
    |_                      → at org.springframework.http.codec.EncoderHttpMessageWriter.write(EncoderHttpMessageWriter.java:203)
    |_                      → at org.springframework.web.reactive.result.method.annotation.AbstractMessageWriterResultHandler.writeBody
(AbstractMessageWriterResultHandler.java:184)
    |_                      → at org.springframework.web.reactive.result.method.annotation.ResponseBodyResultHandler.handleResult(ResponseBodyResultHandler.java:86)
    |_          checkpoint → Handler com.thehecklers.aircraftpositions.PositionController#getCurrentACPositions() [DispatcherHandler]
    |_            Mono.defer → at org.springframework.web.server.handler.DefaultWebFilterChain.lambda$filter$0(DefaultWebFilterChain.java:128)
    |_                      → at org.springframework.web.server.handler.DefaultWebFilterChain.filter(DefaultWebFilterChain.java:119)
    |_                      → at org.springframework.web.server.handler.FilteringWebHandler.handle(FilteringWebHandler.java:59)
    |_                      → at org.springframework.web.server.handler.WebHandlerDecorator.handle(WebHandlerDecorator.java:56)
    |_            Mono.error → at org.springframework.web.server.handler.ExceptionHandlingWebHandler$CheckpointInsertingHandler.handle(ExceptionHandlingWebHandler
.java:98)
    |_          checkpoint → HTTP GET "/acpos" [ExceptionHandlingWebHandler]
    |_                      → at org.springframework.web.server.handler.ExceptionHandlingWebHandler.lambda$handle$0(ExceptionHandlingWebHandler.java:77)
    |_    Mono.onErrorResume → at org.springframework.web.server.handler.ExceptionHandlingWebHandler.handle(ExceptionHandlingWebHandler.java:77)
Stack trace:
    at com.thehecklers.aircraftpositions.PositionControllerTest.setUp(PositionControllerTest.java:68) ~[test-classes/:na] <35 internal calls>
    at java.base/java.util.ArrayList.forEach(ArrayList.java:1510) ~[na:na] <9 internal calls>
    at java.base/java.util.ArrayList.forEach(ArrayList.java:1510) ~[na:na] <23 internal calls>
```

Figure 12-6. Standard checkpoint with description output

ReactorDebugAgent.init()

There is a way to realize the benefits of full backtracing for all `Publishers` within an application—like that produced using hooks—without the performance penalties imposed by enabling debugging using those same hooks.

Within the Reactor project is a library called `reactor-tools` that includes a separate Java agent used to instrument a containing application's code. `reactor-tools` adds debugging information to the application and attaches to the running application (of which it is a dependency) to track and trace execution of every subsequent `Pub lisher`, providing the same kind of detailed backtrace information as hooks with nearly zero performance impact. As such, there are few if any downsides and numerous upsides to running reactive applications in production with `ReactorDebugAgent` enabled.

As a separate library, `reactor-tools` must be manually added to an application's build file. For the Aircraft Positions application's Maven *pom.xml*, I add the following entry:

```
<dependency>
    <groupId>io.projectreactor</groupId>
    <artifactId>reactor-tools</artifactId>
</dependency>
```

After saving the updated *pom.xml*, I refresh/reimport the dependencies to gain access to the `ReactorDebugAgent` within the project.

Like `Hooks.onOperatorDebug()`, the `ReactorDebugAgent` is typically initialized in the application's main method prior to running the app. Since I will be demonstrating this within a test that doesn't load the full application context, I insert the initialization call just as I did `Hooks.onOperatorDebug()`, immediately before constructing the `Flux` used to demonstrate a runtime execution error. I also remove the now-unnecessary calls to `checkpoint()`:

```
//Hooks.onOperatorDebug();
ReactorDebugAgent.init();        // Add this line
Mockito.when(service.getAllAircraft()).thenReturn(
        Flux.just(ac1, ac2, ac3)
                .concatWith(Flux.error(new Throwable("Bad position report")))
);
```

Returning once again to the `getCurrentACPositions()` test, I run it and am treated to the summary tree output shown in Figure 12-7 , which is similar to that provided by `Hooks.onOperatorDebug()` but without runtime penalty:

Figure 12-7. ReactorDebugAgent output resulting from Flux error

Other tools are available that don't directly help test or debug reactive applications but that nevertheless help to improve application quality. One example is Block-Hound (*https://github.com/reactor/BlockHound*), which, although outside the scope of this chapter, can be a useful tool for determining if blocking calls are hidden within your application's code or its dependencies. And, of course, these and other tools are evolving and maturing rapidly to provide numerous ways to level up your reactive applications and systems.

Code Checkout Checkup

For complete chapter code, please check out branch *chapter12end* from the code repository.

Summary

Reactive programming gives developers a way to make better use of resources in distributed systems, even extending powerful scaling mechanisms across application boundaries and into the communication channels. For developers with experience exclusively with mainstream Java development practices—often called *imperative* Java due to its explicit and sequential logic versus the more declarative approach generally used in reactive programming—these reactive capabilities may bear some undesired costs. In addition to the expected learning curve, which Spring helps flatten considerably due to parallel and complementary WebMVC and WebFlux implementations, there are also relative limitations in tooling, its maturity, and established practices for essential activities like testing, troubleshooting, and debugging.

While it is true that reactive Java development is in its infancy relative to its imperative cousin, the fact that they are family has allowed a much faster development and maturation of useful tooling and processes. As mentioned, Spring builds similarly on established imperative expertise within its development and community to condense decades of evolution into production-ready components available *now*.

In this chapter, I introduced and elaborated on the current state of the art in testing and diagnosing/debugging issues you might encounter as you begin to deploy reactive Spring Boot applications. I then demonstrated how to put WebFlux/Reactor to work for you before and in production to test and troubleshoot reactive applications in various ways, showing relative advantages of each option available. You have a wealth of tools at your disposal even now, and the outlook is only getting better.

In this book, I had to choose which of the innumerable "best parts" of Spring Boot to cover in order to provide what I hope to be the best possible way to get up and running with Spring Boot. There is so much more, and I only wish I could have doubled (or trebled) the scope of the book to do so. Thank you for accompanying me on this journey; I hope to share more in future. Best to you in your continued Spring Boot adventures.

Index

About the Author

Mark Heckler is a software developer and Spring Developer Advocate at VMware, conference speaker, Java Champion, and Google Developer Expert in Kotlin, focusing upon developing innovative production-ready software at velocity for the cloud. He has worked with key players in the manufacturing, retail, medical, scientific, telecom, and financial industries and various public sector organizations to develop and deliver critical capabilities on time and on budget. Mark is an open source contributor and author/curator of a developer-focused blog (*https://www.thehecklers.com*) and an occasionally interesting Twitter account (@mkheck).

Colophon

The bird on the cover of *Spring Boot: Up and Running* is a pectoral sandpiper (*Calidris melanotos*).

One of the "grasspipers," these birds are typically found in grassy marshes or wet fields across North America, primarily in the Great Plains with smaller numbers east to the Atlantic Ocean. The name "pectoral" refers to the air sac on the male sandpiper's chest, which puffs out during flight over the tundra, where the birds spend the summer mating season.

These medium-sized shorebirds can be identified by their heavily streaked breast and a bright white belly that forms a sharp border. In order to attract females in courtship, the male will fly above the female, follow her to the ground, and perform an elaborate dance that ends with his wings stretched toward the sky. Once their summers in the tundra end, the sandpipers migrate to South America, with some traveling to Australia and New Zealand for the winter.

Many of the animals on O'Reilly covers are endangered; all of them are important to the world.

The cover illustration is by Karen Montgomery, based on a black and white engraving from *British Birds*. The cover fonts are Gilroy Semibold and Guardian Sans. The text font is Adobe Minion Pro; the heading font is Adobe Myriad Condensed; and the code font is Dalton Maag's Ubuntu Mono.

O'REILLY®

There's much more where this came from.

Experience books, videos, live online training courses, and more from O'Reilly and our 200+ partners—all in one place.

Learn more at oreilly.com/online-learning